Expository
Commentary on
JOHN

Expository
Commentary on
JOHN

J.C. Macaulay

MOODY PRESS

CHICAGO

Formerly entitled *Devotional Studies in St. John's Gospel*

Copyright, 1941, by J. C. Macaulay

MOODY PRESS EDITION 1978

Library of Congress Cataloging in Publication Data

Macaulay, Joseph Cordner, 1900-
  Expository commentary on John.

  First published in 2 v. under title: Devotional studies in
St. John's Gospel.

  1. Bible. N.T. John—Sermons. I. Title.

BS2615.M22   1978   226'.5'06   78-4151

ISBN 0-8024-2420-1

Printed in the United States of America

To
the members, adherents and friends
of the
WHEATON BIBLE CHURCH,
who by their loving confidence
and their high devotion to the Word of God
challenge one's best,
this volume is inscribed by a
grateful pastor.

CONTENTS

PREFACE

When I was a boy at home in Scotland, cans of Nestlés condensed milk were usually part of the pantry supply, and many a good, big spoonful of it disappeared when certain eyes were not watching. We boys liked it. Condensed sermons are apt to be the proverbial "bones" with the meat pared off, but I have really tried to make these more like the condensed milk, hoping that saved and unsaved, minister and layman, young and old, will dip in their spoon and find it to their liking and profit.

The publication of these devotional studies in the gospel at a price within reach of most readers has made impossible the insertion of the text before each study. I suggest, however, that a careful reading of the passage under review will greatly increase the value of the study to the reader. In general I have used the King James Version, but where a literal rendering of the Greek ministered to clarity, I have not hesitated to give it.

One could not produce a series of studies in this glorious gospel without being indebted to many who have gone before. It has been my privilege also to counsel with a number of biblical scholars in Wheaton Bible Church, whose encouragement has been beyond value, not only in this work, but in the whole course of my ministry in that church.

I gladly acknowledge a special debt of gratitude to the Reverend Wendell P. Loveless, former director of radio station WMBI, whose encouragement to the point of insistence is really responsible for this work.

With sincere thanks to God for the aid of the Holy Spirit in these studies, I commit them to His care, praying that the Word who was made flesh for us may be glorified by their wider distribution.

1

JOHN EXPLAINS

JOHN 20:30-31

This introduction deals with:

1. The method of the writing (v. 30)
2. The purpose of the writing (v. 31a)
3. The end of the writing (v. 31b)

MY COPY of Morley's *Life of Gladstone* is in two volumes, and contains 1,444 pages of actual reading matter, exclusive of chronology, index, and other appendixes. The apostle John's record of the Son of God occupies thirty-seven pages of my large type Cambridge Bible. That seems very disproportionate, and can be explained only by the fact that John is not writing a biography, but a gospel. His closing sentence is his disclaimer to any biographical pretensions: "And there are also many other things which Jesus did, the which, if they should be written every one, I suppose that even the world itself could not contain the books that should be written" (John 21:25). That is no idle exaggeration. Remember that John begins, "In the beginning" (1:1). His vision is timeless, cosmic. Certainly our little planet could not house a library large enough to carry such a record.

John's writing, then, is selective. He acknowledges the omission of "many other things." He selects characteristic events. He calls them "signs"—works of Jesus which peculiarly present Him in character. All of our Lord's words and works are characteristic of Him. He is never "out of character." But the apostle John is led of the Holy Spirit to choose such features of His ministry as emphasize the particular character in which he would present the Saviour to us— in His nature as the Son of God, and in His office as the Christ. Even

11

so, the evangelist can give but a representative group of such "signs,"
calculated, when linked together, to show the vast dimensions and the
perfect proportions of our Lord's glory. So John's record is selective,
characteristic, and representative.

The "beloved disciple" did not write for a place in the literary
world. Clement of Alexandria said that he wrote "at the instigation
of men of note." An ancient Latin document says it was "at the request of the bishops of Asia." The Muratorian Fragment tells how
he was "solicited by his fellow-disciples and bishops," and did not
undertake the task till after fasting and prayer. He had no ambitions
for a place among men of letters, but he did have desire to secure
Christ a place in the hearts of men. He wrote, not for entertainment,
but for conviction, just as Luke wrote for confirmation (Luke 1:3-4).
He would have us convinced of the divine office and the divine nature
of Jesus. "These are written, that ye might believe that Jesus is the
Christ, the *Son of God"* (John 20:31a, italics added).

This purpose is stated in a most appropriate setting, with the story
of the conviction and confession of the doubter, Thomas, as background: as if the writer would invite all doubters to review the evidence he has presented, and join Thomas in his exclamation of worship, "My Lord and my God!" (20:28).

I may be thoroughly convinced that an eagle may live out a century,
and that, if it will endure the pain of breaking off its old beak on the
rocks, it will renew its youth and perhaps live well through another
century; or I may be equally convinced that that is all nonsense. Being convinced either way will not perceptibly affect my life. Not so in
the matter before us. What we believe concerning Jesus of Nazareth
has tremendous consequence, and John is bent on convincing us that
"Jesus is the Christ, the Son of God," because the end of such believing is "that ye might have life through his name" (20:31b). Eternal
life is in the question. The believing that he calls for, then, is something more than intellectual assent to a body of evidence; it carries
with it a personal adjustment to the facts presented, which means in
this case an acceptance of, and surrender to, Jesus Christ as Saviour
and Lord. This note of "life through believing" is one of John's ma-
jor themes, and most appropriately it is here stated as the end of his
writing.

The end of any study of John's gospel must be in keeping with the apostle's own statement. The studies presented in this volume are therefore evangelical in purpose. If they serve to strengthen others in the faith "that Jesus is the Christ, the Son of God," and bring some to "life through his name," the end will be fulfilled, and the glory will be His of whom we write.

2

THE DIVINE WORD

John 1:1-4, 14

This chapter presents Christ as:

1. The eternal Word (vv. 1-2)
2. The creative Word (v. 3)
3. The living Word (v. 4)
4. The incarnate Word (v. 14)

WHEN THE HOLY SPIRIT wants to present a truth of unusual vastness, He chooses the simplest words. He can pour eternity into monosyllables. For instance, the whole range of truth is compressed into these words: "For of him, and through him, and to him, are all things" (Rom 11:36). One might spend all his life, and eternity besides, in fathoming that one sentence. So here, when the eternal existence and the divine nature of our Lord are to be declared, our English, apart from the one word "beginning," gives all monosyllables. "In the beginning was the Word, and the Word was with God, and the Word was God" (John 1:1). But now try to explain these primary words, and we shall find ourselves wrestling with philosophical and metaphysical terms. A little tabulation will help us here. The eternal Word is presented in His

1. Eternal being: "In the beginning was the Word."
2. Personal communion: "And the Word was with God."
3. Divine essence: "And the Word was God."

Mark begins his gospel with the ministry of John the Baptist; Matthew starts with Abraham; Luke carries us back to Adam; but John rends the veil of time for his beginning. Genesis and John's gospel have the same first words, "in the beginning," but the New Testament is vaster in its scope than the Old Testament. Moses' "beginning" is related to an act in time, while John's "beginning" refers to an existence filling all eternity. "In the beginning was the Word" is a statement of eternal being, not of a coming into being. Our Lord Himself drew that distinction very clearly when He said to the Jews, "Before Abraham was [came into being], I am" (John 8:58).

Personal communion is indicated in the statement, "And the Word was with God." We believe that God is one, but His oneness is not the solitariness of the unitarian conception. The Word is coeternal with God, realizes personal communion with God, and that communion is eternal as the being of God. There is but one possible conclusion from these two statements, and the apostle John does not hesitate to enunciate it—"And the Word was God." This coexistence and this communion are not between two things, but within one being. Christ did not become God at some point in time, but this interrelation of personality is inherent in the eternal being of God. Thus Eternity, Personality, and Deity are fully attributed to our Lord. This is a moment, not for speculation, but for worship.

The title by which the Lord is presented to us in these majestic phrases suggests an active relationship to God. He is the "Word." Without too much analysis we may say that the title represents God expressing Himself. The activities of God's self-manifestation are wrought in Christ. "The only begotten Son . . . hath declared him" (1:18).

Most appropriately, then, we are immediately introduced to the activity of the Word in the work of creation. "All things were made by him; and without him was not any thing made that was made" (1:3). We are now brought down to that later beginning with which our Bible opens. "In the beginning God created the heaven and the earth" (Gen 1:1). What a flood of light this New Testament revelation pours on the older statement! "And God said . . . and there was," is how the Holy Spirit speaks in Moses. Here we see that God's creative Word was a Person, an eternal, divine, all-glorious Person—the Word. Now also that strange "let us" of Genesis 1:26 is explained. God was not using the royal "we" or the editorial "we," but a bona fide "we," for plurality was there—the "Word" ready to express the mind of God in every act of creation.

There are no exceptions to Christ's agency in creation. Some modern cults, reviving an old heresy, would make Christ Himself an exception, teaching that God first created Christ, who then with bestowed power created everything else. The whole New Testament revelation is dead against that fallacy. He was no more first created before creating the world than He was first redeemed before redeeming the world. He is the eternal, uncreated Mediator in both of these divine activities, and sustains a twofold headship, creational and redemptional, over all things.

This eternal, creative Word is also the living Word. "In him was life" (John 1:4a). Life with Him is not derived, but native. He is the source and fountain of all life, of whatever kind, however expressed. All the "new life" that we see manifesting itself in the spring of the year is from Christ. Our own life is borrowed from Him. But this life in Christ is something to man that it cannot be to beast or flower: "the life was the light of men" (1:4b). There is not a man in all the earth who is utterly devoid of this light. He may not have received "the light of the knowledge of the glory of God in the face of Jesus Christ" (2 Cor 4:6b). He may lack the moral training that many of us boast; he may even be doing his utmost to smother the light; but it is there, and it persists. Even in the darkest heart it shines out its defiance of the darkness, and the darkness can never utterly obliterate it. Received, it is "the light of life"; refused, it is the light of condemnation.

This is the glorious Word who "was made flesh, and dwelt among us" (John 1:14a). Infinite condescension! The incarnation presents a number of contrasts which should help us realize the amazing stoop of the Son of God for our sakes.

A comparison of the verbs in verses 1 and 14 of this chapter is revealing. In verse 1 we have the continuous, eternal imperfect tense to describe the unapproachable glories and divine relationship of God's well-Beloved. In verse 14 the verb indicates the act of becoming. Now look at these verbs with their complements: "was God . . . became flesh" (1-14, ASV). From the infinite sweep of eternal godhood to the narrow limitations of "the likeness of sinful flesh" (Rom 8:3b). It is unthinkable, but it is true!

Contrast again the "was with God" of verse 1 with the "dwelt among us" of verse 14. He abandoned an eternal dwelling before the very face of God for a tent pitching in the midst of sinners. Could condescension be more complete? All for me!

"Veiled in flesh the Godhead see!" There were some anointed eyes that penetrated the veil of flesh and beheld glory: but the glory they saw was not after this world. It was not the glory of pomp and splendor and power and domination. Its distinguishing marks were grace and truth. Have you seen that glory? And what has it done for you? "We all . . . beholding as in a glass the glory of the Lord, are changed into the same image from glory to glory, . . . as by the Spirit of the Lord" (2 Cor 3:18). If we have looked on our Lord as we ought in this study, there should henceforth be more of the glory of grace and truth in our lives.

3

THE ELEMENT OF TRAGEDY

John 1:5-13

In this chapter we learn of:

1. The unextinguished light (v. 5)
2. The unrecognized life (v. 10)
3. The unwanted love (v. 11)
4. The blessedness of accepting the proffered love, life, and light
   (vv. 12-13)

ON A GLORIOUS SUMMER DAY, when the sun is shining in its splendor from a cloudless sky, there is no sense of conflict in the unchallenged reign of the light. But if you have been out at sea in the midst of a great fog, when the ship's strongest lights were piercing the murk and the foghorns were bellowing, then you have sensed the struggle between darkness and light. Since the darkness of sin settled upon this world, the light of God has engaged in unabating combat with it, only to end with the final and complete expulsion of the darkness from God's fair realm. "The light shineth in darkness" (John 1:5).

The light did not leave the field with the entrance of darkness. What finally counts in this statement is that "the light shineth." God has never left Himself without a witness. The Old Testament is a record of increasing revelation and testimony—patriarchal, Mosaic, and prophetic—all an attack upon the darkness, till at last the "Light, which lighteth every man that cometh into the world" (v. 9), appeared in person, and the full revelation of God in Christ was sent upon its age-long ministry of enlightenment. "The true light now shineth," says John in his first epistle (1 John 2:8b).

"And the darkness comprehended it not" (John 1:5b). So reads our

18

King James Version, rather unfortunately. The picture presented is not of a student wrestling with a problem and failing to grasp it; but of an enemy bent on the destruction of the truth and unable to accomplish it. Despite all the assaults of darkness on God's revelation, it is unextinguished and inextinguishable. The powers of darkness have tried many weapons, and at times the light has been obscured almost to eclipse, only to break out again in new glory and splendor. There have been fogs and clouds and mists, but fogs have a way of lifting, clouds of breaking, and mists of dispelling. We think of the Dark Ages, when the pall of Rome lay heavy upon a darkened Europe, and again of the desolations of deism in the eighteenth century; but the Reformation and the evangelical revival were God's effective answers. "The light shineth in darkness, and the darkness overcame it not." Did you ever know when the darkness in your room failed to flee before the switching on of your electric light? It is so in the spiritual world. Light may be rejected, but it cannot be extinguished. Received, it will save; refused, it will consume. But it will always triumph.

"He was in the world, and the world was made by him, and the world knew him not" (John 1:10). Changing the order of the phrases, we see here,

    (a) The Life creating: "the world was made by him."
    (b) The Life sustaining: "He was in the world."
    (c) The Life refused: "the world knew him not."

In the act of creation we are reminded of the transcendence of our Lord, even as every man is apart from the work he accomplishes. But the Creator did not leave the world to itself. "He was in the world." He is immanent in the world as well as transcendent over it. Can we grasp the sorrow of this amazing statement? The transcendent Creator and immanent Sustainer of the world appeared in the world, "and the world knew him not."

Something in us humans gives us a recognition of our own kin. I knew a girl who, as she came up into young womanhood, was gripped with a feeling that those who had brought her up were not her own parents. They were as kind as parents could be, but there was an indefinable something that shouted to her, "Not your own parents!" She started inquiries, and her convictions were sustained. Her mother had died when she was but an infant in arms, and these friends had brought her up as if she had been their own. Recently the newspapers carried the account of a young man who had been brought up by foster parents. His own mother came to live in the same town, and visited the home. Something in his heart said, "That is your mother." He challenged the situation, and soon he was calling her "Mother" who had been all unknown to him till a few days before.

What shall we say, then, of a world which had so wonderful a Parent as the Son of God, its Creator and Sustainer, yet, when He came, did not recognize Him? "The ox knoweth his owner, and the ass his master's crib: but Israel doth not know, my people doth not consider" (Isa 1:3). So God complained of old, and here is the same tragedy on a universal scale. What explanation can be given? One day Jesus said, "The prince of this world cometh, and hath nothing in me" (John 14:30). Must we turn that phrase and say, "The Lord of glory cometh and hath nothing in us"? Is it because sin has so obliterated, or at least so damaged, everything in common between us and our Creator and Sustainer, that when He comes there is nothing in us to flow out to Him, nothing of affinity? "In him we live, and move, and have our being" (Acts 17:28), yet "the world knew him not" (John 1:10*b*).

If tragedy stalks in the rejection of light and in the refusal of life, what shall we say of the spurning of love? "Slighted love is sair to bide" is the telling expression of the Scottish bard. That is what the Son of God endured. "He came unto his own, and his own received him not" (1:11). The first "his own" is in the neuter gender in the Greek, the second in the masculine. He came to "His own things" —His rightful inheritance. The same expression is used of John taking Mary the mother of Jesus to "his own home" (19:27*b*). But with all His rights in this world, with all His proper claims upon Israel as a nation, it was no "home" that He found here, for "His own people" did not receive Him, did not "take Him to their heart." Even in the inner circle of the family He was not at home; "for neither did his brethren believe in him" (7:5). The Messenger from God's heart was thrust from the heart of men.

Nevertheless, the triple blessing of acceptance was realized by some, and still is. "As many as received him, to them gave he power to become the sons of God, even to them that believe on his name: which were born, not of blood, nor of the will of the flesh, nor of the will of man, but of God" (1:12-13). To receive the Lord Jesus means being received into a relationship of love, for the term used for "sons of God" is the love term, referring not so much to official standing as to the tender relation in which children stand with their own parents. "Behold, what manner of *love* the Father hath bestowed upon us, that we should be called the sons [children] of God" (1 John 3:1, italics added).

Nor is this merely an act of adoption, wonderful as that is. It is a relationship of life. We are "begotten of God," so that we are partakers of the very life of God. When we come to the third chapter of this wonderful gospel, we shall see how our Lord relates the new birth and eternal life.

Then this relationship of love and life is also a relationship of light, for no factor is allowed a part in this birth from above that would introduce a strain of darkness. The new birth is "not of bloods" (plural in the Greek), for although mixed bloods are favored for the best breeding in the natural realm, it is not so in the birth of the Spirit. Neither is this birth "of the will of the flesh," for "that which is born of the flesh is flesh; and that which is born of the Spirit is spirit" (John 3:6). "Nor of the will of man" (1:13*b*), for how can the natural man will the things of the Spirit of God? All that is born of bloods and of the will of the flesh and of the will of man is heir to darkness, but those who are born of God are the children of light.

If Christ is unwanted, you are unblessed.

4

THE WITNESS OF THE BAPTIST

JOHN 1:6-8, 15-34

In this chapter we consider:

1. John, the witness:
   - *a)* His divine appointment (vv. 6-7)
   - *b)* His dutiful fulfillment (v. 15)
   - *c)* His definite pronouncement (v. 19)

2. The witness of John:
   - *a)* Concerning himself (vv. 19-27)
   - *b)* Concerning Christ (vv. 29-34)

THREE BRIEF and related statements are made in this section about John the Baptist.

1. "The same came for a witness" (v. 7)
2. "John bare witness" (v. 15)
3. "And this is the witness" (v. 19, ASV)

Try to catch the relation. John came into the world to do a certain piece of work—to bear witness to Jesus Christ. He did what he came for—he gave his witness. His witness was clear, so that it could be recorded.

We all recognize that John was a God-sent man, and that he was honored with a special and unique ministry, as the forerunner of our Lord. But for all the "specialty" of John's work, you and I are as truly called and sent as he, and our office and task are essentially the same as his. We are come as witnesses, to bear witness. "Ye shall be witnesses unto me" (Acts 1:8) stands for every Christian, not only for the original disciples. We are in even better company than that of

22

the Baptist and the apostles in this mission and task of witnessing; we are in partnership with the Holy Spirit. "We are his witnesses of these things; and so is also the Holy Ghost" (Acts 5:32).

The subject of John's witness was "the light." That was no creedal system, no new philosophy, no improved ritual, no human theory, but a glorious Person, who soon would stand in the Temple court and cry, "I am the light of the world" (John 8:12). That is our witness as well as John's. "Ye shall be witnesses *unto Me*," commanded our Lord, and the great apostle echoed in the statement, "We preach not ourselves, but Christ Jesus the Lord" (2 Cor 4:5).

Ian Maclaren, in *Beside the Bonnie Brier Bush*, relates the induction of a young minister, John by name, into the kirk of Drumtochty. He held the Macwhammel scholarship, and felt himself obliged to make a "deliverance," which meant a scholarly statement. Five years before, his mother had died, and in her last words had committed him to a life of consecration. "If God calls ye to the ministry," she had said, "Ye'ill no refuse, an' the first day ye preach in yir ain kirk, speak a gude word for Jesus Christ." It was now the day before the great occasion, and the minister's aunt was burdened. Had the laddie forgotten? Tactfully and lovingly she reminded him of the needs of the rustic villagers, and ended with an echo of his mother's words, "but oh, laddie, be sure ye say a gude word for Jesus Christ." The minister remembered. That night a manuscript found the fire, and the next morning a word was spoken that kindled fire. It was "a gude word for Jesus Christ." That was John's mission. It is ours.

John did what he came to do. "John bare witness" (John 1:15). Have you ever gone from one room to another to do something, and straightway forgotten what you came for, perhaps by distraction, or through absentmindedness? Too many Christians are like that regarding their duty to witness for Christ. Not so John. He did what he came for, and did it continuously, as the tense of the Greek verb indicates. No matter what the specific topic of the hour, it was a witness for Christ.

The apostle Paul, writing the the Colossians, commanded that the letter be read to the church in Laodicea, with a special message to Archippus, the young minister at the latter place: "And say to Archippus, Take heed to the ministry which thou hast received in the

Lord, that thou fulfil it" (Col 4:17). That word goes for every one of us. For whether we be preachers or farmers, salesmen or teachers, factory hands or doctors, we are commissioned to be His witnesses.

"And this is the witness" (John 1:19, ASV), says the Spirit of inspiration, whereupon He sets down for all generations a record of John's witness. I wonder how many of our sermons would bear the test of being written down! A stenographic transcription of a sermon will indicate how clear the witness has been. Perhaps such a test would call for some discipline on the part of many a preacher. To make records on the hearts of men, we need to be clear and plain in our declarations. When John MacNeil, the Scottish evangelist, was studying in Edinburgh, he was one day surrounded by his Latin, Greek, and Hebrew texts. His young sister, looking over his shoulder, said, "Your Latin and your Greek and your Hebrew are all right, but they all have to be translated into English to understand them." "The best of gospels in the best of English," was Alexander Whyte's description of Hooker's sermons. Some men are hard to "pin down." Their deliverances are eloquent vacuities. Let us witness so that the simplest may be able to record, "This is what he preached."

Consider, then, the content of the Baptist's witness.

First, he gave an account of himself. He did not come to bear witness of himself, but every servant of God must be willing to let the world take his fingerprints. When a man tries to hide his identity and his association, we become suspicious that he is a vendor of some heresy. John had to "clear the decks" for his testimony to Christ by stating quite plainly his own relation to the entire divine economy. Negatively, he denied that he was himself the Christ, Elijah, or "that prophet" (1:21). The denials became ever briefer, as if he were growing impatient to talk about his Lord rather than about himself. Positively, he called himself "the voice of one crying in the wilderness, Make straight the way of the Lord" (1:23). That was a far better statement than a direct use of the term "forerunner." It cast his hearers back upon the Word of God, that great pronouncement of Isaiah (Isa 40:3). His credentials were in the pages of Holy Writ, not just on a parchment from the ecclesiastical authorities.

It was of Jesus, however, that John continually spoke; and it was no uncertain sound that this trumpet voice uttered. A sevenfold witness to the Lord Jesus is discernible in the passage before us.

1. *The divine superiority* of Jesus is stated in verse 27: "He it is, who coming after me is preferred before me, whose shoe's latchet I am not worthy to unloose." This was said by one of whom the Lord Himself declared, "Among them that are born of women there hath not arisen a greater than John the Baptist" (Matt 11:11). Behold, a greater than the greatest is here!

2. *The divine sacrifice* is indicated in verse 29: "Behold the Lamb of God." Patriarchal sacrifices and Levitical offerings alike had waited for this day. What measure of sacrifice was involved in the great holocausts of the Temple compared with this one sacrifice of heaven—the Lamb of God?

3. *The divine redemption* is announced in connection with the sacrifice of the Lamb—"which taketh away the sin of the world" (1:29*b*).

> Not all the blood of beasts
> On Jewish altars slain
> Could give the guilty conscience peace
> Or wash away the stain;
>
> But Christ the heavenly Lamb
> Takes all our guilt away;
> A sacrifice of nobler name
> And richer blood than they.

4. *The divine preexistence* is declared in verse 30: "After me cometh a man which is preferred before me: for he was before me." Actually Jesus was born six months after John the Baptist, but John says, "He was before me," using the imperfect tense of the verb "to be," not the aorist tense of the verb "to come into existence," so indicating the continuity of eternal being, as the apostle John declares in the opening words of the gospel.

5. *The divine anointing* is described in verse 32: "I saw the Spirit descending from heaven like a dove, and it abode upon him." All the anointings of Old Testament ritual looked forward to this anointing which identified the Messiah, the anointed One long promised.

6. *The divine prerogative* is proclaimed in verse 33: "The same is he which baptizeth with the Holy Ghost." The Spirit of power, wisdom, grace, truth, and love is at the disposition of this Man! If this is so, we are not surprised at the final statement in the Baptist's witness, concerning

7. *The divine Person:* "This is the Son of God" (v. 34). What a witness! And hallelujah, what a Saviour!

5

A CHAPTER OF GREAT FINDS

JOHN 1:35-51

In this chapter our thoughts will follow this course:

1. The Law of seeking and finding
   - *a)* Finding necessitates searching
   - *b)* Searching assures finding

2. The experience of seeking and finding
   - *a)* What the seeking sinner finds in Christ
   - *b)* What the seeking Christ finds in the sinner

3. The method of seeking and finding
   - *a)* Three spheres of personal witnessing
   - *b)* Three elements in personal witnessing

"HE THAT SEEKETH *findeth*" (Matt 7:8, italics added). Our habit is to emphasize the finding. We ought to lay equal stress on the seeking. "He that *seeketh* findeth." In the spiritual realm there are no chance finds. Any really worthwhile discovery is the end of diligent search.

Jesus findeth Philip, we are told. He did not stumble on him by chance, take a liking to him, and invite his company. He had come to seek and to save that which was lost, and in the pursuit of His holy task He found Philip and Andrew and Simon and John and Nathanael. Furthermore, the Lord's search was not of a general nature, in the course of which He made particular finds. The seeking was as particular as the finding. He sought John, and found him. He sought Philip, and found him. And so for the rest. In the fifteenth chapter of Luke's gospel, it is a particular sheep that is sought, a particular piece of silver that calls for lamp and broom, a particular son that is

27

yearned over and welcomed home. "He sought *me,* blessed be His name!"

This also is true—that there is no accidental finding of Jesus. "If thou seek him, he will be found of thee" (1 Chron 28:9*b*), said David to his son, Solomon. The prophet Azariah stated it as a matter of history that "when in their distress they turned unto Jehovah, the God of Israel, and sought him, he was found of them" (2 Chron 15:4, ASV). Jeremiah is equally explicit. "Ye shall seek me, and find me, when ye shall search for me with all your heart" (Jer 29:13). And our Lord Himself sums it up in few words: "Seek, and ye shall find" (Matt 7:7). For how does the Lord find His lost ones? By causing them to seek after Him! What were John and Andrew doing as they followed the baptizer? They were seeking the Messiah! What were Philip and Nathanael doing all those evening hours and all those Sabbath days that they spent together poring over the sacred rolls or thinking deeply under their favorite fig tree? They were seeking "him, of whom Moses in the law, and the prophets, did write" (John 1:45). No wonder these earnest men were able to cry one to another that blessed day, "Eureka! We have found!"

You hope some day to know the Lord, for you have heard it said that "this is life eternal, that they might know thee the only true God, and Jesus Christ, whom thou hast sent" (17:3). Only you do not exert yourself about it, not realizing that every moment you do not have life eternal you are hanging on the brink of eternal ruin, loss, and damnation! As you hope to enter the paradise of God, as you hope to stand uncondemned in the presence of the thrice-holy God, I bid you, "Seek ye the LORD while he may be found, call ye upon him while he is near: let the wicked forsake his way, and the unrighteous man his thoughts: and let him return unto the LORD, and he will have mercy upon him; and to our God, for he will abundantly pardon" (Isa 55:6-7). Seek Him, more eagerly than man ever sought for gold: hasten after Him with more zeal than ever explorer sought the poles or scientist the secrets of nature. Seek until the song breaks from your lips:

> I've found the pearl of greatest price;
> My heart doth sing for joy!
> And sing I must, for Christ is mine:
> Christ shall my tongue employ.

This brings us to consider the end of the search. When these men of Galilee found Jesus, their seeking days were over. True, henceforth they sought to know Him better, in His love, His grace, His wisdom, His glory, His purposes; but they never sought beyond Him. "Ne plus ultra," they might have emblazoned on a sacred miter to adorn His brow, and we too know, as by a God-given instinct, that there is nothing beyond Him. When we have found Him, we have arrived at finality. "All that I want is in Jesus!" "All my springs are in thee" (Psalm 87:7). Did we seek after righteousness? "Christ is the end of the law for righteousness" (Rom 10:4). Did our hearts cry for peace? "He is our peace" (Eph 2:14). Or did we pant for life? "He that hath the Son hath life" (1 John 5:12). Did we crave light in our darkness? "The life was the light of men" (John 1:4). Were we seekers after the Father? "He that hath seen me hath seen the Father" (14:9). All reality is summed up in Him. "It pleased the Father that in him should all fulness dwell" (Col 1:19). "In him all things consist" (Col 1:17, ASV). Yes, in Christ there is infinite scope for growth in knowledge, understanding, wisdom, power, love—but there is nothing beyond Him: our search for the ultimate, for the real, for the true, ends at His feet.

What fullness dwells in Him! I am amazed that in the beginning of the gospel such heights and depths and lengths and breadths of vision should be attained! See what titles crowd this early page—titles indicative of what these first disciples found in Him. John and Andrew, helped by the enlightened baptizer, see in Jesus the Lamb of God. Andrew, after that first afternoon with his new Master, proclaims Him to his brother Simon, as the Messiah. Again Philip, the fellow student of Nathanael, reports of Him that He is the one "of whom Moses in the law, and the prophets, did write" (John 1:45). Nathanael in turn lifts up his wondering eyes to behold "the Son of God . . . the King of Israel" (1:49). Now all these titles indicate needs that have been met in Jesus, longings that have been satisfied, burdens that have been lifted, hopes that have been realized. Is your heart burdened, weary, seeking, dissatisfied? If only we could have John and Andrew and Simon and Philip and Nathanael and the rest here! How they would witness and say, "Jesus Christ proved to be all that I needed. My heart was wholly satisfied in Him!" John and Andrew would say, "My soul was weighed down with the burden of my guilt, but I saw the Lamb of God bearing away my sin, and my heart leapt for very lightness." Then would Andrew and his brother Simon Peter continue, "We were strongly bound in the fetters of our sin, and could by no means release ourselves, till we found the Messiah, God's chosen Deliverer, and lo! He set us free." And Philip would take up the word, and say, "I was fallen into great despair because of the apparent hopelessness of life, and of the world; but I found Him of whom it was written in the Holy Scriptures, and He filled me with abounding hope." While Nathanael would add, "As for me, I thought that vision was clean gone forever, that God had altogether withdrawn Himself, until I looked in the face of Jesus and saw the very glory of God."

What is your need? What is the big question of your heart? Oh, that you would believe the testimony that Jesus is abundantly able, and He alone is able. "Come unto me," He cries, "and I will give you rest" (Matt 11:28).

In the mystic East there are many seekers. Their solemn, mournful greeting to one another often is, "We have not found." I have heard of some among them who made a solemn covenant between themselves that if one should find—find the truth, find rest, find God—he would hasten to tell the others. Happy are we if we can say, "I have found! I have found Him!" Are we telling the rest? But more of that in a moment.

We have tried to tell you that

> Those who find Him find a bliss
> Nor tongue nor pen can show:
> The love of Jesus, what it is,
> None but His loved ones know.

But what did Jesus find when He found Andrew and Peter and you and me? Was the find worth the search? He got a son of thunder in John—a man of fiery spirit, daringly covetous of power and ready to bring down the damnation of fire on first provocation. In Andrew He got a very common man—just a common sinner. Simon Peter was an impetuous fellow, unstable as water; well intentioned, but blown with the wind. Philip was slow, calculating, unimaginative.

Nathanael was a victim of narrow prejudices. No, Jesus did not find an army of full-fledged saints when He lighted on these Galileans. I think they would compare more favorably with the motley crew that assembled to David in the cave of Adullam than with a band of angels. Yet the Lord made a great find in these men. He would not have gone seeking them had He not thought them worth all the travail and humiliation to find them. And right here let us stop and remember that the Lord would not have gone the dark, hard way of the cross to find you and me had He not considered us worth the awful price. The value, however, lies not in what we are, but in what He can make of us. He takes a son of thunder and makes him into an apostle of love. He finds a very common man (his name just means "a man"), and enables him at last to crash the gates into the inner circle of the apostolate. He undertakes for the unstable Simon and transforms him into a mighty rock fit to take a foundation place in His church. He sanctifies the cautious, calculating disposition of a Philip until he is written down in tradition as "that holy and glorious apostle and theologian." A prejudiced Nathanael he delivers from his narrow groove and makes him a man of heavenly vision, a guileless Israelite.

Left to ourselves, we are of little account, but found by the Lord Jesus, we can become under His hand something for His everlasting delight and glory. Macaulay the historian tells of an apprentice who gathered the pieces of glass which his master threw away in making stained-glass windows, and out of the scrap pieces made a cathedral window far surpassing the work of his master, who, in a rage of jealousy, committed suicide. The Lord Jesus can take up the common clay of our humanity, the broken earthenware, and make sons of God, fashioned after His own image. Of us also He can make living stones for His temple, new sharp threshing instruments for the beating down of mountains, vessels unto honor, meet for the Master's use.

There is something very personal in all this finding. Not only is it the individual who is found, but the method is, the individual finding the individual. You have noticed, have you not, that the two who left John the Baptist and followed Jesus did so, not on the day he preached the public sermon on the Lamb of God, but the following day when he pointed out the Lamb to them personally. That is worth remembering. Andrew then went out after his brother with the good news of their wonderful find. Jesus Himself went out to find Philip, but I have an idea that Andrew and Peter had something to do with preparing the way. Finally Philip sought out his friend Nathanael. So the apostolic band was gathered.

Brethren, I believe in preaching, else I should not be here today: but I am firmly convinced that preaching, to be effective, requires both the preparation and the follow-up of personal witnessing. The mighty sermon of the day of Pentecost, at the close of which three thousand professed the name of the Lord, was preached after, and in conjunction with, the witnessing of the one hundred and twenty. May God give us all tongues of fire for this sacred task! The preacher wants the Pentecostal power, but do every one of you crave it also, that we may have many tongues singing and speaking of our great Redeemer in the power of the Spirit!

See in what circles the witness may go forth. Our text shows witnessing in the circles of discipleship, kinship, and friendship. John tells his disciples, Andrew informs his own brother, and Philip invites his friend. All our relationships with our fellowmen constitute openings for gospel witnessing. Relationship involves responsibility, and no responsibility exceeds this—to make the Saviour known. We are all inclined to shift the task and ask others outside these relationships to do it for us. Perhaps we are conscious that within these spheres we are coming short in living demonstration. If so, let us get right, live right, and witness right.

Do you inquire how to go about it? That is a very big topic in itself. But see what we have in this chapter from beginners in the task of personal witnessing. First comes John the Baptist's bold declaration—"Behold the Lamb of God." Then comes the personal testimony of Andrew and Philip—"we have found" (John 1:41). Finally there is the persuasive invitation of Philip—"Come and see" (1:46). These three elements—declaration, testimony, and invitation—will enter into all true witnessing. Fearlessly state what Christ is set forth in Scripture to be; tell what you personally have found Him to be in your experience; then gently but firmly urge the claims of Christ and invite to personal acceptance. You cannot improve on that technique.

6

THE BEGINNING OF HIS SIGNS

JOHN 2:1-11

In this chapter we shall break the multiple sign of the incident related into its constituent parts, and consider:

1. The sign of the wedding bells (vv. 1-2)
2. The sign of the failing wine (vv. 3-4)
3. The sign of the stone waterpots (vv. 6-8)
4. The sign of the reversed order (vv. 9-10)

THE ENTIRE gospel of John could be comprehended in the words of 1:14, "We beheld his glory." The sum of this beautiful incident is that He "manifested forth his glory" (2:11). The apostle's end in writing his gospel was: "that ye might believe that Jesus is the Christ, the Son of God" (20:31). The effect of the sign enacted in Cana was that "his disciples believed on him" (2:11*b*). We seem to be dealing, then, with a miniature of the whole. This event is specially representative and characteristic, and becomes not only the "beginning of his signs" (2:11*a*, ASV), but in some respects the chief. It is a multiple sign, and may well be studied in its component parts.

It is significant that our Lord wrought the first miracle of His earthly ministry, not in the house of mourning, but in the place of rejoicing; not at a funeral, but at a wedding. He came indeed to comfort our sorrow, but also to sanctify our joys. He came, not to call a fast, but to spread a feast. He gives the best robe, not a garment of sackcloth. He brought, not a doctrine of ascetic severity, but "joy unspeakable and full of glory" (1 Pet 1:8).

It is equally significant that the first miracle was wrought in the home rather than in the Temple; for while we worship in the Temple, we live in the home. Moreover, Christ wrought for the home at its founding, not at its crumbling. "Home, home, sweet home," we sing: but its sweetness is determined by the place which Jesus occupies in it, by the measure in which He is allowed to mold it. Without Christ, home can very readily become a place of disillusionment and bitterness, but with Christ it is a "little bit of heaven." The time to invite His presence is not when ruin begins to threaten or the breakup has already come (although He can heal and rebuild even then), but at the beginning, so that it may be built securely. I have read of an ancient temple which was noted for its fragrance. The secret of the sweet perfume was that the builders had saturated the mortar with attar of roses. A home built by Christ is like that—it is "home, sweet home."

"The wine failed" (2:3) says our American Standard Version. That is true always of the world's wine, of earthly provision. Is it the wine of pleasure?

> Pleasures are like poppies spread—
> You seize the flower, its bloom it shed;
> Or like the snow falls in the river—
> A moment white, then melts for ever;
> Or like the borealis race,
> That flits ere you can point their place;
> Or like the rainbow's lovely form
> Evanishing amid the storm.

Wealth, pomp, and power are equally uncertain and transitory, and they never give the mead of satisfaction that they promised.

It has been suggested that the presence of Jesus and His disciples was responsible for the shortage of wine. It does appear from verse 2 that they were last-minute guests. Add six men unexpectedly to a little village feast, and one may expect a strain on the provisions! However that may be, I know that the coming of Jesus into the life soon discovers the poverty of previous provision. The things of this world, which before seemed supremely desirable, pale and fade and fail. But does Jesus leave us impoverished? A thousand times, no! His presence at the wedding feast was the guarantee of an unfailing supply. Under His hand, common water became "the best wine"

(2:10, author's trans.), and there was no lack. So the common things of life, sanctified by the Lord Jesus, are richer and more enduring in their ministry of pleasure and joy, than the most elaborate provision of wealth and luxury.

The sign of the stone waterpots teaches us the nature of Christ's provision. These waterpots were set, we are informed, "after the manner of the purifying of the Jews" (2:6). Washing with the Jews was religious more than hygienic. It was part of their daily ritual. The waterpots, then, stood as symbols of all that elaborate system of outward ceremony and ablution which could not wash away sin nor satisfy the deep yearnings of the soul. Jesus transformed them into symbols of inward reality. Instead of water for outward washings, there now came from them wine for inward consumption, to make the heart glad and the spirit rejoice. That is exactly the difference between religion and Christ. The world is full of religion, but all its ceremonials, sacrifices, and oblations, genuflections and prostrations, chantings and processionals, can never accomplish salvation. But the Lord Jesus, who drank the gall of wrath for us, gives the wine of salvation to all who will receive.

Brimful obedience brings brimful blessing. When Jesus said to the servants, "Fill the waterpots with water" (2:7), they did not reply, "How full will do?" They just filled them to the brim, and then drew off wine. How full is your waterpot of consecration? How full is your cup of obedience? If we desire "the best wine," we must render full obedience. In measure as we obey shall we know the joy of the Lord. Those who are not realizing the more abundant life would do well to examine themselves on this point. I have seen young people holding out on God on certain issues, and the disharmony created was evident; but when they have yielded to the will and call of God, a new light shone from their eyes, indicating that they had already partaken of the good wine.

Now look at the sign of the reversed order. The way of the world is, "Every man at the beginning doth set forth good wine; and when men have well drunk, then that which is worse" (2:10). How true! You go to buy an automobile. The dealer shows you all the good points until you are sure that you must have this car and no other. After you have driven it awhile, you find that there are conditions under the hood which had not been told you. Your car is burning oil. It has a jumpy motor. You were left to find that out for yourself. The world puts on its beautiful garments, and the youth is allured by the promise of thrills, popularity, gaiety. He is left to find out for himself the sorrow of a broken body, a ruined career, a smashed home, and all the misery that follows sin. Temptation does not present the shame, the remorse, the despair at the end. After the poor dupe has well drunk, he comes to these bitter dregs.

Christ operates after a different order. "Thou hast kept the good wine until now" (2:10*b*). Sometimes He gives a bitter cup to begin with—the cup of conviction of sin—but that is to induce us to take His cup of salvation. This cup of salvation is good from the beginning. How sweet is the draught of forgiveness, of assurance, of peace, of first love! We are sure that we are drinking heaven's best wine when we first come to the Saviour. But it is not so. He has wine of still richer quality for us as He prepares us to receive it. Till always we are saying in wonder, "Thou hast kept the good wine until now."

> To Jesus every day I find my heart is closer drawn;
> He's fairer than the glory of the gold and purple dawn;
> He's all my fancy pictured in its fairest dreams, and more;
> Each day He grows still sweeter than He was the day before.

And the best is still to come.

> Oh! Christ He is the Fountain, the deep sweet well of love;
> The streams on earth I've tasted, more deep I'll drink above:
> There to an ocean's fullness His mercy doth expand,
> And glory, glory dwelleth in Emmanuel's land.
>
>   ANNE R. COUSIN

7

JESUS, THE ICONOCLAST

John 2:13-22

In this chapter, dealing with the first cleansing of the Temple, we shall consider:

1. The occasion of the cleansing: the abuses connected with the Passover worship
2. The significance of the cleansing: that it was at once an attack, a claim, and a prophecy
3. The failure of the cleansing: in that it had to be repeated later
4. The sign of the cleansing: the sanctuary of His body, and ours

THE PASSOVER, even more than other feasts, drew multitudes of Jews from all the world of that day. It was a matter of necessity that sacrificial animals should be available for purchase in or near Jerusalem. In addition, the Temple taxes and gifts were payable only in the sacred coin, the shekel of the sanctuary, so it was necessary to establish bureaus at which the Roman money could be exchanged for the sacred. So far, so good. But the point of legitimacy was passed when these conveniences were placed right within the precincts of the Temple, and religion was made easy for everybody. When worship loses the elements of discipline, it has lost its value. When it no longer costs, it no longer counts. It becomes a weakening luxury instead of a fortifying exercise.

The whole business of exchange and sale had come to be a racket. Monopolies were sold, prices were fixed, rake-offs were given for certain privileges; and the priestly family was foremost in collecting the spoils. Sacrificial animals had to be approved, and only those on sale by the privileged vendors were approved; therefore, monopoly prices could be charged. Edersheim relates how Simeon, the grandson of Hillel, led a reform against these abuses, and reduced the price of two sacrificial doves from $3.75 to eight cents! Clearly the house of prayer had been turned into a den of robbers.

The place chosen for all this illicit traffic was the court of the Gentiles. This court had been built as an invitation to all Gentiles to come and worship the God of Israel. The Jew, however, was not much concerned about the salvation of the Gentile, and rather resented his presence in or near the Temple. The Jew must have the whole Temple for himself, so the Gentile's place of prayer was taken over for the fraudulent gains of the traders and their sponsors.

The significance of our Lord's act, then, becomes very clear. It was an attack on these three abuses of secularization, vested interests, and sectarianism. Our Lord is still against these things, wherever they are found. He is against popularizing His church and making His worship a luxurious appeal to the senses rather than an exercise of the soul. He is against privileged classes in His church, who would lord it over His heritage and make merchandise of His people. He is against such exclusiveness as will regard neither the rights of a fellow believer nor the needs of the lost about us. It would not be surprising if some of our churches need a touch of the Lord's whip!

The Lord did not come to the Temple as did the prophets of old, saying, "Thus saith the LORD, your worship is corrupt," and so on. He entered as Lord of the Temple, and acted on His own right. He called it, not "the temple of the LORD," but "My Father's house" (John 2:16). He was not "as one of the prophets" (Mark 6:15). The Jews understood His language better than the critics. They perceived His high claims in His words and deeds, and made them the basis of His condemnation as a blasphemer. On that day Jesus fulfilled the Scripture which says, "The Lord, whom ye seek, shall suddenly come to his temple . . . and he shall sit as a refiner and purifier of silver" (Mal 3:1-3).

I am sure, too, that Jesus with the whip in His hand was setting forth a prophecy of another day of greater terror, when men shall cry out to the mountains and rocks, "Fall on us, and hide us from the face of him that sitteth on the throne, and from the wrath of the

Lamb: for the great day of his wrath is come; and who shall be able
to stand?" (Rev 6:16-17). In that day He shall exchange the whip for
a rod of iron, and His enemies shall be broken in pieces. But that
day need hold no terror for us, if we can say with Zinzendorf, and his
translator, John Wesley:

> Jesus, Thy blood and righteousness
> My beauty are, my glorious dress;
> 'Midst flaming worlds, in these arrayed,
> With joy shall I lift up my head.
>
> Bold shall I stand in Thy great day
> For who aught to my charge shall lay?
> Fully absolved through these I am,
> From sin and fear, from guilt and shame.
>
> NICOLAUS L. ZINZENDORF

This cleansing of the Temple, heroic and magnificent as it was,
was a sad failure. Is it blasphemy to call any act of Jesus a failure?
We are speaking the language of men to bring forth more vividly
divine truth. This cleansing took place at the first Passover of our
Lord's public ministry. At His last Passover He found the very conditions reestablished which He had attacked three years before, and He
repeated the purging. Even that was no permanent cleansing. Jesus
Himself witnessed to the Jews, "Behold, your house is left unto you
desolate" (Mark 13:35). The double purging did not save it from
destruction.

Here is a striking example of "what the law could not do" (Rom
8:3)! The Law can enforce a temporary reformation, but it cannot
regenerate. Reformation and regeneration are not identical twins.
Did the eighteenth amendment cleanse America from the curse of
liquor? Did the abolition of slavery make all men free? Our Lord has
most vividly summed up the history of reformation in what is sometimes called a parable. "When the unclean spirit is gone out of a man,
he walketh through dry places, seeking rest, and findeth none. Then
he saith, I will return into my house from whence I came out; and
when he is come, he findeth it empty, swept, and garnished. Then
goeth he, and taketh with himself seven other spirits more wicked
than himself, and they enter in and dwell there: and the last state of

that man is worse than the first" (Matt 12:43-45). More than the whip of reformation, more than the scourge of the Law, is needed for thorough and permanent cleansing.

> What can wash away my stain?
>   Nothing but the blood of Jesus.
> What can make me whole again?
>   Nothing but the blood of Jesus.

I am sure that was in the mind of Jesus when, in response to the Jewish demand for a sign to vindicate His right to act so imperiously, He said, "Destroy this temple, and in three days I will raise it up" (John 2:19), speaking of the sanctuary of His body. Not the whip of the Law, but "the offering of the body of Jesus Christ once for all" (Heb 10:10), sanctifies, cleanses, and makes whole. Do not lay hold of the Ten Commandments, the Sermon on the Mount, the Golden Rule, the example of Jesus, for salvation. An evil heart, native to us all, can never rise to such heights, nor will these high standards bestow forgiveness. There is one hope only for the sinner. "The blood of Jesus Christ His son cleanseth us from all sin" (1 John 1:7). That is the sign of the cleansing.

When Jesus spoke of His body as a "temple," He used the word which signifies the innermost sanctuary, the place of the dwelling of God. "Know ye not," says the apostle to us, "that your body is the sanctuary of the Holy Ghost?" (1 Cor 6:19, ASV margin). If the outer court of the material Temple must needs be cleansed, how much more must the inner shrine be kept holy for the indwelling of the Holy Spirit! After knowing such a sanctuary as the body of Jesus, so pure, so undefiled, how can the blessed Spirit dwell with us? May the Lord of the Temple purge us for His own dwelling!

> Spirit of purity and grace,
>   Our weakness, pitying, see:
> O make our hearts Thy dwelling-place,
>   And worthier Thee!

8

A MIDNIGHT INTERVIEW

JOHN 2:23—3:21

In this chapter we perceive:

1. The divine discernment of men (2:23—3:2)
2. The divine demand on men (3:3-8)
3. The divine dealings with men (3:9-16)

BELIEVING MEN and an unbelieving God—that is the amazing situation that confronts us in the closing verse of chapter two. "Many *believed in his name* . . . but Jesus did not *commit* himself unto them" (John 2:23-24, italics added), is our English translation, but where we have two verbs, "believe" and "commit," the Greek has the same verb in both places. There surely must be a good reason why our Lord did not answer faith with faith. It was a spurious type of believing that He perceived in the Jerusalem crowd. They were sign believers, carried away with a display of power, but having no fundamental conviction. When I was in Los Angeles some time ago, some of the inhabitants told me that anyone who comes to that city with a novel idea—whether in amusement, eating, or religion—will have a great following. Whether this be correct let those who know the famous Western city judge, but one is reminded of the Athenians of Paul's day, who "spent their time in nothing else, but either to tell, or to hear some new thing" (Acts 17:21). The belief of the Jews was akin to that spirit, and the divine Searcher of hearts did not "fall" for them. He saw in their belief no turning from sin, no acknowledgment of His lordship, no committal of their lives to His command, no sense of need. To open His heart to them, therefore, would be casting pearls before swine, giving that which was holy to the dogs.

41

There was one man there to whom the Lord did commit Himself. That man was Nicodemus. A little Greek particle at the beginning of chapter three is ignored in the King James Version and translated "now" in the American Standard Version. I believe it ought to be rendered "but," for the whole story of Nicodemus stands in striking contrast with the statement of 2:24. Knowing what was in man, Jesus perceived something in this leading Pharisee which was lacking in the multitude of shallow sign believers.

"The same came to Jesus by night" (John 3:2*a*). "Coward!" cry the harsh judges of human action. "Slander!" I reply. Why put the worst interpretation on the action of one who afterward raised a lone protesting voice in the Sanhedrin in defense of the Lord Jesus, and later ministered lovingly and lavishly in the burial of the sacred body? The whole story suggests rather the earnestness of the man in coming when the conversation would not be interrupted by the curious multitude. He felt that in the presence of Jesus he was facing spiritual reality which he had not discovered in all the minutiae of the Law.

He was a cautious man. "Rabbi," he called Jesus. Of the three titles indicating three degrees of teachers—Rab, Rabbi, and Rabban—he gave Jesus the middle one. Then he declared the conclusion at which he and his fellow Sandhedrinists had arrived, at least tentatively, on the basis of the works of Jesus. "We know that thou art a teacher come from God: for no man can do these miracles that thou doest, except God be with him" (3:2*b*). There had been no direct voice from God to Israel for a long time. None spoke with authority. But now the type of works that Jesus did carried the stamp of divine power and gave authority to His teaching. That was as far as Nicodemus and the others could go at the present stage; and Nicodemus came, as the chief of the rabbinical staff, to make inquiry for his own hungry heart, if not on behalf of the council, regarding the authoritative message which the "teacher come from God" had brought. The Lord saw the hunger, and committed Himself in the great gospel teaching that follows.

The "teacher come from God" began the lesson with a statement of the divine necessity for men. "Ye must be born again" (3:7), He exclaimed. What a radical demand! Had He said, "Ye must be reformed," "Ye must get a new outlook on life," or a thousand other things, He would have been readily understood. But "born again"! That is as much beyond possibility as it is beyond reason! Yet there it is stated, and not as an arbitrary demand, but as a basic necessity. The Teacher did not say, "Except a man be born again he shall not be granted entrance into the kingdom of God," but, "Except a man be born again [or, from above], he *cannot see* the kingdom of God" (3:3, italics added). The demand is based, not on arbitrary appointments of the divine King, but on the native ability of man. The unregenerate man simply lacks capacity for the things of God, just as Paul says, "Now the natural man receiveth not the things of the Spirit of God: for they are foolishness unto him; and he cannot know them, because they are spiritually . . . [discerned]" (1 Cor 2:14, ASV). We lived in the rugged country of the north for ten years. I have been out there in the great wilds reveling in the beauties of rocks, hills, forests, lakes, birds, flowers, and sky, adoring the wisdom and might of the eternal Creator. I used to take my good fox hound out with me. Had he any response to all this majesty and glory? None in the least. His nose was most of the time to the ground, searching out the tracks of game animals. We were just born different, with different capacities and responses. So "that which is born of the flesh is flesh; and that which is born of the Spirit is spirit . . . Ye must be born again" (John 3:6-7).

The spiritual birth must be by spiritual means. If we hold to that fundamental maxim we shall be saved from error and confusion when we read further, "Except a man be born of water and of the Spirit, he cannot enter into the kingdom of God" (3:5). Material water will add nothing to spiritual ends, so I am satisfied that the "water" here connected with the new birth is a spiritual element described figuratively. The explanation most satisfying to my own mind is that which, linking Scripture with Scripture, sees the water as a figure of the Word. Paul tells us in the great church epistle that we are sanctified and cleansed "with the washing of water by the word" (Eph 5:26), and again in his letter to Titus he calls regeneration a washing. And after all, is not the new birth effected by the Holy Spirit's use of the Word, making it live in our conscience and heart? Peter also very definitely links regeneration with the action of the Word: "being born again, not of corruptible seed, but of incorruptible, by the Word of

God, which liveth and abideth for ever" (1 Pet 1:23). Sovereignly, inscrutably, like the wind, the Spirit works through the holy Word, and men are born again.

All that is mysterious, awful. But when we come to God's method of bringing men to the new birth, we reach the "simple gospel." In a word, God's way of salvation is Christ—Christ sent into the world (John 3:17), Christ given to the world (v. 16), and Christ lifted up for the world (v. 14). Christ is the Messenger of God to an estranged world, the gift of God to an impoverished world, the Lamb of God to a lost world. He came to reveal the Father. He came to assume our nature and be our Representative before God. He came to bear our sin and become the sinner's Substitute in the place of judgment.

The other aspect of the divine method concerns our response— "that whosoever believeth in him should not perish, but have everlasting life" (3:16b). What is it, then, to believe? He is God's Messenger; then acknowledge Him with an obedient hearing; He is God's gift; then receive Him with a grateful heart; He is God's Lamb; then trust Him for the taking away of your sin. Do not be merely fascinated by His miracles and entranced by His peerless life and intrigued by His matchless teaching; but commit yourself to Him as one whose eternal destiny is bound up in His life, death, and resurrection.

> Upon a life I did not live,
>   Upon a death I did not die:
> Another's life, another's death,
>   I stake my whole eternity.

By that you have eternal life; by that you are born again.

9

RECESSIONAL AND PROCESSIONAL

JOHN 3:22-36

In this chapter we consider two magnificent statements:

1. John the Baptist delivers his own retiral address (vv. 22-30)
2. John the evangelist delivers an inaugural address for Christ (vv. 31-36)

OCCASION LENDS meaning to men's statements. We shall better understand John the Baptist's great utterance in the light of the events which called it forth.

He had been preaching and baptizing. The refrain of his message had been, "Repent . . . for the kingdom of heaven is at hand" (Matt 3:2). To his baptism Jesus had come, receiving the rite despite the Baptist's protest. Not long after, Jesus Himself was engaged in a ministry so similar to that of John that it looked like a rivalry. His preaching echoed the same call to repentance on the same ground that the Kingdom of heaven was at hand, and He carried out the same ordinance of baptism, only at the hands of His disciples—a mark of assumed superiority. The seeming rivalry became more apparent when some of John's disciples turned from him to follow Jesus. One scarcely wonders that a tinge of jealousy began to color the thoughts of John's followers. Just then a cantankerous Jew came at John's disciples on the question of ceremonial purifications, perhaps questioning the validity of John's baptism. The relation between baptism and the many Jewish ablutions would be a natural question. Whatever this questioning Jew said, his remarks seem to have fanned the flame of jealousy in the followers of the Baptist for their master's prestige. They could no longer contain themselves, but vented their resentment. "Rabbi, he that was with thee beyond Jordan, to whom thou barest witness, behold, the same baptizeth, and all men come to him" (John 3:26).

Moses was faced with the same type of jealous loyalty when Eldad and Medad, two of the seventy newly appointed elders, were heard prophesying in the camp, and Joshua offered the suggestion that they be forbidden to do that which would affect Moses' monopoly of the sacred gift. What a noble answer Moses gave! "Enviest thou for my sake? Would God that all the LORD's people were prophets, and that the LORD would put his spirit upon them!" (Num 11:29).

The reply of John the Baptist to his followers' complaint is of the same noble spirit. First he states the sovereignty of divine appointments, a recognition of which must abolish envy. "A man can receive nothing, except it be given him from heaven" (John 3:27). If John received his ministry from heaven, and Jesus in turn received His from heaven, what dispute could there be? Each one must fulfill his own ministry, his responsibility being to please Him who commissioned him. Using the apostle Paul's classic figure, the relation between servants of God must be that of the several members of the body, eye, ear, foot, hand, and the others, fulfilling their several functions without strife or envy, and every one essential.

John's answer goes further, showing the particular relation between him and the newcomer, his apparent rival. First, "I am sent before him" (3:28b). We think of Elijah girding up his loins and running ahead of the chariot of Ahab from Carmel to Jezreel in the drenching rain. The gorgeously caparisoned heralds who precede a royal procession may capture the fancy of children, but the massed throngs hold their shouts of greeting for the king himself. Originally a forerunner went ahead to see that the way of the noble personage was clear and smooth. So John affirms that he is the forerunner of the One who is now eclipsing him—sent to prepare His way and to turn men's eyes and hearts to Him.

There is yet another relationship. John calls himself the Bridegroom's friend, whose office is to present the bride, according to Oriental custom. The bride's father usually fulfills that office now, and when he answers the minister's question, "Who giveth this woman?" with his brief, "*I* do," he quietly retires to his seat, as much as to say, "I have handed this woman, my daughter, over to this man, who now becomes her husband, to be first in her affection, esteem, and devotion. From this moment I accept the minor place in her life." In like spirit John the Baptist said, "I have heard the Bridegroom's voice come to claim His bride, whom it was my business to present. My task is done, and my joy is full in the joy of my Friend, the Bridegroom. Most gladly do I withdraw, that the beloved Bridegroom may be all in all. Do we perform our service in such a spirit?

The last word is the retiring bow of a most noble knight. "He must increase, but I must decrease" (John 3:30). It was, so far as the record goes, the last public utterance of John. Next we see him in prison, sending a private message to Jesus—and after that, the execution to satisfy the revenge of a hateful woman. Here is the self-effacement of the true servant. I have been told that when a harp is in perfect tune, its strings vibrate invisibly, as if they would hide themselves in the melody. When we are rightly attuned to Jesus, we are hidden in Him. Michelangelo used to say, "The more the marble wastes, the more the statue grows." So it is only as this self of ours wastes and retires and goes out to the cross that the form and likeness of the Son of God can be seen. His increase is by my decrease. And it is only thus we find ourselves.

After that brief but magnificent retiring statement of the Baptist comes the even more vital presentation of the office and witness of the Christ.

First we are told His rank. He is "above all" (3:31a). If we consider His place among men, He towers as a mighty Everest above them all. If we contemplate Him surrounded by heavenly beings, angels, cherubim, and seraphim, He is still above all. Men and angels are alike creatures. Jesus finds His rank in the realm of the uncreated. No place is worthy of Him short of the eternal throne. No one stands His equal outside the Godhead. He belongs to that glorious, holy Trinity of Father, Son, and Holy Spirit, of one substance and in eternal equality. Whether we view Him as the Babe of Bethlehem, the Stranger of Galilee, the Lamb of Calvary, the High Priest in the heavenly sanctuary, or the returning Lion of Judah, He is still "above all," Lord of men and angels, Lord of all worlds, Lord of time and space, Lord of all.

Next we are informed that His testimony is an immediate one, not a relayed communication. "What he hath seen and heard, that he testifieth" (3:32a). In these words we are thrown back to the times of our Lord's preexistence in the presence of God. He brought His message from heaven. But He received it in two movements. The Greek verb translated "hath seen" is in the perfect tense, whose "basal significance is the progress of an act or state to a point of culmination and the existence of its finished results." Our Lord had a whole eternity of seeing, when the whole being of God and all the wonders of creation and the entire divine plan lay before Him as an open book. He came into the world with the fruit of all that seeing. But in the companion verb "heard," the Greek uses a different tense, which by contrast suggests that amazing moment when the eternal, equal Son divested Himself of the robes of His glory and stood before the throne as "the servant of Jehovah," and there "heard" from the lips of His Father, as in a commission, the things that He must speak on earth. In verses 26 and 38 of chapter eight, our Lord uses the same two tenses of the same two verbs to bring out the same difference of idea. The harvest of eternal open vision coupled with a specific command from the Father—that constitutes the testimony of Jesus. No wonder "he . . . [spake] as one having authority, and not as the scribes" (Matt 7:29).

The supreme-ranking but self-abasing Messenger was not bereft of communion with the Godhead during His humiliation. The Holy Spirit rested upon Him mightily. "For he whom God hath sent speaketh the words of God: for God giveth not the Spirit by measure" (John 3:34). The Holy Spirit wrought at the birth of Christ, was with Him in youth, came upon Him in a mighty anointing at His baptism, rested upon Him in His ministry, energized Him for the supreme sacrifice, and quickened Him from the dead. Jesus attributed His mighty works to the Holy Spirit, and now the same Holy Spirit is shown to be in the words He spoke.

It was no measured enduement that Christ enjoyed. "It pleased the Father that in him should all fulness dwell" (Col 1:19), and the fullness of the Spirit was included. Our blessed Lord, with His divine nature and His perfect attunement with God, had full capacity for the Holy Spirit, so His realization of the Spirit's fullness was unlimited, unmeasured. Now it is written, "Of his fulness have all we received" (John 1:16). Yes, He is willing to share that fullness of grace and truth, that fullness of the Spirit; but we are limited in our capacity, both by the deficiencies of our nature, and by our lack of submission to the perfect will of the Father. Lord, increase our capacity, and fill us with Thine own fullness!

10

THE MASTER SOUL-WINNER AT WORK

JOHN 4:1-30

In this chapter we look on as a soul is won by the tender love of Christ:

1. Jesus deals with a thirsty soul (vv. 7-15)
2. Jesus deals with a sinful soul (vv. 16-19)
3. Jesus deals with a seeking soul (vv. 20-26)

JUST AS I AM: Thy love unknown has broken every barrier down."
How heartily this woman of Samaria might have sung those lines. For if ever the Son of Man broke through barriers to reach a soul, it was in this very instance. No Jewish rabbi would have debased himself by teaching a woman, but Jesus did not allow the sex barrier to deter Him from His saving mission. What Jew would have stooped to converse intimately with a Samaritan? "The Jews have no dealings with the Samaritans" (John 4:9*b*), but Jesus, "being a Jew" (4:9*a*), began by asking a favor of this Samaritan woman. Had the Pharisees been around, they would have said, "This man, if he were a prophet, would have known . . . what manner of woman this is . . . for she is a sinner" (Luke 7:39). Jesus knew, and spoke to her just the same. So the sex barrier, the race barrier, and the moral barrier were all broken down by the Saviour. He will break down every barrier for you, too.

There are three distinct stages in our Lord's dealings with the woman of Samaria. First He dealt with her as a thirsty soul, then as a sinful soul, and finally as a seeking soul.

See how He used His own physical thirst as a means of approach to her spiritual thirst, and also how He disarmed prejudice by making a request which apparently left Him at her mercy. In soul-winning, as in all ministry, contact is a most important factor. We cannot tabulate methods of approach, but we can learn principles and seek wisdom from above for the application of them in individual cases. Two principles are in operation here. First, seek common ground. In this case thirst was that common ground. Second, set the party at ease. The Jew hated the Samaritan from his ground of superiority, while the Samaritan equally hated the Jew from his place of conscious inferiority. See, then, how the request for a drink would deliver this woman from that inferiority bond, set her at ease, and disarm much of the prejudice.

Of course the woman raised objections, but they were not the rebuffs that would have followed a less wise approach. They rather lent themselves to our Lord's progressive revelation and offer of the true, living water. Always try to discern between the objections of the willful unbeliever and the questionings of the longing soul. Jesus makes two statements, one of which the woman knew only too well from experience to be true; so that strong presumption would be aroused in her mind as to the truth of the second. The first was "Every one who keeps on drinking of this water shall thirst again" (John 4:13, author's trans.). Right well she knew that, and she knew also that all the earthly wells out of which she had constantly drunk had left her unsatisfied, disillusioned, unhappy. The second statement offered hope: "Whoso takes a drink of the water which I shall give shall never thirst for evermore" (4:14*a*, author's trans.). Our Lord made big claims and big offers, and the blessed thing is that He would substantiate them. We should so present the gospel that men will feel we have just what they need and what they must have. Let us do justice to our gospel and to our Saviour in our dealings with needy sinners. No wonder the Samaritan woman blurted out, "Give me that water!" (4:15, author's trans.).

In the fascinating account of their terrible journey across the Gobi Desert, Mildred Cable and Francesca French tell of coming across a man in the mule tracks so nearly dead that they had to lift him by the shoulders before he showed any sign of life. His one faint murmur

was "A drink of water and I am your slave for life!" Many around
us are just as desperate with spiritual thirst, but they do not know
the nature of their thirst, nor the cure. If only we could tell them
of the living, satisfying water as attractively as Jesus did, how many
of them would cry out, "Give it to me, give it to me!"

But thirsty souls are sinful souls, and sin must be dealt with before
salvation can be known. What is Calvary but the great divine necessity to deal with sin, fully, finally, eternally, in order to cope with
the whole range of human need? It is just at this point that all purely
human efforts at alleviation and uplift fail. They try to counteract
the effects of sin without dealing with sin. God, both out of His own
righteous nature and out of the necessity of the case, must and does
begin at the root. The cross of Christ is His all-sufficient answer.
Pardon, life, deliverance, reconciliation, peace—all come in the blood-
stream of Calvary.

Even as God must face the sin question in order to meet the needs
of men, so each man for himself must face his own sin question if he
would know the blessings of God's salvation. Immediately this
woman, then, made her request for the living water, Jesus brought
her face to face with her sin by one simple demand: "Call thy husband" (John 4:16). That touched the cancer, and brought to view
the whole panorama of sin, so that she afterward said to the men of
Sychar, "Come, see a man, which told me all things that ever I did"
(4:29).

Wise parents are careful not to punish their children until they
have some realization of wrongdoing. Forgiveness should never be
granted apart from a like sense of guilt, with an accompanying sorrow for the wrong. In the divine economy this is an absolute rule.
Even the gracious prayer of Calvary, "Father, forgive them; for they
know not what they do" (Luke 23:34), will be answered first by
bringing the guilty nation to a realization of what they have done.
"They shall look upon me whom they have pierced, and they shall
mourn for him" (Zech 12:10). Confession and repentance are involved in faith. Just as Joseph spoke roughly to his needy brothers
to bring them to a confession of their former sin before revealing
himself in reconciliation, so the Holy Spirit reproves first of sin in
order to lead to repentance and salvation. It is the hungry man who

values bread, and it is the guilty man who values pardon. Gospel preaching must include the notes of sin and repentance.

Did the woman at the well try to evade the sin question by posing a query on ritual and authority? Perhaps her question was a buffer to absorb some of the shock of Christ's unmasking statement. Even so, she did not deny the charge, nor did she put up any defense, but rather confessed her guilt in saying, "I perceive that thou art a prophet" (John 4:19). Then she revealed that with all her sin she was not wholly irreligious. Despised among her co-religionists for her brazen looseness of morals, there was yet a seeking spirit underneath it all. In her dark mind, worship was bound up with locality and tradition and ceremony. She was a seeking soul, and to her, in all her thirst and sin and darkness, Jesus gave that high, spiritual definition of true worship, whose full content the most enlightened and most spiritual among us has not yet apprehended. "God is Spirit," He announced, "and they that worship him must worship him in spirit and truth" (4:24). That was more than her groping mind could receive all at once, and in a sort of despair of any present deliverance she gave expression to a deep, perhaps long-smothered hope of the Messiah's coming, to which our Lord replied with a self-revelation more pointed than He was wont to give: "I that speak unto thee am he" (4:26).

It was a long step from a request for a drink of water to that declaration of Messiahship. He began with her thirst—that was most immediate in her consciousness. He proceeded to her sin—that must be unbared and put away. He encouraged her search, and rewarded it with a final "I am." No wonder she "left her waterpot" (4:28) in her haste to tell of her newfound Saviour! And while it was an act of forgetfulness in the excitement of a great moment, it was a symbolic act; for with a spring of living water bubbling up in her soul, no more would she have to trudge her weary way to polluted, unsatisfying wells of the world.

> I heard the voice of Jesus say,
>   "Behold, I freely give
> The living water; thirsty one,
>   Stoop down, and drink, and live."

I came to Jesus, and I drank
   Of that life-giving stream;
My thirst was quenched, my soul revived,
   And now I live in Him.

HORATIUS BONAR

11

THE SATISFACTION AND THE
URGENCY OF GOSPEL SERVICE

JOHN 4:31-38

In this chapter we are given a glimpse of the true spirit of service, as exemplified in our Lord:

      1. He has a heart to do the will of God
      2. He has eyes for the harvest of souls

CONVERSATION increases hunger. Jesus, hungry before meeting the woman of Sychar at the well, had carried on a long, earnest conversation with her, which would normally quicken the appetite; yet when the disciples returned with provision and the woman was gone, He did not turn to the basket with the expected zest. Indeed, He seemed to have forgotten His hunger, and the disciples were perplexed. With natural solicitude for their Master's comfort, they urged Him, "Master, eat" (John 4:31). His answer puzzled them still more: "I have meat to eat that ye know not of" (4:32). They did not for a moment suspect that the Samaritan woman had given Him food, so in their lack of spiritual understanding they could only wonder if somebody else had come along during their absence in the village. It was in answer to their perplexity that He made this wonderful statement, "My meat is to do the will of him that sent me, and to finish his work" (4:34).

Men can become so absorbed in a pursuit which holds them in suspense that they forget to eat. For the time being the fascination of their occupation seems to lend that satisfaction which food ordinarily imparts. I doubt if any people in the world relish food more or eat more ravenously than the Eskimos. Gontran de Poncins declares that he has seen half a dozen of them eat fifty pounds of meat at one "sitting," yet they will stand motionless, bent over a seal hole, for many hours, even into days, forgetful of hunger, in their intense eagerness to spear a great seal. If it be so with an ordinary mortal in an ordinary pursuit, can we wonder that the Son of God forgot the need of His body in the blessed occupation of leading a soul from darkness into light? Would that we had more of such a spirit!

I have heard preachers say, "I would rather preach than eat." I am not much of a gormandizer myself, so that I personally derive more pleasure from preaching than from eating. But our Lord did not say, "My meat is to preach," or "My meat is to do personal work," or even, "My meat is to save souls." He said, "My meat is to do the will of him that sent me." My pleasure in preaching may be very selfish, however orthodox and fervent the sermon may be. Your thrill in singing may be equally selfish, although your song may be the most spiritual and uplifting. It was not some particular form of service suited to His gifts and disposition that was meat to the Lord Jesus, but simply doing the will of the Father. Ordinarily God's will for us will be an occupation for which we have aptitudes, so that there will be a degree of natural pleasure in the task; but our real satisfaction is not to be simply in the exercise of our aptitudes, but in fulfilling that which we know to be the will of our Father. Then, if in the course of our service we are called upon to do that against which the flesh rises up in rebellion, the discipline of taking delight in the will of God will not be found so severe. We shall rather be able to rejoice that we are counted worthy to have fellowship in the sufferings of our Lord. If in such an hour also we can say, "My meat is to do the will of Him that sent me," we have learned the lesson of Gethsemane and Calvary.

There is an element of tragedy in Jesus' word to His disciples: "I have meat to eat that *ye know not of.*" The disciples were not wholly unspiritual, but they were yet only babes in spiritual attainment. This secret of satisfaction, so real to their Master, was still unknown to them. Is not our Lord's statement a foreign tongue to many of us today? Which is nearer the truth—"My meat is to do the will of God," or, "My meat is to have my own way"?

I asked the new day for some motto sweet;
Some rule of life by which to guide my feet:
I asked and paused: it answered soft and low—
　　God's will to *know!*

Will knowledge then suffice, new day? I cried;
But ere the question into silence died,
The answer came; Nay, this remember, too—
　　God's will to *do!*

Once more I asked: Is there still more to tell?
And once again the answer softly fell:
Yes, this one thing, all other things above—
　　God's will to *love!*

Lessons crowded in fast that day. Perhaps, on their way from the village to the well, the disciples had been remarking on the state of the crops, and reckoning four months to harvest. Now as the Lord spoke to them of the secret meat which was His, He lifted up His eyes toward Sychar and saw a group of men flocking toward Him, led by the woman. "Look!" He cried. "Harvest! You say four months to harvest? I have but newly sown, and already see the harvest white for reaping!" How often a season of harvest has looked remote, but God has laid hold on one key person, through whose conversion there has been a sudden turning of many to the Saviour. "Four months!" we have cried in despair. "White unto harvest!" has been God's answer.

What eyes our Lord had for harvest! When that excited group of men came hurrying from the village toward the well, what do you think was in the minds of the disciples? Rather likely they were saying, "Another interruption! Just when we are all ready to eat! As if we were not already positively famished!" On more than one occasion the disciples showed resentment at the intrusion of the crowd. But where they saw intruders, Jesus saw souls; where they saw only a crowd, He saw harvest. What do we see in the untimely caller? In the one who sells us gasoline and mends our tires? What do we see in the milling throngs of the great city? Oh for anointed eyes, to see as Jesus saw! If we have harvest eyes, we shall be keeping our sickle sharp and ready.

Too often our cry of "four months" is indicative of our spirit of procrastination. Being unready ourselves, we transfer our unreadiness to the souls we ought to win. I know the danger of "plucking unripe fruit," but there is equal danger of being "futurists" when the Lord is a "now-ist." "White already to harvest" (4:35*b*) is a warning as well as a statement, for whitened harvest, if neglected, can very quickly become blackened harvest. A few years ago, in a section of southern Ontario, in Canada, just when it was time to take in the harvest, rain started, and continued day after day, week after week, till wherever one looked in that whole countryside, grain lay blackened and ruined in the fields. No one could blame the farmers, but we may learn from that. Neglect of whitened harvest means blighted, blasted, blackened harvest.

Dr. Boreham of Australia tells how Donal Hunter made proposal very clumsily to Jean Cameron when he was about to leave Scotland for the Antipodes, and, meeting with rebuff, finally asked her, if ever her heart turned to him, to send him a sprig of the white heather that grew by the burn they both knew so well. Now Jean loved Donal, and every time she went down by the burn the impulse came to send that sprig of heather, but pride, or something, held her. Fifty years of delay on her part were matched with fifty years of watching on his part. Then she fell mortally ill. Lying at the point of death, she begged a niece to send a sprig of white heather to Donal, with news of her illness. That little bit of heather was laid on a grave in Australia, just three months old. The harvest of love, once white, had blackened.

If the call of the Lord Jesus, the call of His love and salvation, is upon you, act now, lest you be part of a blackened harvest when you cry, "Too late! Too late!" "Behold, now is the accepted time; behold, now is the day of salvation" (2 Cor 6:2*b*).

12

HOW FAITH GROWS

JOHN 4:43-54

In this study of a nobleman's faith we consider:

1. The request of faith (vv. 43-47)
2. The test of faith (vv. 48-50)
3. The reward of faith (vv. 51-53)

THE GALILEANS received him" (John 4:45), we read, but apparently their receiving was like the believing of those in Jerusalem, based on the thrill of seeing miracles. As in Jerusalem, Jesus did not commit Himself to the crowd. The similarity of situations is further accentuated by the emerging of a true believer as the Galilean counterpart of Nicodemus. This was a nobleman, or king's man, of Capernaum, an honorable servant at the court of Herod. The reason for his different attitude to Jesus is not far to seek—he had a personal need which he knew only Jesus could meet.

If a noted specialist in cancer were to make his home in our town, all our townsfolk would receive him as an asset to our community. Whether or not I became one of the famous physician's personal friends, I should share the general gratification at having him as a fellow citizen. Now if my beloved wife were in the advanced stages of this terrible disease, and her case had baffled all to whom she had gone for help, do you not think my attitude to this newcomer, the conqueror of cancer, would be something other than general esteem? I know I should be after him before ever he got his shingle hung out, pressing him to take over my wife's care immediately. It was, then, personal, conscious need which set this nobleman apart from the other Galileans, and brought him into a relation to Christ which so many others never knew. The same is true today. To multitudes Jesus Christ is a great historic figure whom they hold in sincere reverence and high admiration, knowing that He has turned the tides of history more effectively, and for greater good, than anyone else. That would sum up their whole attitude to Him. While others, conscious of a deep personal need, borne down with a burden of fear, of sorrow, of sin, have turned to Him as their only hope, and have entered into an experience of Christ unknown to the complacently interested. *Your* need may be a personal, spiritual one; it may be a home problem; it may be a straying son or daughter; whatever it is, fall behind the Galilean king's man, bring your need to Christ, pour out your request to Him, and you will know that "Jesus never fails."

The nobleman's faith was neither very vigorous nor very enlightened. Jew though he was, his faith could not match that of the Gentile soldier of the same town. But he had faith enough to bring his request to Jesus, and to make it urgently. Do not wait for more faith, or the "right kind" of faith. Bring what faith you have. Rather, bring your need, and the faith will be taken care of.

Faith must be tested. The faith of the Syrophenician woman was sorely tried, but with blessed results. The Lord does not try our faith to discourage us, but to add "praise and honour and glory" (1 Pet 1:7*b*).

The Lord's first answer to the urgent plea of the care-driven father was, "Except ye see signs and wonders, ye will not believe" (John 4:48). Did you notice that the Lord said "ye," not "thou"? Jesus did not set this man apart and accuse him as an individual of being a wonder-seeker. Rather, He took occasion to rebuke the shallow multitude, making this nobleman the channel. At the same time it was a searching of the man's own heart, to see whether he would dissociate himself from the cheap curiosity and selfishness of the crowd and cling to Christ.

The response was magnificent. He did not make any attempt to parry the stroke, to deny the charge, or to justify himself. He simply pressed his need, as much as to say, "If thou, Lord, shouldest mark iniquities, O Lord, who shall stand?" (Psalm 130:3). I ask only mercy. My need is my plea. "Come down ere my child die" (John 4:49). God cannot resist that kind of pleading. So long as a man will justify himself, God will find an answer of condemnation; but let a man say "Amen" to the divine judgment, and plead mercy, that man will be justified.

While honoring the cry of need, the Lord still further tried the suppliant's faith. The nobleman could think of only one method of deliverance for his child, namely, the actual, visible presence of Jesus in the home. "Come down ere my child die!" he cried. Jesus would have him learn that he could not dictate the divine method. Have not we been guilty of that many times? "Lord, do this for me; and in case You don't know, here is the way to go about it!" Absurd, is it not? Then, too, Jesus would teach this nobleman the true essence of faith—complete reliance on the bare word of the Lord. "No, I shall not go down, but go thy way; thy son liveth. Art thou willing to rest upon My word alone?" That was the final test; and while a test, it was also a mercy. If the nobleman would receive it, his mind would be immediately eased; whereas, had Jesus gone with him as requested, would not the father's fear have increased every moment that they might be too late? God's way is always best, and God's way is always the faith way. If we would know real peace, the end of carking anxiety, we must learn to accept and lean upon His sure word, not waiting for feelings and evidences.

It was a different faith which the nobleman carried home from that which he brought to Jesus. It was a tested faith, a sifted faith, an intelligent faith, and a victorious faith. That in itself is a great reward of faith, but other rewards awaited.

Halfway home, or more (for I think the eager father had speedier feet that day than the servant!), he was greeted with an echo of the words of Jesus, "Thy son liveth!" (John 4:51). This time it was the report of the accomplished fact, given by an eyewitness. That was not enough for a man who had stepped out into the life of faith. Sir Henry Jones, for many years the professor of moral philosophy in Glasgow University, Scotland, wrote a book which he entitled, *A Faith that Enquires*. All true faith inquires. Faith launches us on a great ocean of inquiry. The rejoicing father's next query, then, was not the question of doubt, but the inquest of faith. "What time did the boy begin to improve?" (see 4:52). The answer was better than his faith. He expected to hear that improvement became noticeable shortly after that seventh hour when Jesus had said, "Thy son liveth," but the truth was more wonderful than that. It was not a matter of "beginning to mend," but the boy had felt the fever depart, as if he had awakened from a bad dream, and the immediate recovery had sent the servant hurrying to report to his master. "So the father knew that it was at the same hour, in the which Jesus said unto him, Thy son liveth" (4:53).

Are such answers to prayer known today? In Sault Ste. Marie, Canada, a few years ago, a Salvation Army officer of my acquaintance became greatly burdened for his unsaved son away from home, whereabouts unknown. He gave himself to prayer on a certain day, until the Holy Spirit put a great assurance in his heart. Two days later he received a letter from his boy, to this effect: "Yesterday I was on the train going from Toronto to Windsor, when it suddenly struck me that I was going to hell as fast as the train was taking me to Windsor. I could not shake it off, so I knelt down on my knees in the railway coach and asked God to save me." Later inquiry, like that of the Capernaum nobleman, discovered that the boy's experience on the railway train was "at the same hour, in the which Jesus said unto him [the father], Thy son liveth."

"Jesus Christ the same yesterday, and to day, and for ever" (Heb 13:8). Hallelujah!

13

THE CONTROVERSY BREAKS

JOHN 5:1-18

In this chapter we observe how a simple occasion had complex results:

1. The occasion—gracious ministry (vv. 1-9)
   - a) Jesus seeks out His man (vv. 1-5)
   - b) Jesus deals with His man (vv. 6-9)

2. The results—prejudiced accusations (vv. 10-18)
   - a) Sabbath-breaking (vv. 10-16)
   - b) Blasphemy (vv. 17-18)

WHERE THERE IS a predisposition to controversy, the storm can break on very slight provocation. The prejudices of the Jews did not require much of a spark to make a conflagration, and, as we shall see, Jesus supplied the spark in the course of His most gracious ministry.

This simple incident is illustrative of still more principles put in operation by the master Worker, from whom we must learn if we would well serve. First, in seeking out His man, Jesus goes to the congregation of the needy, and there picks out the neediest of the congregation. Where would He be more likely to find someone needing His healing touch than among the crowd of "sick, blind, halt, withered" (John 5:3, ASV) at the pool of Bethesda? And what more needy one could He choose for healing than this man, thirty-eight years an invalid, and always too late to reach the water when its healing quality was present and active? "The Son of man is come to seek and to save that which was lost" (Luke 19:10) is His own statement of the principle, beautifully illustrated here. A good fisherman fishes where there are fish. It is all right for a little child to hold a hookless, baitless line tied to a little stick over a fishless puddle of water in a pretence to be fishing, but a man so engaged would be considered "peculiar." I remember seeing one of my fellow townsmen practicing his casting in one of the quieter streets, and I did want to laugh. It was only practice, and no doubt that same man was wise enough to go where the fish were when he really went fishing. Many of the evangelistic services held in our churches these days are efforts to fish where there are no fish. What about getting out to some pool of Bethesda where the lost are?

Jesus went directly to the neediest of the needy. There is no case beyond His practice, and the greater the sinner, the greater demonstration of His grace. "Where sin abounded, grace did much more abound" (Rom 5:20). Tackling some really hard cases would be good for many a Christian worker. I am not prepared to say that the deliverance of a man who has spent many years far down in sin is a greater miracle than the salvation of a child and the preservation of the life from sin's defilements, but we must not confine our efforts to children because they are more easily reached. The big sinner needs Jesus too.

Watching our Lord's method with this man, important principles emerge. He first grapples with the man's will. That is the citadel of the soul, and in this instance Jesus made a frontal attack. "Wilt thou be made whole?" (John 5:6b) is a question referring to the action of the will, not to the presence of a passive wish or desire. When the leper came to Jesus for healing, he said, "If thou *wilt*, thou canst make me clean," and Jesus answered, "I *will*; be thou clean" (Matt 8:2-3, italics added). The same verb is used here. God will never save a man against his will. Every man must say, "I will," to the Saviour. A hope to be saved someday will not suffice. With the man at the pool it was most necessary to stir up the will to be healed which he had well-nigh lost over the long years of disappointment.

The very recounting of his case, coupled no doubt with the inspiring presence of the Lord Jesus, stirred again the slumbering will, and Jesus next called the man's faith into play by the command, "Rise, take up thy bed, and walk" (John 5:8). It is noticeable that He did not give this man's faith any outward assistance beyond the word of command. He did not take him by the hand and lift him up.

Like the nobleman of Capernaum, this cripple was cast upon the bare word of the Lord. He must act in faith; and he did. As he obeyed he discovered the new strength, just as the ten lepers realized their healing in the path of obedience.

Will, and faith: that is the order. A man's will to be saved must be aroused, then the way presented upon which his faith can lay hold. All this is equally applicable to ailing Christians. Whatever spiritual blindness, lameness, dumbness, deafness we may have, the Lord challenges us to will to be made every whit whole, then bids us rise and walk the path of obedience, in doing which we shall find our strength renewed, our vision clarified, our stumbling cured.

What a furor was created by this act of healing! We admit that the Sabbath was not ordinarily the proper day for moving furniture, but occasion lent propriety to the act. What better day to give the evidences of Christ's power to heal and save? However, Pharisaic interpretation of the Law would not allow it, although the Law itself provided for the watering of beasts or the rescue of an endangered animal on the Sabbath. Since, then, the penalty for Sabbath breaking was death, and the rulers took him to task on such a grave offense, the healed man trembled, and shifted the responsibility onto the One who had healed him. Now Jesus had so quickly been swallowed up in the crowd that the man had not had opportunity to identify Him. It would seem, then, that the persecutors threatened the poor fellow that he had better help them to spot the Sabbath breaker or else he would have to answer for his own crime. At any rate, he was properly scared, and almost wished he had never been healed. While in that state of confusion, Jesus met him, and warned him not to continue in his sin, lest a greater evil than his former ailment should come upon him. Apparently his paralysis had been the fruit of his own sin. What an opportunity he had to cast himself upon the care of his Saviour, but instead he went right back to the Jews with the report that it was Jesus who had healed him, knowing right well that they were not interested in Jesus as a Saviour and Benefactor, but as a Sabbath breaker. He would expose his Deliverer to the wrath of the Jews to save his own skin.

The persecutors then turned on Jesus with their charge of Sabbath breaking. Already they were thirsty for His blood. He answered their threats magnificently: "My Father worketh hitherto, and I work" (John 5:17). He told them in effect that if they charged Him with Sabbath breaking they would have to include His Father in the charge, with whom He was working in the closest possible cooperation.

The Jews perfectly understood to whom Jesus was referring when He spoke of "My Father," for now they "sought *the more* to kill him, because he had not only broken the sabbath, but said also that God was *his own Father,* making himself equal with God" (5:18, italics added). They had determined on His death for Sabbath breaking, now all the more for blasphemy.

Did Jesus claim deity when He called Himself the Son of God and God His Father? The Jews so understood Him, and crucified Him for it. Had he meant otherwise, how easily He could have corrected their error and saved Himself! Why did He not say, "I am simply using these terms to teach you that God is the Father of all men and all men sons of God?" Because He was not so using the terms. He was calling God His own Father in such a sense that if He were not very God of very God, the Jews did right to put Him to death. Our Lord never disputed the charge, but went to His death as One who claimed to be, as none else, the Son of God. What is your answer to His claim? "Crucify him!" (John 19:15), or, "My Lord and my God"? (20:28). As for me, I worship with convinced Thomas.

14

FATHER AND SON

JOHN 5:19-20

The remainder of the fifth chapter of the gospel is rich in revelation:

1. The relationships of the Son (vv. 19-20)
2. The prerogatives of the Son (vv. 21-30)
3. The witnesses to the Son (vv. 31-47)

We shall consider these in three consecutive chapters, and in the present one deal with

The relationships of the Son:
1. Dependence on the Father
2. Equality with the Father
3. Communion with the Father

OUR STUDY has brought us to a passage of Scripture so sublime that it leaves the maturest and most enlightened believer panting for very wonder. Yet those words of astounding revelation were spoken to a group of unbelievers who were bent on the destruction of the Lord Jesus, whom they were charging with Sabbath breaking and blasphemy. Was Jesus then casting His pearls before swine? By no means. These representatives of Jewry must hear the claims of the divine Messiah, whether the testimony became to them the instrument of illumination and life or of confusion and death.

We who believe approach this chapter of revelation with awe, dazzled as by the glory of the throne room. How can we scale such heights? "Such knowledge is too wonderful for me; it is high, I can-

67

not attain unto it" (Psalm 139:6). Let us pray that the Holy Comforter may take of these things of Christ and reveal them unto us.

In this address of our Lord's to the Jews, which some think was given as an official answer before the Sanhedrin to the charges laid against Him, I find three main topics dealt with: the relationships of the Son, the prerogatives of the Son, and the witnesses to the Son.

In the matter of relationship, we are first informed of the Son's dependence on the Father. "The Son can do nothing of [or from] himself, but what he seeth the Father doing" (John 5:19, ASV). This is not the dependence of impotence, nor that of inferiority, but the dependence of unity and of voluntary subservience.

A railway car can do nothing without the engine. It has no power in itself to speed across the continent. The power has been built into the locomotive, and when that is operated and controlled it will pull a hundred cars. The dependence of the Son on the Father is not that of the railway car on the engine. "All power is given unto me" (Matt 28:18), He says. His being unable to act "on His own" is not for want of power or ability.

On the human plane we might think of two people entering into a solemn agreement that neither one will ever act without the other in certain defined matters. Within the sphere of that agreement one of the parties may be brought under pressure to act, but he will say, "I cannot act on my own in this matter. My agreement with my partner makes it imperative that we act together." Only the case between our Lord Jesus and the Father is not merely one of mutual covenant. The agreement is written into the very divine nature, so that if the Son acted "from Himself," He should not simply be breaking a contract, but belying the divine nature in which He and the Father are one.

There is, however, a covenant involved here also. The mighty undertaking of redemption necessitated a rearrangement of relationship within the Godhead. The Son, foreordained to execute the task, assumed the role of Servant. Here is the apostle Paul's tremendous statement: "Christ Jesus . . . being in the form of God, counted it not a prize to be on an equality with God, but emptied Himself, taking the form of a servant" (Phil 2:5-7, author's trans.). As the perfect Servant, He had no independent will, but had one will with the Father. "I can of myself do nothing" (John 5:30, ASV) was His constant attitude.

Are we also, by His infinite grace, servant sons of our heavenly Father? Then it is our privilege, as also our highest duty, to sink our will in the will of God, to refuse independence of action from God, to hold body, mind, all, sacred to His "good, and acceptable, and perfect, will" (Rom 12:2).

In this sphere of holy relationship we read next of the equality of the Son with the Father. "What things soever he [the Father] doeth, these the Son also doeth in like manner" (John 5:19, ASV). The dependence and the equality are not contradictory or mutually exclusive. It is here clearly indicated that our Lord's voluntary humiliation did not affect His essential and eternal equality in the Godhead. When Paul tells us that "Christ Jesus . . . being in the form of God, thought it not a prize to be on an equality with God," he does not imply that Jesus gave up that equality. He simply undertook to express that equality in a new relationship, in the form of a Servant rather than in the form of God. The God character and the Servant character were always His. In the outshining of the God character, with all its glory and majesty, His equality with God was manifest to all the heavenly host. When He chose to assume the servant place and give the servant character full expression in the work of redemption, that equality must of necessity be hidden in the garment of humiliation. His rights to full expression of divine glory He voluntarily laid aside, but that did not touch the fact of equality. It is this fact which is indicated in these words our Lord, "What things soever he [the Father] doeth, these also doeth the Son likewise" (5:19).

Think into that tremendous claim. Here is a Man standing before a group of Jews who have already accused Him of blasphemy and are seeking His death, pressing home His claims with the statement that there is no work of God of which He is incapable or which lies beyond the sphere of His own activity. That man is either mad, or He is God. What say you?

Have we not a mighty Saviour? When we trust the Lord Jesus for our salvation, we commit ourselves to the One in whom all God's works are wrought. He who created the heavens and the earth out of nothing, who hangeth the earth on nothing, who brought order and beauty out of our universal chaos; He who sustained divine equality in human flesh, who burst the bands of death, who carried His own conquering humanity right up to the throne of God: is not He able to meet our need and save our souls? He has borne heavier loads. He bears along the ages, He bore the sin of the world. The bridge that can carry the transcontinental train will bear a mouse. And Jesus can carry me! "He is able also to save them to the uttermost that come unto God by him, seeing he ever liveth to make intercession for them" (Heb 7:25).

Last in this category of relationship is communion. "For the Father loveth the Son, and sheweth him all things that himself doeth" (John 5:20). Here is love in all its divine perfection and in its most glorious expression. God is the ultimate source of love, and love is His ultimate character. "God is love" (1 John 4:8). Here, too, is the perfect object of love—the Son, the full outshining of God's glory and the exact image of His person. "The Father loveth the Son" (John 5:20a). This is love's supreme relationship. It is impossible for us to comprehend the ineffable bliss of this interflow of love within the Godhead. With the infinite capacity for love in God, its absolutely unrestrained and unlimited expression; with the infinitely perfect object upon which to bestow it, no shadow of sin or disappointment or fear to cloud it: oh, we are lost in the very attempt to ponder such love!

This love knows no secrets. "The Father loveth the Son, and sheweth him all things that himself doeth" (5:20). The Father finds a perfect sympathy and understanding in the Son which heightens the joy and glory of all His works. What communion is this! The nearest to perfect love in this world looks on from far distances. Happy are we if in any of the love relationships of life we realize the faintest echo, the merest shadow, of such complete communion. And to think that a Man once walked this earth who knew such fellowship with God!

What can it mean? It must surely mean that God is seeking to draw man up to Himself to share this love, this communion. Does not our Lord speak to us in such a strain? "As the Father hath loved me, so have I loved you" (John 15:9). "Thou didst send me, and lovedst them, even as thou lovedst me" (17:23, ASV). "He that loveth me shall be loved of my Father, and I will love him, and will manifest myself to him" (14:21). "No longer do I call you servants; for the servant knoweth not what his Lord doeth: but I have called you friends; for all things that I heard from my Father I have made known unto you" (15:15, ASV). Can we catch the awful, blessed reality of it all? Love set upon us like to that which interflows within the Godhead: loved by both Father and Son as the Father loves the Son—and we shall not forget the love of the Spirit which is ours too: loved with a love which yearns to lead us into every mystery, every secret of God!

> Loved with everlasting love,
>   Led by grace that love to know;
> Spirit, breathing from above,
>   Thou hast taught me it is so!
> Oh, this full and perfect peace!
>   Oh, this transport all divine!
> In a love which cannot cease,
>   I am His, and He is mine.
>
> WADE ROBINSON

What was the purpose of the equal Son's assumption of a Servant's dependence, but to bring this love to you and to me—by way of the cross? Not apart from the sharp pangs, the deep darkness, the bitter cup, the awful load, could we be brought to God in reconciliation and into the fellowship of sons. "Behold, what manner of love the Father hath bestowed upon *us,* that *we* should be called the sons of God" (1 John 3:1, italics added). What response have we given Him for all this?

15

THE PREROGATIVES OF THE SON

JOHN 5:21-30

In this chapter we consider the claims of Jesus Christ to three divine prerogatives:

1. Life: inherent, sovereign
2. Resurrection: of life and judgment
3. Judgment: as Son of man

IT IS THE PREROGATIVE of the Son of God to have life in Himself. "For as the Father hath life in himself, even so gave he to the Son also to have life in himself" (John 5:26, ASV). Tremendous statement! Remember, it is a Man who is speaking: the Son of God indeed, but speaking as the Son of Man. How can life be both derived and inherent? How can it be both bestowed and essential? In the mystery of the divine Being, in the community of the Godhead, life must be inherent in the Son as in the Father, for They are one. How, then, *gave* the Father to the Son to have life in Himself? I can see no other explanation than that the Father gave to the Son the right to carry over that inherent life of His divine nature into His assumed humanity. By this life of God the humanity of Jesus is glorified. Surely our partaking of the life of God is made possible only because of its transmission to humanity in the person of the Son of God. Does not this cast light on that wonderful verse, "God hath given to *us* eternal life, and this life is *in his Son*" (1 John 5:11, italics added)?

Electrical power comes across country from the great power plants in cables carrying as heavy a load as 133,000 volts. Suppose that were directly shot into our homes, with the equipment that we have generally installed. Every lamp, every element, every fuse would be blown,

72

and perhaps more serious damage would ensue. To introduce this great electrical power into our homes, the current is passed through transformers which break down the high voltage to 110, and then the living current rushes safely and efficaciously to every room of the house, to operate our motors, light our lamps, cook our meals, clean our rugs, and minister in a hundred ways.

What alienated sinner could come into contact with the power of the life of God, and endure? It would be to us as consuming fire. But Jesus Christ is the Transformer of the current of divine life. It is inherent in His deity. He transmits it to His humanity and by uniting us with Himself sends that life of God in human voltage coursing through our souls. It enters every part with its mighty regenerating and sanctifying power until it is written, "If any man be in Christ, he is a new creature: old things are passed away; behold, all things are become new. And all things are of God" (2 Cor 5:17-18).

This life may be had by all. It costs to carry the electric current into a home, to install the wiring, the outlets, and all the rest of the equipment. But "the *free gift* of God is eternal life in Christ Jesus our Lord" (Rom 6:23, ASV, italics added). The Lord tells us in this chapter how the contact is made. "The hour cometh, and now is, when the dead shall hear the voice of the Son of God; and they that hear shall live" (John 5:25, ASV). Later on He will speak of physically dead people. Here He has in view the spiritually dead, "dead in trespasses and sins" (Eph 2:1). There is life for every one of them—eternal life, divine life—just for the hearing. It is no idle hearing, however, that will secure such great gain: not the kind of hearing that you give to the radio when you are barely more than conscious of its being turned on. This is the hearing of attention, the hearing of obedience, the hearing of faith. See what the immediately preceding verse says: "He that heareth my word, and believeth on him that sent me, hath everlasting life" (John 5:24). Give heed to the call of Jesus Christ, let all your resistance against Him cease, commit your soul and your life over to His care and keeping, and that moment you will come to life with the surge of the life of God. Make the contact of faith with the Lord Jesus and the current will flow—the power of divine life, the illumination of divine light, the warmth of divine love.

The voice of the Son of God cries aloud today, but its quickening power is known only by those who give heed. One day that voice will ring with a new note of universal command, and every ear will awaken, every mortal respond. "The hour cometh, in which all that are in the tombs shall hear his voice, and shall come forth" (John 5:28-29, ASV). No longer is it the voice of invitation, but the voice of summons.

The day came when this same Jesus stood before a sepulcher from which the stone had, by His command, been rolled away. He lifted up His voice in imperious tones: "Lazarus, come forth" (John 11:43). And Lazarus walked forth from the tomb which had held him for four days. It was a discriminating cry, particularizing one man. Had it not been so, every grave would have cast forth its dead that day. I have no doubt that our Lord called forth His friend Lazarus in demonstration of this declaration now before us. If He can summon one from the dead by name, He can summon all.

But there is discrimination here also. Two resurrections are stated to result from the shout of the Son of God—the resurrection of life, and the resurrection of judgment. True, if we had this passage only, we should think that it was one general resurrection, in which the good and the wicked were to rise together, to receive respectively at the hands of the Judge their commendation unto life and their condemnation unto death. In the light of other Scriptures, however, we see that here we have another instance of a very common phenomenon in prophecy, two far distant events being seen together, as if one.

I remember being tested in judging the relative distances of cars. The testing case looked like an automobile game in a slot machine. The glasses through which one looked from the side of the case made the tiny toy cars seem very far away. The one being tested was to stop the machine when the two cars appeared side by side. Generally they turned out to be some distance apart. Prophecy frequently gives us events in one view that actually are separated in fulfillment, sometimes by long periods. In the Old Testament, the two comings of Christ are often seen in perspective as if they were one. The "day of the Lord" (1 Thess 5:2), which actually covers a whole era, is seen from the distance as an event. So here, the Lord's purpose is not to indicate the temporal relation of the two resurrections, but the fact of them, with this emphasis, that it is His voice that will call all men, good and bad, from the tomb.

No man can afford to turn a deaf ear to the voice that will call him at last either to life or to death, to commendation or to judgment, to a share in the Holy City or to a part in the lake of fire. It is the part of wisdom to listen to that voice now when it invites to life, to salvation and peace and rest, lest you at the end hear its resistless tones summon you to stand in confusion and nakedness before the great white throne. "To day if ye will hear his voice, harden not your hearts" (Heb 3:15). "Hear, and your soul shall live" (Isa 55:3).

All this leads naturally to this last-mentioned prerogative of the blessed Son of God—that of judgment. "For neither doth the Father judge any man, but he hath given all judgment unto the Son" (John 5:22, ASV). There is a false conception abroad that would characterize God the Father as a stern, vindictive Judge, demanding vengeance on every slightest mistake of men, and God the Son as tender and merciful, seeking to appease the Father's wrath and to mitigate His judgments. That is horribly false. It is true that *the Son of God . . . loved me and gave himself for me*" (Gal 2:20, italics added), and that "we have not an high priest which cannot be touched with the feeling of our infirmities; but was in all points tempted like as we are, yet without sin" (Heb 4:15). But it is also true that *"God so loved the world, that he gave his only begotten Son*" (John 3:16, italics added). How many Scriptures bear witness of the love, mercy, tenderness of the Father! Then we have this further testimony, that judgment is given over to the Son. Do you think, then, that the lowly Jesus will be light in judgment and give you an easy go-by, after all your rejection of Him, your multiplied sins that have cried out to heaven? You are forgetting another side to the character of the blessed Lamb of God. He is also the Lion of Judah. When once He sits for judgment, you will face the Lion, not the Lamb. If you have trodden underfoot the blood of the Lamb, you will be trodden under the feet of the Lion. Then I counsel you and beseech you, "Kiss the son, lest he be angry, and ye perish from the way, for his wrath will soon be kindled" (Psalm 2:12, ASV).

For two reasons the right of judgment is given to the Son. The first is, "that all may honor the Son, even as they honor the Father" (John 5:23, ASV). Many are willing to give a certain honor to God in the abstract, but refuse to acknowledge Christ. That will never please the Father. We used to have a crude expression, "Love me, love my dog." Without irreverence let me apply it. God says, "Love Me, love My Son," "Honor Me, honor My Son"; and to ensure that "at the name of Jesus every knee should bow, . . . and . . . every tongue should confess that Jesus Christ is Lord" (Phil 2:10-11). God has bestowed on Him this divinest of all prerogatives—universal judgment.

Judgment is given to the Son that no mouth shall ever be opened to question the justice *and the mercy* of the judgment. "He gave him authority to execute judgment, *because he is a son of man*" (John 5:27, ASV, italics added). No man will ever be able to answer when the sentence of eternal death is passed upon him, "God, You don't understand. You are passing judgment on creatures whose temptations and weaknesses You have never known. You have judged poor, frail men by impossible standards of divine power and holiness." There will be no such answer, for He who bears the scepter of judgment bears also the scars of those days when "He . . . suffered being tempted" (Heb 2:18), when He "was in all points tempted like as we are, yet without sin" (4:15), when He "suffered . . . the just for the unjust, that he might bring us to God" (2 Pet 3:18). A man, even the Son of Man, will be your Judge. Therefore I say unto you in His name, "Agree with thine adversary quickly, whiles thou art in the way" (Matt 5:25). Turn the Judge into your Friend, as He seeks now to be. Accept Him as your Saviour, as He died to be. Hear now the word of the Judge Himself! "He that heareth my word, and believeth him that sent me, hath eternal life, and *cometh not into judgment, but hath passed out of death into life*" (John 5:24, ASV). Will you now hear and believe?

16

WITNESSES TO THE SON

JOHN 5:31-47

In this chapter four witnesses are cited to substantiate the claims
of the Lord Jesus:

1. John the Baptist (vv. 32-35)
2. The works of Christ (v. 36)
3. The Father Himself (v. 37)
4. The Holy Scriptures (vv. 39, 40, 46, 47)

SUCH CLAIMS as Jesus made for Himself in the foregoing verses require substantiation. The Mosaic Law required two or three witnesses to establish a matter. Our Lord went beyond the requirements
of the Law and cited four witnesses. The first of these was John the
Baptist, who was universally regarded as a prophet. The Sanhedrin
had sent an official delegation to him to inquire into his mission, and
the report of his declaration at that time was in their possession. He
had disclaimed Messiahship but had proclaimed the Messiah. John's
witness was official in the double sense of his having been definitely
sent by God to herald the coming of Christ, and his having delivered
his message to an official committee of the Sanhedrin.

Our Lord put the stamp of His approval upon John's witness.
"Truth," He called it, challenging the Jews to believe it, and so believe in Him. He recalled the intensity of John's ministry. "He was
a burning and a shining light" (John 5:35a). He spoke the truth
clearly, and he spoke it with warmth. There was no dead, cold ortho-
doxy in the Baptist. He was willing to be consumed in the heat of his
own witness—and so he was. Ice cubes may be very clear, but they are
very cold. On the other hand, heat is no guarantee of clarity. The

clear mind and the warm heart are both needed for effective witnessing.

John's ministry stirred quite a revival in Israel. They were "willing
for a season to rejoice in his light" (5:35b). There was a great shaking
of the dry bones, expressed in much confessing and repenting and
baptizing, as expectation grew for the coming of Messiah. But it was
only seasonal. Today we would blame the revivalist, saying, "He just
stirred folks' emotions, and there was nothing to it!" We should have
to go counter to our Lord's estimate, however, to blame John. The
fault was not with the preacher, but with the people. They were glad
of the light he brought them, but when the light began to burn down
into the sin cancers like an acetylene torch, they objected to the heat
of it. Many today are quite willing for the shining, but refuse the
burning.

John's witness had its limitations. He was but a man, and how can
a mortal fully witness to One who, being very God, is utterly beyond
human comprehension? Would a common private be able to gauge
an officer's qualifications for general rank? No more can a man, even
sent from God, fully witness to the glories of the Son of God. Other
witness must be called. Jesus next cites His works. "The works which
the Father hath given me to finish, the same works that I do, bear
witness of me" (John 5:36). This is not a reference simply to the
occasional miracles of our Lord. It is the works in their totality,
the works as they must finally be manifested in their finished state,
that are the great witness that "Jesus is the Christ, the Son of God"
(20:31). Every deed of mercy, every word of grace, was contributing
its part as Jesus wrought and taught, but it is in view of the finished
whole that "every knee shall bow, . . . and . . . every tongue . . . confess
that Jesus Christ is Lord" (Phil 2:10-11). He was engaged in these
works before He came to earth, He continued them in the days of His
humiliation, they occupy Him now in the glory, and one day the
finished work of Christ will appear in the new heaven and the new
earth.

But there is in every part the essence of the whole. We are told that
a drop of water contains all the essential phenomena of the ocean, and
an atom is a universe in itself. Every work of Christ bears the character of the great whole, and the divine imprint is discernible for all

who have eyes to see. Divinely authorized and dutifully accomplished, they all carry distinctly evidential value. The very fact that gospel sermons can be preached so consistently from the words and works of Jesus indicates their redemptive worth, and shows that they are all part of the great divine whole.

The third witness is "the Father himself" (John 5:37). Does this refer to the voice of approval at the baptism and the transfiguration? It would seem that only John and Jesus heard the first, while only three disciples, with their Lord, heard the second. It must be something more universal. The perfect tense used in this regard suggests a witness which God put into the world with abiding effects. I believe it is a witness which is implanted in every man, and which intuitively recognizes the truth concerning Christ when it is presented. Call it conscience if you will. It is the ally within every man of the testimony of the gospel, and which all who reject the gospel must fight down, whether with reasonings, excuses, or outright refusal. It is this inward pressure that accounts for the strenuous reactions in many, so different from their reactions to an insurance or book salesman. The witness of the Father is surely that inner voice which keeps saying its "Amen" to the testimony of Christ, and which will not be silenced.

The last witness cited is the Scriptures. "[Ye] search the scriptures; for in them ye think ye have eternal life: and they are they which testify of me" (5:39). That Christ is the grand subject of Scripture is an axiom with us. "In the volume of the book it is written of me" (Heb 10:7). The reference is, of course, to the Old Testament Scriptures. There we have Christ foreshadowed in the histories, typified in the ordinances, anticipated in the songs, predicted in the prophets: and we can add, manifested in the gospels, proclaimed in the Acts, interpreted in the epistles, unveiled in the Apocalypse.

Despite this clear witness, it is possible to search the Scriptures and not find Him. The scribes were diligent searchers of the sacred volume, yet they missed Christ. To preserve the accuracy of Holy Writ, they would count the words in every book, determine the middle word, and see that every copy conformed. Destructive critics do much searching in the book. They can tell what chapters, verses, and parts of verses were written by J, E, D, P, R, ad infinitum. But scribes and critics seem to be alike in their "great omission." The pages do not present to them the "Christ, the Son of the living God" (John 6:69). We may be neither scribes nor critics, yet miss the vision, but if we sit at the feet of the Holy Spirit, He will take of the things of Christ and reveal them to us.

While the Scriptures are the great abiding witness of Christ, they do not of themselves impart life. The scribes thought that the handling of the sacred Word had sacramental value for salvation. Jesus corrected their error, showing that the value of the Scriptures lay in their pointing to Him, that men might come to Him and live. Knowledge is not life, but knowledge is responsibility. Our responsibility is the greater if we know the Scriptures and do not come to Him of whom they speak. "*I* am the way, the truth, and the life: no man cometh unto the Father, but by *me*" (14:6, italics added).

How many redeemed souls since Jesus spoke these blessed words could rise up and say, "Let one more attest. I have known this Jesus, and His power and grace in me bear witness that He is the Son of God." And still another witness every believer has, proof against all specious reasonings and subtle temptations: "He that believeth on the Son of God hath the witness in himself" (1 John 5:10) —the constant assurance of the indwelling Holy Spirit.

17

HOW TO HAVE PERENNIAL REVIVAL

JOHN 6:1-13

In this chapter one of Christ's great miracles is seen to be a parable of life on the highest plane:

1. Vision: seeing the multitude with the eyes of Jesus (v. 5)
2. Provision: what is enough for one is enough for all (v. 9)
3. Distribution: multiplying hands and multiplied hands (v. 11)
4. Collection: the law of compensation (v. 13)

JESUS LIFTED UP His eyes. That was habitual with Him, as it was with His father David. The hills used to draw David's eyes upward.

> Hills draw like heaven,
> And stronger sometimes, holding out their hands
> To pull you from the vile flats up to them.

So sang Elizabeth Browning, and David found it so. The hills were God's prophets to him, speaking of the divine encircling and protection. The dome of heaven with its starry hosts also called to the sweet singer of Israel, until he sang, "The heavens declare the glory of God; and the firmament sheweth his handywork" (Psalm 19:1). Then his vision mounted still higher, and he cried, "Unto thee do I lift up mine eyes, O thou that sittest in the heavens" (Psalm 123:1, ASV). Great David's greater Son had this habit also. Twice it is recorded that He lifted up His eyes to God, and twice upon men. We shall never see far if we are continually grubbing. Vision is for those who will lift up their eyes.

On this occasion it was a great multitude that Jesus saw on lifting up His eyes. But real vision consists in the *how* of the seeing. The

81

disciples saw the crowd too, but they did not see what Jesus saw. Some count men as they count cattle—so many head. Others, thinking in terms of labor, count so many hands. To others the multitude is the gauge of success, the criterion of popularity. Holy eyes read something else: they see need. "When he saw the multitude, he was moved with compassion on them, because they fainted, and were scattered abroad, as sheep having no shepherd" (Matt 10:36). Unshepherded sheep, distressed and scattered—that is what Jesus saw. Again, with the men of Sychar hurrying toward Him, He cried to the disciples, "Lift up your eyes, and look on the fields; for they are white already to harvest" (John 4:35). Needy sheep, whitened harvest—that is what Jesus saw. Put in a word, the crowd spelled to our Lord *need*, great need, unspeakable need. Do we wonder that He who could sense the hunger of a Nicodemus, who could discern the thirst of a Samaritan woman, who could appreciate the longings of a Zacchaeus, would read multiplied need in a great crowd? Once we have apprehended the worth and the need of the individual in the light of eternity and of Calvary, we shall have the correct vision of the multitude—such vision as Spurgeon had when he wept at the sight of thirty thousand gathered to hear him preach in the Great Crystal Palace. May the Holy Spirit anoint our eyes so to look upon men!

He who envisions the need will seek provision for it. Our Lord immediately broached the subject, first asking Philip's thought. Philip was the calculator, the arithmetician. Moreover, he was not figuring on a too lavish scale. A little for all was the limit of his reckoning. Timorous Andrew came a bit nearer the mind of the Lord, for he had a serious thought about meeting the need of the hungry crowd. His first thought seems to have been that perhaps Jesus could do something with the little fellow's lunch, but as soon as he mentioned it, either his faith caved in with the apparent grotesqueness of the thought, or he feared he was making a fool of himself before the other disciples, so he retreated with an apologetic "but what are they among so many?" (John 6:9).

The five bannocks and two sardines were sufficient for one healthy boy's lunch. Now we know that barley increases and fish multiply in the normal processes of nature, but that does not apply to baked loaves and dead fish. Our Lord's miracle, then, was not any speeding

up of nature's processes. It was a parable of the principle that provision for one is provision for all. God has not provided a separate
sun for every individual, but one sun for all, yet each one of us needs
all there is of the sun. If there were only one man in the earth he
would need the whole sun. Yet what is required for one is enough
for all. That is God's way in salvation. If there were but one sinner
on earth, he would still require the whole mighty plan of salvation.
Anything short of it would not avail. Yet that provision required
for one is sufficient for all. That is why "whosoever will may come."
Of that great truth Jesus gave us a parable when He made one boy's
lunch adequate to the needs of over five thousand people.

We must remember that it was only when the lad gave up his few
sandwiches that they multiplied into provision for all: that it was
only when the widow of Zarephath yielded to the strange demand of
the prophet, "Me first," that her store became perpetual: and that it
is only as we hand ourselves over in glad consecration to God that He
can use us to bless those about us.

Where did the multiplication take place. I am very sure that was
done in the hands of Jesus. His are the miracle-working hands. Yet
He required multiplied hands to distribute the multiplied loaves.
When the widow came to Elisha with her distress, telling how her
late husband's creditors were about to take her two boys in payment
of debts, he told her to gather as many vessels as she could find and
fill them with oil out of the one cruse she had left. So long as there
were vessels to receive it, there was oil to fill them. The supply staid
only for lack of vessels. Likewise, lack of distributing hands stays
the miracle-working hands of our Lord.

The disciples could not do the multiplying, but only the distributing. They would soon exhaust what they carried in their arms from
the hands of Jesus. How could they replenish their store for distribution? By going back to Jesus: and so long as they kept in touch
with that source of supply, they continued to bless the multitude with
food. If we, as ministers and Christian workers, are not "feeding"
the hungry folks around us, it is just because we are not keeping
in touch with Jesus. Sermons may be orthodox, and Bible teaching
a marvel of "rightly dividing," but these will not feed the hungry
unless they are being brought straight from the hands of our blessed

Lord. We cannot easily breathe out twice without breathing in. We cannot minister without constant returning to the reservoir of all power. Dr. Alexander Whyte preached an unusually solemn and impressive New Year's sermon in Free St. George's, Edinburgh. One of his devoted members followed him to the vestry, and said, "It went to my heart as if you had come straight from the Audience-Chamber." "And perhaps I did," replied the minister.

A collection was made at the end of the meeting. "Gather up the fragments that remain, that nothing be lost" (John 6:12). Prodigality marks all the divine economy, but this also, "that nothing be lost." And a little later in the chapter we read, "This is the Father's will which hath sent me, that of all which he hath given me I should *lose nothing*" (v. 19, italics added). I feel safe in the hands of such a Saviour!

What was done with the crumbs? No, I don't think they all went to the disciples. I am sure the little fellow who gave up his lunch carried home, with the help of strong Peter, enough to keep himself and his little and big brothers and little and big sisters eating for several days. For that is in keeping with the divine law of recompense.

> We lose what on ourselves we spend:
> We have as treasure without end
> Whatever, Lord, to Thee we lend,
>   Who givest all.

To be continually rich in revival blessing, keep the vision clear, keep the consecration unbroken, keep in touch with Jesus, and keep giving.

18

A STORMY CROSSING

JOHN 6:15-21

In this chapter we consider a typical interpretation and a practical application:

1. Typical interpretation:
   - *a)* A view of the cross
   - *b)* A view of the ascension
   - *c)* A view of the church
   - *d)* A view of the return

2. Practical application:
   - *a)* The *meaning* of the storm
   - *b)* The *Master* of the storm

THIS INCIDENT of the stormy crossing followed immediately the feeding of the five thousand. In all the synoptic accounts it is specified that Jesus *blessed and broke the bread,* which recalls the manner of His institution of the Lord's Supper. In the latter case He immediately said, "This is my body" (Matt 26:26), and while He did not so speak about the distribution to the five thousand, the next day He made that distribution the basis of His teaching on the living bread, which He declared was His flesh. This is sufficient justification for considering the miraculous feeding, with its blessing and breaking and distributing of bread, a parable of the cross.

After the miracle, seeing the rising tide of clamor among the people to make Him king, He sent His disciples, unequal to such a situation, to the other side of the lake. All by Himself He subdued the spirit of the crowd and dismissed them, and immediately ascended the mountain to give Himself to prayer. We cannot but associate this with His ascension into "the hill of the Lord," into heaven itself, to the very throne, after His passion, where "he ever liveth to make intercession" (Heb 7:25) for us. So we have a view of the ascension.

If this incident gives us a glimpse of our ascended, interceding Saviour, our living "advocate with the Father" (1 John 2:1), we shall not be surprised if we find some representation of the church during that advocacy. Just before going up to His place of prayer on the mountainside, Jesus sent His disciples out onto the sea. The sea in Scripture is often used as a symbol of the nations in all their restlessness and confusion. Into that very sea our Lord sent His church, represented in the group of disciples around Him, just before ascending to the Father. "Go ye therefore, and teach all nations" (Matt 28:19). "Go ye into all the world, and preach the gospel" (Mark 16:15). "Ye shall be witnesses unto me both in Jerusalem, and in all Judea, and in Samaria, and unto the uttermost part of the earth" (Acts 1:8).

The sea did not receive the twelve very kindly that day. The storm burst upon them, whipping the waters to fury, until they were "tormented in rowing." The parable was acting according to the pattern. It was a furious reception that the world gave the infant church as it launched on its agelong mission. All down the centuries the storm of opposition has continued with varying force. The stones, the scourge, the cross, the stake, the torture chamber, exile—these are but a few of the weapons that the nations have used against the church of Christ; but the Lord, sending His church forth as sheep in the midst of wolves, gave a guarantee that "the gates of hell shall not prevail against it" (Matt 16:18). The sea could beat against the little ship, but it could not engulf it. Once before the disciples had faced storm that threatened their boat, but then Jesus was asleep in the stern, and

> No waters can swallow the ship where lies
> The Master of ocean, and earth, and skies.

Now they were as safe with Jesus praying on the mountainside as they had been with the beloved Master on board. So the church is as secure in the midst of all its foes, with its great Head praying at the right hand of God, as if it were already the church triumphant and at rest.

The end of the story, then, is not shipwreck, but the appearing of the Lord. He came to them on the water. He came to them through the storm. Immediately He stepped on board, they found themselves "at the land whither they went" (John 6:21), not a fraction off their course! The moment He arrived, they arrived. What a blessed picture of the return of the Lord Jesus, coming to and for His harassed, persecuted, tempted, tormented church! Then immediately, the storm will be over, the port reached, heaven gained, and "so shall we ever be with the Lord" (1 Thess 4:17).

Coming now to application, we consider the meaning of the storm. On the part of the disciples there was reaction. They had just witnessed, and had a part in, one of the greatest of our Lord's miracles. Their hearts had been fired with wonder, adoration, exultation. From that mountaintop of exhilaration they were quickly plunged into the trough of fear, despondency, and despair. Their impotence and torment in the midst of the waves were but aggravated after the uplifting experiences of the day. We do not read that they exhorted one another to faith in the One who prayed for them on the hillside! We are told only of their torment. In our human experience the juniper tree is not far from the peak of Mount Carmel. We must be very thankful that God does not dismiss His servants as soon as they get "down in the dumps." True, He cannot use us while the cloud of despondency is on us, but He sends His angels to prepare special diet for His run-down ministers, brings them back to Horeb, the mount of God, and sends them forth recommissioned and renewed. God knows how to save us from the storms of reaction.

What may be regarded as reaction on our part may be as truly counterattack on Satan's part. Our Lord did not yield to despondency as we so quickly do, but storm followed blessing in His experience. After the voice of loving approval at Jordan, acclaiming Him the beloved Son, came the forty days of fiery temptation in the wilderness. If Satan would so attack the Son Himself after a special blessing, he certainly would try to rob the disciples of all the blessing of that day of glorious participation in miraculous distribution. Hence the storm with its threatening and tormentings. We had better be well girded after times of unusual blessing and triumph. The counterattack will come. But fear not: "When the enemy shall come in like

a flood, the Spirit of the LORD shall lift up a standard against him"
(Isa 59:19).

God has something to do with the storm. The Lord knew that the
squall would rise in vicious fury that night, yet He sent His disciples
into it. For their destruction or hurt? On the contrary, for their
highest good. He must test them. After the demonstration He has
given of His power and (in symbol) of His cross, He must see whether
they will trust Him in the dark, in the storm, when they cannot see
Him. "When he hath tried me, I shall come forth as gold" (Job
23:10).

> When through the deep waters I cause thee to go,
> The rivers of sorrow shall not overflow;
> For I will be with thee, thy troubles to bless,
> And sanctify to thee thy deepest distress.
>
> JOHN RIPON

After all, Satan, though "prince of the power of the air" (Eph
2:2), is not master of the storm. The Master was up there on the
hillside. He was watching, seeing every toilsome stroke of the impotent oars. He was praying lovingly, availingly. In due time He came,
the great Deliverer. He is Master of our storms, too, and "he stayeth
his rough wind in the day of the east wind" (Isa 27:8). He is our
prevailing Advocate, faithful in His intercessions though all earthly
friends should forget us. And, even as He joined Himself to the three
Hebrews in their furnace of affliction, and came to His tormented
disciples in the midst of their storm, so He makes His presence, love,
and power known to us in all our afflictions. "Be of good cheer; it is
I; be not afraid" (Matt 14:27). That is the still, small voice that
quiets the tempest.

19

THE BREAD OF LIFE

JOHN 6:22-40

In this chapter we trace our Lord's answers to a series of Jewish errors, leading to the first "I am" of this gospel:

Error 1. Putting the passing in place of the permanent (vv. 26-27)

Error 2. The religion of DO (vv. 28-29)

Error 3. The philosophy of "seeing is believing" (vv. 30-33)

Error 4. Asking without apprehension (vv. 34-35)

AT THE BURNING BUSH God declared to Moses His ineffable name, I Am. It seems at first like an incomplete name, but actually it is the name of infinite, eternal, absolute Being (the name of Being without modification, without qualification, without boundary, without limit).

Coming over into John's gospel, we again find the great name, I Am, compounded in such a way as to relate it to human needs. What does man need? Being "dead in trespasses and sin" (Eph 2:1), he needs life. Walking in darkness, he needs light. Straying like a lost sheep, he needs a shepherd. Soul hungry, he needs living bread. Groping in a maze of error, he needs truth. Lost in a trackless wilderness, he needs a way that leads to God. In this gospel, then, the mighty God comes down and once again pronounces the name of infinite Being, but this time linked to these very needs. "I am the way, the truth, and the life" (John 14:6), "I am the good shepherd" (10:1), "I am the light of the world" (8:12), "I am the bread of life" (6:35).

The section now before us brings us to the first of these "I Am" declarations. What leads up to this remarkable name is a dialogue in which our Lord answers a whole series of Jewish errors. Here is grace indeed, that Jesus would recompense all their folly and blindness and prejudice with such a blessed revelation of Himself.

We shall consider the errors of the Jews in order to appreciate our Lord's answers. First, they put the passing in place of the permanent. "Ye seek me," said Jesus, "not because ye saw the miracles, but because ye did eat of the loaves, and were filled" (6:26). They had full stomachs yesterday, and they liked the feeling, so they were coming back for more. It would be no hardship to follow Jesus if He would run a free miracle restaurant for them!

The apostle Paul wept over certain "enemies of the cross of Christ" (Phil 3:18), whose particular mark was that their god was their belly. The term in Scripture is used to signify the natural appetite. Of all the things that men seek after, how many are for the satisfaction of natural appetite? Is not that practically all that most men live for? Yet it is a bad bargain, for it all passes away, and even while it lasts does not give the satisfaction it promised. "Wherefore do ye spend money for that which is not bread? and your labour for that which satisfieth not? Hearken diligently unto me, and eat ye that which is good, and let your soul delight itself in fatness" (Isa 55:2). By such words the prophet Isaiah sought to turn the men of his generation from the passing things to the permanent, from the merely sensual to the spiritual.

The "Prodigal Son" of Luke fifteen went into the far country, seeking what? Fine clothes, good shoes, sparkling jewelry, lots to eat, and a merry time. Did he find these things? Instead, he got rags, bare feet, starvation, wretchedness. When he returned home, however, he found all that he had reckoned on finding in the far country. He received the best robe, shoes, the ring, the fatted calf, while it was his own father who said, "Let us . . . be merry!" (v. 23). The far country had only substitutes to offer, with the sting at the end. The reality was found in the Father's house. Only in Christ shall we find what the soul needs—the "meat" which endureth unto everlasting life" (John 6:27).

The second error of the Jews was their clinging to the religion of DO. "Then said they unto him, What shall we *do*, that we might work the works of God?" (6:28, italics added). The essence of the Law is, "If ye *do* these things, ye shall live by them" (see Lev 18:5). The elders and scribes added to the Law, thinking to add more merit and make sure of salvation, until it was an unbearable load. "This *do*" could well sum up all human religion. Sometimes it is a moralistic DO, and sometimes it is a ritualistic DO. A few weeks ago, the theosophical society announced that the ritual of the Mystic Dawn would be performed in their national headquarters right close to us. This ritual, they assured us, brought to people a deeper realization of God. Ritual never has, never will, bring men to God. Neither will moral living make men pleasing to Him. God is interested neither in our religious performances nor our good behavior until we come to the one thing needful. "This is the work of God, that ye believe on him whom he hath sent" (John 6:29). Believing on His Son is the first act of man that is well pleasing to God. After that there will be lots of doing, but instead of the works of man offered to God for salvation, they will be the works of the Holy Spirit wrought in and through the already saved man—and these are acceptable to God. Let us keep things in God's order. "By grace are ye saved through faith; and that not of yourselves: it is the gift of God: not of works, lest any man should boast. For we are his workmanship, created in Christ Jesus *unto* good works, which God hath before ordained that we should walk in them" (Eph 2:8-10, italics added).

The third error was the philosophy of "seeing is believing." "What sign shewest thou then, that we may see, and believe thee?" (John 6:30). That is a false philosophy. For one thing, the contrary is far more true, that "believing is seeing," and then, as Jesus reminded them, believing does not invariably follow seeing: "Ye also have seen me, and believe not" (6:36). It is not more seeing, more evidence, that is required, but the will to believe. God has given abundant evidence, in the works of nature, in the testimony of history, in the practical effects of the gospel, in the millions of lives transformed, to satisfy anyone who has the will to believe. If anyone will not believe, then, the cause is not lack of evidence, but "an evil heart of unbelief" (Heb 3:12).

The Jews suggested to Jesus what they would accept as satisfactory evidence of His claims to their faith and allegiance. He had given

them one meal, but Moses, they hinted, had fed them for forty years
with bread from heaven. It really was not more evidence they were
looking for, but just more full stomach. In replying, Jesus corrected
them on three points. "Moses gave you not that bread from heaven;
but *my Father*" (John 6:32, italics added). That was point number
one. The second one went still further: "The bread of God . . .
giveth life" (6:33, italics added), which the manna did not do. Angel's
food as it was, it only sustained temporarily the physical life. "Your
fathers ate . . . manna in the wilderness, and they died" (6:49, ASV).
In the third place, "the bread of God . . . giveth life *unto the world*"
(6:33, ASV, italics added). It is universal in its scope, not national
or racial.

Jesus had made it clear that the bread He offered was God-given,
life-giving bread, yet they were still thinking in terms of stomach-
filling bread. Notwithstanding their carnal thought, our blessed Lord
proceeded to the great revelation, giving them full opportunity to
correct their error and receive Him. "I am the bread of life: he that
cometh to me shall never hunger; and he that believeth on me shall
never thirst" (6:35). Can we really fathom that statement? Some
truths lie on the surface. Here it is indicated that the bread of life
is a Person, that the fountain of all human satisfaction is a Person,
that all need finds its supply in a Person. And that Person is Jesus,
our Lord. *Things* can never fill the soul of man, whether things to
eat, things to see, things to wear, or things to do. Neither can the
human soul be filled with another human soul, even as one empty
vessel cannot fill another empty vessel. Only by living touch with the
infinite fullness of God can the deep hunger of man be satisfied. God
made it so in creating us, as St. Augustine put it, "Thou hast made
us for Thyself, and our restless hearts can know no rest until they
rest in Thee." That divine fullness is conveyed to us in the divine-
human person of our Lord Jesus, in whom all fullness dwells.

The way of realization is so simple. No elaborate ritual needs to
be learned, no initiation into secret mysteries undergone. Come,
believe in Jesus as able and ready to meet your need; that is the end
of your hunger, the last of your thirst. The fountain of all satisfaction, nourishment, and life is in Him. "O taste and see that the
LORD is good" (Psalm 34:8).

20

EATING FLESH AND DRINKING BLOOD

JOHN 6:41-71

In this section our Lord advances three further thoughts in elaboration of the statement, "I am the bread of life." The unfavorable reactions of His hearers are made the stepping-stones of these new stages of revelation:

1. "The bread . . . is my flesh" (v. 51)
2. "And my blood is drink" (v. 55)
3. "The words . . . are spirit" (v. 63)

UP TO THIS POINT in the chapter Jesus has made two great statements: (1) that He *gives* the bread of life (v. 32), and (2) that He *is* the bread of life (v. 35). All the wonderful revelation surrounding these statements was given in face of prejudice and misunderstanding. Despite the increasingly unfavorable reaction of the crowd, which finally affected even a large group of His own followers, Jesus continued to enlarge on this deeply spiritual truth until He had fully expounded it. Every renewed evidence of antagonism was made the occasion of further illumination, which, if it did not profit them that heard it because of their unbelief, has come down to all generations to enrich and bless untold millions.

Our Lord's declaration of His heavenly origin met with much murmured dissent among the Jews. How could a fellow Galilean, whose whole family connection they knew thoroughly, be other than themselves? It is related that a later contemporary of Thomas Carlyle visited the hometown of the famous man of letters. On making inquiries regarding the Carlyle family, he received rather grudging admissions from some of the old-timers that there was a "Tammas in the family, who went to London and wrote books and things," but the real man among all the brothers was one who had made a record in driving hogs to the Ecclefechan market! That same spirit of refus-

ing to recognize one of ourselves as in another category from ourselves
dictated the dissent of the Galilean Jews from our Lord's claim to
heavenly origin.

Jesus answered the murmuring with another statement packed full
of gospel truth. First, He showed the process of the work of grace.
The Father does a twofold work. He draws (v. 44), and He teaches
(v. 45). The sinner gives a twofold response. He comes (v. 45),
and he believes (v. 47). Whoever then will give this appropriate
response to the divine plea "hath eternal life" (v. 47, ASV). The
striking aspect of all this process is that it centers in Jesus Christ. It
is to *Him* the Father draws men, of *Him* the Father teaches men; to
Him sinners come, in *Him* sinners believe; and through *Him* men
have eternal life.

Reverting to the figure of bread, Jesus reiterates His claim, "I am
the bread of life" (6:35), and definitely draws the contrast between
the manna, which could not keep the fathers from dying in the wilderness, and Himself, the bread that makes men immortal, deathless.
Then He defines the bread more closely as His flesh, given in sacrifice for the life of the world. We have been told in the great Logos
chapter, that "the Word was made flesh" (1:14), a phrase indicating
our Lord's assumption of our humanity. This giving of His "flesh"
for the life of the world, can only refer to His yielding Himself as
Son of Man to the death of the cross for the redemption of man.

If our Lord's declaration of His divine origin disturbed the Jews,
His statement of divine purpose and mission properly roused them.
Their dissension grew from a murmuring to a bitter contention.
"How can this man give his flesh to eat?" (6:52). The idea of eating
the sacrifice was not at all foreign to them, and they could not but
see in the words of Jesus a reference to that well-known practice.
Their reaction to the thought was utter repudiation, so that they
almost had a "free-for-all" over it.

Once again the imperturbable Christ answered the dissent by carrying His doctrine still further, now adding the blood to the flesh, in a
triple proposition. Negatively, eating the flesh and drinking the
blood of the Son of Man is the "sine qua non" of life for men (v. 53).
Positively, thus partaking of the flesh and blood of the Lord Jesus
imparts eternal life and assures a place in the resurrection of life

and blessedness (v. 54). Further, eating and drinking of this sacred meat are the means of communion, through mutual indwelling (v. 56).

The question pressingly arises. What does it mean to eat the flesh and drink the blood of the Son of Man? One will suggest that we do this at the Holy Communion, the ordinance of the Lord's Supper, in instituting which our Lord said of the bread and the wine, "This is my body" (Matt 26:26), and "This is my blood" (v. 28). While indeed these phrases suggest the ordinance, I am persuaded that they do not refer to it, but that both refer to a common third which is the fulfillment of both. The communion service is not an end in itself, but is a fingerpost, pointing to the same spiritual reality spoken of by our Lord in the words now before us. We do not have to go far afield for an explanation of this mystical language. Eating is to satisfy hunger, and drinking is to quench thirst. The meat which Jesus offers is His flesh, the drink He provides is His blood. How do we eat of His flesh and drink of His blood? He has Himself told us in verse 35 of this chapter: "He that *cometh to me* shall never hunger; and he that *believeth on me* shall never thirst" (John 6:35, italics added). If the coming to Him is the end of our hunger, and the believing on Him the end of our thirst, then the coming and the believing are the eating and the drinking. But it is a coming to Him and a believing on Him *as the sacrificed One,* the crucified One, the One who *in His death* accomplished all that the ancient altar taught of substitution, atonement, reconciliation. That same sacrifice we recall at every partaking of the simple communion feast, and there we renew our faith and love.

In adding the blood to His former statement, our Lord introduced an astounding thought. Blood-covenanting is a primitive rite of well-nigh universal practice. The intermingling of blood, either by mutual tasting or by intertransfusion, made men blood brothers, closer than natural brothers. Fifty times Henry Stanley exchanged blood with African chiefs, so sealing friendship with them, until H. Clay Trumbull wrote in his remarkable book, *The Blood Covenant:* "The blood of a fair proportion of all the first families of equatorial Africa now courses in Stanley's veins; and if ever there was an American citizen who could appropriate to himself preeminently the national motto, 'E pluribus unum,' Stanley is the man."

The blood covenant was not unknown to the Jews. God's covenant with Israel was essentially a blood covenant, as every sacrifice testified. There was, however, this difference, that partaking of the blood was strictly prohibited among them. The prohibition went even further than the blood of the sacrifices, to include the blood of animals eaten in ordinary fashion. When Jesus, then, spoke of Himself in terms of the altar, and added the requirement that they must drink His blood as well as eat His flesh in order to secure life and fellowship, not only the already dissenting Jews, but many who had received Him and were following Him as disciples, shrank from His teaching. "This is a repulsive saying" (John 6:60, author's trans.), they exclaimed. They are not the last who have found the teaching of the blood repulsive. The trend of "modern" Christianity is to get rid of this "slaughter-house religion," as it is called. For myself, there is something more repulsive in the sin that needs washing away than in the blood that cleanses it; nor do I regard those whose "delicate sensibilities" are offended by the doctrine of the blood as more refined than my blessed Lord who taught that we must eat His flesh and drink His blood in order to live.

The Saviour's answer to the murmurings of His disciples is equally an answer to all modern objections to His teaching. He was not talking, He declared, in physical or sacramental terms, but spiritual. The full content of His words we may not explore while still in the body, but it becomes evident that our Lord regarded His redemptive work as centering in His death, and He would focus our attention there.

The cross is always a weapon of division. The stream always divides there. So as our Lord held up His death as the instrument of life, "many of his disciples went back, and walked no more with him" (John 6:66), but Peter, spokesman for a loyal group, reaffirmed an unshakable faith: "We believe and are sure that thou art that Christ, the Son of the living God" (v. 69). On which side are you?

> Whoso has felt the Spirit of the Highest
> Cannot confound nor doubt Him nor deny:
> Yea with one voice, O world, though thou deniest,
> Stand thou on that side, for on this am I.
>
> Meyer's *Saint Paul*

21

CHRIST'S UNBELIEVING BROTHERS

JOHN 7:1-10

The seventh chapter of our gospel revolves around the Feast of Tabernacles, and falls into three sections:

1. The going up to the feast
2. The middle of the feast
3. The last day of the feast

The incident concerned with the going up to the feast tells us of the unbelief of Christ's brothers:

1. The *fact* of the unbelief (v. 5)
2. The *expression* of the unbelief (vv. 3-4)
3. The *answer* to the unbelief (vv. 6-8)

WERE IT NOT STATED unequivocally in the Scriptures, I should not accept it. That these men should have had the Lord Jesus for a big Brother, should have grown up in the light of His always perfect character and known the benefits of His never failing kindness, and then not believe in Him, is well-nigh unthinkable. Some of us have loved ones in our family circle who do not believe. Perhaps that is because we are failing in our testimony. But if we are living as we ought and faithfully praying and witnessing, we may draw comfort from this, that "neither did his brethren believe in him" (John 7:5), despite His utter perfection. There is further encouragement in this, that they did not remain unbelievers forever, but after His resurrection they rallied round Him and became humble worshipers and servants of their divine Brother. We may still hope and pray for our kinfolks.

Why did they not believe in Him while He was still a member of their common household? There is only one explanation—the evil heart of unbelief. It was no lack of opportunity, it was no defect in Christ; it was just that sinful bent which was as native to them as to us. Their being born of the same mother as our Lord did not make them saints, or exempt them from the depravity common to our race. Indeed, their unbelief, in face of such unparalleled privilege and blessing, is one of the greatest proofs of that natural depravity.

This lack of sympathy and understanding in the home is an indication also of the awful solitariness of Jesus. Taking the widest view, "He was in the world, and the world was made by him, and the world knew him not" (John 1:10). Narrowing it to His own nation, "He came unto his own [things], and his own [people] received him not" (v. 11). Think of the attitude of the rulers and of the vast majority of the common people. Within the circle of His followers He was still a lonely Man. As He set His face to the cross, He could not arouse the sympathetic understanding even of His closest disciples. Now we see that even the home roof was not hospitable to Him. His zeal was mistaken for madness, and "neither did his brethren believe in him" (7:5). In all the world He found no asylum from His loneliness. There came a time when, for our salvation, He must suffer being bereft of the Father's staying presence, becoming in that dark hour the one God-forsaken Man.

We shall never know such solitariness. In times when we are misunderstood, maligned, misinterpreted, and we seem to be very much alone, He will say to us, "I will never leave thee, nor forsake thee" (Heb 13:5*b*), and He understands.

Christ's brothers expressed their unbelief in a strange fashion. At first their words would appear more like an expression of faith, urging Him on, but the Holy Spirit says they were the words of unbelief. "Depart hence, and go into Judea, that thy disciples also may see the works that thou doest" (John 7:3). It was rather presumptuous, to say the least. Their words were evidence that they did not believe in His wisdom, His plan, His program, His methods. He was acting foolishly according to their view. How then could they regard Him as the "Christ, the Son of the living God" (6:69)? What assumed the form of good advice, then, was really a definite expression of unbelief.

The world will always have good advice to offer to God's servants, sometimes very friendly and well meant, sometimes subtle and with ill intent. Our Lord's great prototype, Moses, fell into the snare of accepting advice from the best-intentioned father-in-law in the world on how to run God's business. He set up, without consulting God about it, the organization that Jethro proposed for distributing the responsibilities of leadership. It was not long till he had to scrap it in favor of God's own plan of seventy Spirit-filled elders. The Spirit of God is a better Counselor for the direction of the work of God than all the worldly-wise about us. It is the part of true wisdom to submit all proferred counsel to God for His approval or otherwise.

The advice given our Lord by His brothers smacked very much of the temptation in the wilderness. Here is the reasoning of the brothers: "There is no man that doeth any thing in secret, and he himself seeketh to be known openly. If thou do these things, shew thyself to the world" (7:4). Put alongside that: "Then the devil taketh him up into the holy city, and setteth him on a pinnacle of the temple, and saith unto him, If thou be the Son of God, cast thyself down: for it is written, He shall give his angels charge concerning thee: and in their hands they shall bear thee up, lest at any time thou dash thy foot against a stone" (Matt 4:5-6). There is the same thought—make a big demonstration, do something sensational, and the crowd will accept you. And this—don't go the hard way; avoid the cross. Even Peter urged the same counsel on his Master: Pity Thyself, do not go the cross way! But whether the lips were a brother's, or a disciple's, the Lord recognized the hiss of the serpent, and thrust the self-saving and self-advertising advice from Him.

Our Lord's reply to His brothers' unbelieving and presumptuous suggestion was twofold. First, He told them that He was living a divinely timed life. He was going by God's clock. That word, "My time is not yet come" (John 7:6a), may have ultimate reference to the cross, for our Lord often referred to His suffering and death by that term. Here, however, it has primarily to do with His going up to the Feast of the Tabernacles. Everything in His life was timed from above, every day was gauged, every hour measured, every minute marked on the divine chart. That is why He arrived at the well of Sychar just in time to meet the needy woman there; that is why He went into the synagogue just when the man with the withered hand was there—and so all through His life. Perhaps the reason we find so few opportunities for service is that our lives are not finely adjusted to the divine schedule, not timed by the divine clock. Like the brothers of Christ, our "time is alway ready" (7:6b) in that we have no set time. We act according to custom, according to popular demand. We are driven by the winds of necessity, whim, chance, popularity. The will of God can never be realized in an irresponsible life like that. The biographer of Robert Morrison, Marshall Broomhall, says of the great pioneer missionary that he "filled each unforgiving minute with sixty seconds' worth of distance run." That could only be possible by living a God-directed, God-timed life. Otherwise we may have sixty seconds worth of action, but not of distance run.

The second item in our Lord's answer was equally telling: "The world cannot hate you; but me it hateth, because I testify of it, that the works thereof are evil" (7:7). Lord Chesterfield, that supreme type of the man of the world, gave us a maxim which is universally true: "If you would make men think well of you, make them think well of themselves." The Lord Jesus came to make men face their sins until they should cry out, "God be merciful to me a sinner" (Luke 18:13b). Until they came to that, they certainly did not take well to Him or His teaching. When you are one with the world, you do not require to time your contacts with it; but when you are making an assault upon its hypocrisy and godlessness, the accurate timing of warfare is demanded. We may be sure of our full twelve hours if we allow God to control the minutes.

22

ANSWERING JEWISH PREJUDICES

JOHN 7:14-36

In this chapter three distinct prejudices of the Jews come to light, and our Lord answers them:

1. Prejudice concerning His teaching (vv. 14-18)
2. Prejudice concerning His works (vv. 19-24)
3. Prejudice concerning His mission (vv. 25-36)

THE FEAST is now in full swing, and Jesus, having gone up to Jerusalem, is boldly teaching in the Temple. "The Jews marvelled" (John 7:15a), we are told, but their wonder took the form of offense. "How knoweth this man letters, having never learned?" (7:15b), they murmured. That He knew learning, they had to admit; but He had not received it in the rabbinical schools, He was not a seminary-trained man, so He could be regarded only as an unauthorized, self-made upstart.

There has always been a strong element of prejudice against unlicensed preachers, or those who have not received the approval of the hierarchy. England has its own epic story of the struggle of the free churches. How their ministers, not having episcopal license or ordination, were persecuted, imprisoned, even beheaded, in the conflict for freedom! John Bunyan spent years in Bedford Jail just because he preached without authorization of the state church.

Christ's answer to this prejudice began with a blunt denial that He was a self-made, self-taught Man. "My teaching is not mine, but his that sent me" (7:16, ASV). He had both learned in a higher school and received ordination from higher hands than any of the rabbis and scribes. His teaching was from God, and God had sent Him to pro-

101

claim it. Even today, if an unlettered man has listened to the voice
of the Spirit of God, and his heart is fired by the zeal of the Spirit, he is
more learned in divinity and is more authorized to preach than the
finest product of our finest seminary if the latter be lacking that personal enduement from God.

Christ's further answer to this prejudice against His unlicensed
preaching turned on the Jews themselves. There is one way, He told
them, by which you may certainly discover whether My teaching is
unauthorized, self-authorized, or God-authorized. "If any man will
do his will, he shall know" (7:17a). The phrase "will do" is not the
future tense of the verb "to do." It is the present subjunctive of the
verb "to will" plus the present infinitive of the verb "to do." If any
man set himself determinedly to do the will of God, is Jesus' statement, he will come to know concerning the teaching, whether it is
(out) from God, or whether I speak from Myself. The will is parent
to the understanding. How much Greek will a student ever come to
understand if he does not "will" to learn it? It is equally so in the
things of the Spirit of God.

The second prejudice of the Jews was directed at the works of our
Lord. It was not vocally expressed at the moment, but it had been
brewing in their minds for a long time, especially since the episode
of the healing of the impotent man by the pool of Bethesda, and Jesus
knew their thoughts. That incident had established Him in their
minds as a habitual Sabbath breaker (see Greek of John 5:16, 18).
They were bent, therefore, on His death.

Answering people's thoughts before they utter them puts them on
the defensive, and in days of war the merest child learns what tremendous advantage is on the side of an army that can hold the
offensive. Christ certainly wrested the offensive from the Jews when
He answered their unspoken thoughts. He accused them of being
Law breakers—every one of them. This robbed them of their right
to press an indictment against Him. As they took a defensive position in their question, "Who goeth about to kill thee?" (7:20),
Jesus pressed the assault home. Even in their attempts to keep the
Law they broke it, for in order to administer the ordinance of circumcision they frequently broke the Sabbath. It was a choice between
circumcising on another than the eighth day and doing it on the

Sabbath. Is it any worse, asked Jesus, to make a man every whit whole on the Sabbath than to cut him on the Sabbath?

The application was clear. "Judge not according to appearance, but judge righteous judgment" (7:24). In the course of his long, brilliant career as prime minister of England, Gladstone determined to do away with the system of purchase, by which commissions in the army were bought—a system open to much abuse and detrimental to the efficiency of the service. He introduced an abolition bill, which the House of Commons passed, but at which the upper house balked. While the lords quibbled, Gladstone presented to the queen an act of the reign of George III, which empowered the crown to abolish this system, and asked her to use her prerogative. She did so, and the startled lords found the thing done while they disputed. Gladstone's political enemies called him every kind of lowdown rascal for stooping to such "trickery," but those who knew Gladstone realized that it was characteristic of his determination to chase abuses wherever he could, and he did it in all good conscience. "Trickery" was the judgment of appearance. The nobler judgment was the righteous judgment. Samuel had to learn the lesson in his day, that "man looketh on the outward appearance, but the Lord looketh on the heart" (1 Sam 16:7b). We shall be safer to avoid passing judgment where it is not demanded, remembering such Scriptures as "Who art thou that judgest another man's servant?" (Rom 14:4a), and, "Let us not therefore judge one another any more" (14:13). Then, when judgment is required of us, let us give it with charity.

> Who made the heart, 'tis he alone
>   Decidedly can try us;
> He knows each chord, its various tone,
>   Each spring, its various bias.
> Then at the balance let's be mute,
>   We never can adjust it;
> What's done we partly may compute,
>   But know not what's resisted.
>
>   BURNS

Knowing that the rulers had decided on the death of Jesus, the crowd wondered that He was allowed to go on teaching without interruption. The rumor began to go the rounds that the rulers had perhaps changed their minds and were beginning to think that this Jesus was the very Christ. "But," they continued, gratified with their superior discernment, "we know better than that. The Christ is to come surrounded with mystery, while this man is one of ourselves. We know all about him, so he cannot possibly be the Christ." Their ignorance was colossal. The Scriptures clearly indicated that the Christ was to come from Bethlehem of Judea, and Jesus came from that little town, although they took Him for a Galilean because He had been brought up in the northern province. We have all listened to men who dogmatized on the basis of what they did not know. Perhaps we have all been guilty.

Whether our Lord's answer was an acknowledgment that they knew *something* about Him, or whether the words were shot back at them in the form of exclamatory negation with a vein of sarcasm, I am not prepared to say, but it finally amounts to this: "Whatever you know of Me is all on the human plane. You are totally ignorant of my true origin, my divine origin. You are not acquainted with the Father who sent Me." Apart from His divine origin we cannot know Christ.

The taunt of the common people aroused the rulers to action, but Christ's answer to their step of violence was a warning to all that their opportunity was brief as it was great. Soon He would pass from their sight, and they would be left in darkness, infinitely deeper than their former state. Opportunity was represented among the ancients as a beautiful maiden with long hair flowing forward, and arms and wings all stretched forward, so that there was nothing by which to seize her the moment she passed. Gospel opportunity does not last indefinitely. "Seek ye the LORD *while he may be found,* call ye upon him *while he is near*" (Isa 55:6, italics added).

We know that our Lord referred to His return to the Father. The Jews, however, asked, "Will he go unto the dispersed among the Gentiles, and teach the Gentiles?" (John 7:35*b*). There was more truth in their question than they knew. The Jewish rejection of Christ and His gospel opened the door of faith to the Gentiles, and the Jews as a race have remained in spiritual darkness while the Gentiles have received "the light of the knowledge of the glory of God in the face of Jesus Christ" (2 Cor 4:6*b*). Don't let prejudice rob you of your heritage in the Saviour.

23

FULL AND RUNNING OVER

JOHN 7:37-39

These three verses express three distinct thoughts concerning the divine provision for our lives:

1. The divine satisfaction (v. 37)
2. The divine overflow (v. 38)
3. The divine method (v. 39)

THIS WAS THE EIGHTH and culminating day of the Feast of Tabernacles, the most joyous of the Jewish feasts, commemorating the wonderful provision God had made for their fathers during the forty years when they lived in tents and booths in the wilderness. On each of the seven days proper of the feast, a priestly procession went to the pool of Siloam and carried thence water in golden vessels, which they poured out by the brazen altar. This ritual commemorated the water from the flinty rock in the desert. It would seem that the water ceremony was not repeated on the added eighth day, which climaxed the seven. Surely this omission was symbolic, whether the Jews so intended it or not, of the inadequacy and exhaustion of the Old Testament economy. Their fathers ate manna in the wilderness, and died; they drank water from the smitten rock, and died. There were no eternal springs, or springs of eternal life, in the ancient ritual. They offered sacrifices continually, and were not cleansed from their sins. It was on that day, then, which by its omission declared the incompleteness and imperfection and failure of all former provision, that Jesus cried out in great passion of soul, "If any man thirst, let him come unto me, and drink" (John 7:37*b*).

It was a universal offer, implying ability to substantiate it. Jesus was here claiming to meet every man's need, to quench human thirst, of whatever sort. Most people have grown wise to the extravagant claims of "cure-alls," yet here is such a claim which cannot be met with the indulgent smile. We know that there is in man a thirst too deep to be satisfied by anything this world has to offer; we know too that somewhere there must be that living water which will answer to human need. Jesus' claim to supply it looks good, and multitudes bear witness that it *is* good.

But does Jesus really satisfy every kind of thirst? Are there not some thirsts which are illegitimate? The thirst itself is basically right, but men judge wrongly concerning what will satisfy their thirst, and develop wrong appetites for those things. Let us, however, call these appetites thirsts for the moment. Will the Lord Jesus satisfy a man's pleasure thirst? Assuredly! "In thy presence is fulness of joy; at thy right hand there are pleasures for evermore (Psalm 16:11). "Thou shalt make them drink of the river of thy pleasures" (Psalm 36:8*b*). Will He satisfy the thirst for wealth? Yes! "He that spared not his own Son, but delivered him up for us all, how shall he not with him also freely give us all things?" (Rom 8:32). "All things are yours; whether Paul, or Apollos, or Cephas, or the world, or life, or death, or things present, or things to come; all are yours; and ye are Christ's; and Christ is God's" (1 Cor 3:21-23). Will He satisfy the thirst for power? "Ye shall receive power, after that the Holy Ghost is come upon you" (Acts 1:8), until "as a prince hast thou power with God and with men, and hast prevailed" (Gen 32:28). "So we might go on to cover knowledge, love, and every other thing man craves, sublimated and fulfilled in Jesus Christ.

Whatever our Lord does, He does in superabundance. When He made the heavens, He did not count out half a dozen stars as their portion, but made the stars "a great multitude, which no man could number" (Rev 7:9). So it is not enough for Him merely to quench our thirst. He must put within us springs that will overflow the channels of our own personality and bring blessings to others. "He that believeth on me, as the scripture hath said, out of his belly [innermost being] shall flow rivers of living water" (John 7:38).

This overflowing life is a life of faith. There was faith in the preceding verse. The coming to Jesus to receive the living water is an

act of faith, but here we have the continuous exercise of faith that
insures the more abundant life. Three times in the New Testament
we have the words, quoted from Habakkuk, "The just shall live by
faith." Tradition has it that these words came to Martin Luther as
he was laboriously climbing the Scala Sancta in Rome, and they became the watchword of the Reformation. Remarkably enough, they
occur in the three books on which Luther wrote his greatest works,
Romans, Galatians, and Hebrews. Some have suggested that the emphasis in Romans is, "The *just* shall live by faith," in Galatians, "The
just shall *live* by faith," and in Hebrews, "The just shall live by *faith*."
If so, we shall take the Galatian emphasis here, for it is the continuous
faith for living which means overflow.

Ezekiel pictures for us a wonderful river, having its source at the
altar and flowing through the land to the sea, first ankle-deep, then
knee-deep, then loin-deep, then over the head. After describing the
beneficial effects of these holy waters, the prophet adds, "and every
thing shall live whither the river cometh" (47:9). Apart from the
prophetic value of the passage, we certainly have in it a picture of the
life of blessedness and power. I heard Andrew Gih of China once
describe the various depths of the river as having to do with the sanctified walk, the prayer life, power for service, and full communion.
That is very suggestive, but it is the last phrase that intrigues me.
"Every thing shall live whither the river cometh."

When motoring across one of the vast stretches of western desert,
we noticed a green band would come near and then recede, breaking
the monotony of the treeless wastes. Later, climbing the face of a
mountain, we looked back over the immense plain, and saw this band
of green, like a huge snake, winding across the country. One does not
require to say that it was following a river, and "everything lived
whither the river went." It is the Lord's intention that we should
carry with us everywhere such potency to bless, revive, and sweeten.
The more abundant life is not one of selfish enjoyment of spiritual
blessings, but one of bestowal, making fertile and beautiful the desert
lives around us.

The divine method of bringing this to pass is given in the interpre-
tative parenthesis. "This spake he of the Spirit" (John 7:39). Our
Lord spoke, John tells us by inspiration, with Pentecost in mind. He

was speaking prophetically. The Holy Ghost had not yet come to assume His temporal mission in the age, the church, and the individual believer; nor could He so come till the glorification of Jesus in heaven after His earthly humiliation. "It is expedient for you that I go away," He said later to the inner group, "for if I go not away, the Comforter will not come unto you; but if I depart, I will send him unto you" (16:7). Our Lord lived in a perpetual realization of the Holy Spirit for Himself, and in the faith of a coming Holy Spirit for His people. We know that the coming of the Holy Spirit did make a remarkable difference in the apostles. What is the explanation of their new boldness, their new discernment, their new power, their new victory over self, their new steadfastness? All is explained in one word, "filled with the Holy Ghost" (Acts 2:4). That is the secret of apostolic triumphs. The rivers of living water were flowing.

Has the Holy Spirit grown old and decrepit? Is He unequal to the problems of our advanced twentieth century? Or is He still able to make an overflow in the life of the believer? Why, then, are so many of us content with a little trickle of blessing when Jesus says *rivers?*

> Lord God, the Holy Ghost,
> In this accepted hour,
> As on the day of Pentecost
> Descend in all Thy Power.

24

A SINNER FREED

JOHN 8:2-11

In this chapter we have prosecution and defense:

1. The watertight case for the prosecution.
   - *a)* The evidence complete (v. 4)
   - *b)* The Law clear (v. 5)
   - *c)* The dilemma perfect (v. 6)
2. The invincible answer for the defense.
   - *a)* Law answers Law (v. 7)
   - *b)* Grace answers Law (vv. 10-11)
   - *c)* Grace answers grace (v. 11)

THIS IS ONE of the disputed sections of the New Testament. Despite its weak documentary authority, I am glad it has been retained, for it is so like Jesus, and such a shining example of the triumph of grace over Law.

The scribes and Pharisees are not found in very good humor here, and it is not to be wondered at. Their Feast of Tabernacles had been properly spoiled, the fly in the ointment being Jesus of Nazareth. First there had come to their ears the rumor that the people were suspecting them of changing their minds concerning Jesus, and that whipped them to action. Then they perceived a rising tide of faith in Him on the part of the populace, as they saw His wonderful works. The officers whom they sent to arrest Him in the middle of the feast did not report till the last day, so they were kept in session, waiting on tenterhooks. Finally they came without Him, not with any report of a clever escape, but with the statement that His words fascinated them, paralyzed them, and rendered them incapable of laying hands on Him. The last straw came when Nicodemus, one of their leading Sanhedrinists, cautioned them not to be hasty in their judgment, but to reserve it until they had given Jesus the hearing which the Law demanded. The meeting broke up in pandemonium, and there was not much sleep for the well-trounced scribes and Pharisees.

They vowed to get Him yet, and the discovery of a woman in sin suggested their next move. Where they found her, and who was the other party, we are not told. At any rate, early next morning they dragged their victim into the treasury, where Jesus was teaching. The let-down atmosphere on the day after the excitement of the feast was rudely disturbed by this new commotion.

The scribes certainly had a watertight case against the offender. For one thing, the evidence was complete. A few years ago a young girl was murdered in a sporting camp in northern Ontario. The case was tried in the town where I was then pastor. Everybody was sure that the accused was guilty, but the evidence was incomplete, and the jury was instructed to bring in a verdict of not guilty. So the man left our town, a murderer in the eyes of the people, but in the eyes of the law, clear. Sometimes circumstantial evidence is strong enough to determine a case, even where direct evidence is lacking. The Pharisees had no lack that day. The woman had been caught in the act.

In addition, the Law on the case was perfectly clear. Often cases are tried in the courts where difficulty is experienced in determining what law should apply. Decisions in such cases are frequently made on a basis of precedent. There was no such uncertainty here. The Law was clear. "Moses in the law commanded us, that such should be stoned" (John 8:5). Only the man, who must have been caught in the act too, should have been there to be stoned with her. One wonders if it were not one of the hypocrites themselves! The absence of the man, however, did not affect the case of the woman. The Law said she should die.

Why did they bring the case to Jesus? He was not the official judge of Israel, was not even a member of the Sanhedrin. They thought they could commit Him to an opinion, and whichever way He decided they would have Him trapped. If He said, "She must be stoned according to the Law," that would be rebellion against Rome, for the Romans had wrested the *jus gladii* from the hands of the Jews, as they admitted to Pilate in the case of Jesus Himself. If, on the other hand, He forbade the stoning, He would be dishonoring the Law of God, and repudiating His Messianic claims. The dilemma was, as they thought, perfect. He must choose Moses or Caesar, and in either case would be condemned.

As the excited Pharisees chattered away, Jesus stooped down and wrote on the ground. What did He write? I am sure it was something pertinent to the matter on hand. Being pressed for answer, He answered Law with Law. An executioner must be found, only he must be one who has a right to condemn this woman. It will not do to have dwellers in glass houses throwing stones. "He that is without sin among you, let him first cast a stone at her" (John 8:7). Then again He stooped down, and began to spell out with His fingers the sin of the senior member of the Sanhedrin, the one who thought he was so well covered: till he slunk away to hide his confusion. Then Jesus began on the second, and he suddenly remembered a business appointment in the city. So Jesus answered Law with Law, until not a man of them was left to carry on the case against the poor adulteress.

When they were all gone, I think Jesus, in order to quiet the woman's fears and give her new hope, added this to His writing: "If thou, LORD, shouldst mark iniquities, O Lord, who shall stand? But there is forgiveness with thee, that thou mayest be feared" (Psalm 130:3-4). He was beginning now to answer Law with grace. "Did no man condemn thee?" (John 8:10, ASV), He asked her on looking up. "No man, Lord." "Neither do I condemn thee" (v. 11, ASV).

Will the Lord condone sin? No, but He will forgive the sinner. As He stooped that day, His shoulders felt the weight of this woman's sins, and, almost involuntarily, His finger traced the form of a cross. Then He spoke to her as the Man of Calvary, as the "Lamb of God bearing away the sin of the world" (see John 1:29). What condemnation could there be for this stricken, broken, penitent sinner when He was already "bearing her sin in His own body up to the tree" (see 1 Pet 2:24)? "Who is he that shall condemn? Shall Christ Jesus that died?" (Rom 8:34, author's trans.). With her sin laid on Himself, He saw her no more in her sin, but in Himself, and "there is therefore now no condemnation to them that are in Christ Jesus" (8:1, ASV).

Grace never comes singly, but in twins. There is always grace for grace. The grace of free forgiveness alone might be thought of as inducing license to further sin, although even in human relations that is not the tendency. But a second grace comes to support the first, expressed in the Lord's further word to the woman, "Go, and sin no more" (John 8:11). One who has experienced the wonder of divine justification does not go on sinning, for the grace of sanctification answers to the grace of justification. "If any man be in Christ, he is a new creature: old things are passed away; behold, all things are become new" (2 Cor 5:17). The woman who was brought to Jesus in shame and condemnation went away in peace, forgiven, cleansed, a new creature. Shall we make the truth of this lesson personal? The case against us is complete. "All have sinned, and come short of the glory of God" (Rom 3:23). God has lots of evidence against us. The Law is clear, too. "The soul that sinneth, it shall die" (Ezek 18:4). If Law is the last court of appeal, we are forever lost. Just here is where the Lord Jesus comes in. He bowed His head to the full demands of the Law against us, stepping into the sinner's place, assuming our debt of sin, and going out to death for us. The only One who was worthy to execute sentence against us has accepted the sentence in His own person. The demands of the Law have been fully granted in His death, and fully exhausted by His death. Now grace reigns, answering Law by the cross of Christ, and bringing the word of pardon, justification, and life to the sinner. The same One who died for us, being the risen and ever living Saviour, brings to us further grace, to deliver us from the power and allurement and bondage of sin, and to lead us on in the power of God to be "more than conquerors through him that loved us" (Rom 8:37).

25

JESUS BEARS WITNESS OF HIMSELF

JOHN 8:12-59

In this chapter, after a word about the validity and the confirmation of Christ's self-attestation, we shall consider the content of the witness:

1. Concerning His person
   - *a)* The name which attests deity (v. 58)
   - *b)* The name which illumines the cross (v. 28)
   - *c)* The name which commands destiny (v. 24)
   - *d)* The name which meets human need (v. 12)

2. Concerning His work
   - *a)* Giver of light (v. 12)
   - *b)* Giver of liberty (v. 36)
   - *c)* Giver of life (v. 51)

"THOU BEAREST RECORD of thyself; thy record is not true" (John 8:13), taunted the Jews. Is our Lord's witness concerning Himself valid? That is the question. Who of all Adam's race could bear an adequate witness concerning a divine being? Divine things being outside the scope of native human experience and observation, no man can give original testimony regarding them. They must first come by revelation of God. If Jesus Christ is "God . . . manifest in the flesh" (1 Tim 3:16), He is the only One among men who can give original testimony regarding Himself. All others must bear such witness as they receive of and from Him by the Holy Spirit. "For what man knoweth the things of a man, save the spirit of man which is in him? Even so the things of God knoweth no man, but the Spirit of God" (1 Cor 2:11). How much valid testimony could be presented by a conclave of puppies on the subject of man? No more could man give valid testimony about divine things except he received it from God. Here, then, in Christ, we have the original witness. If His testimony is not valid, we are left without any true word.

The Law of Moses demanded that every testimony be at the mouth of two witnesses to be accepted. So our Lord, after claiming that His personal testimony was valid because it was original, cited the Father as the second, corroborating Witness. The Father's witness is found in the Old Testament Scriptures, in the divine works which He gave the Son to perform, and in the immediate testimony of every man's conscience.

In this self-attestation, both the person and work of Christ are dealt with. His divine nature is presented by the use of the Greek equivalent of the divine name as revealed to Moses—I AM. Muhammad claimed that the angel Gabriel had given him ninety-nine names of God. We may be certain that all of them put together do not exhaust the nature of God, nor equal the divine comprehensiveness of this simplest word in all language—I AM. It is a name which embraces all time and fills eternity, a name infinite in its range, absolute in its priority. Yet fourteen centuries after the revelation of that august name to Moses at the burning bush, a simple Galilean stood up in the Temple courts of Jerusalem and quietly but unequivocally assumed that name, saying, "Before Abraham was, I am" (John 8:58). These words express more than priority in time. Two distinct verbs are used, indicating a coming into being for Abraham, but an eternal existence for Christ. The Jews apparently recognized the claim to deity in the words of Jesus, for they immediately took up stones to stone Him for blasphemy.

This is the name which illumines the cross. "When ye have lifted up the Son of man, then shall ye know that I am" (8:28). Frequently our Lord used the term "lifted up" with reference to His death. "As Moses lifted up the serpent in the wilderness, even so must the Son of man be lifted up" (3:14). "And I, if I be lifted up from the earth, will draw all men unto me. This he said signifying what death he should die" (12:32). Now if our Lord had said, "When ye shall see the Son of man coming in the clouds of heaven with the glory of His Father and of the holy angels, then shall ye know that I am," we should have easily understood. But Jesus is continually saying something other than we would expect! He calls upon the cross to attest His deity. And indeed that is the divinest act wrought by God—when the eternal Son emptied Himself and stooped to the shame and burden and anguish of the cross for the redemption of a lost world. I think that was a diviner act than the creation; it certainly unfolded more of the divine character. In heaven itself, God the Creator is not forgotten, but the song is forever celebrating the Lamb and the blood and the cleansing and the redeeming. By all that His cross has wrought we know Him as our Redeemer-God.

This is the name that commands destiny. "If ye believe not that I am . . . ye shall die in your sins" (8:24*b*). On all sides we hear that it does not matter what we believe as long as we are sincere. Strange that men should apply a principle to the important matter of eternal life which they would repudiate as utterly false in any other relation. Do men do business on such a principle? Is industry run on such a maxim? Does it go in the laboratory of science? It certainly did not work in that Chicago hospital a few years ago when the nurses emptied the wrong bottle into the food for the babies in the maternity section, and all Chicago and the entire country sent up a wail as if the whole world had been bereaved. The nurses were sincere, but that did not save the babies, nor their own positions. There is something which every man must believe in order to be saved: that Christ is the eternal God. Failing to believe that, he will die in his sins, and that means to be lost eternally. Only the great I AM can take away our sins, and if we do not come to Him as the mighty, covenant-keeping, everlasting God of our salvation, we must carry our sins up to the great white throne, and hear the awful words, "Depart from me!" (Matt 25:41). Eternal destiny is wrapped up in this name.

In the Old Testament the ineffable name—held so sacred by the Jews that they would not utter it, until we do not know the correct pronunciation—was often written in compound form, indicating that the eternal God was entering into relation with His people to meet their need. Thus we have Jehovah Tzidkenu, Jehovah-Rophi, Jehovah-Nissi, Jehovah-Jireh, Jehovah-Shalom, speaking of the Lord our righteousness, our Shepherd, our banner, our Provider, and our peace. When Jesus came, He made the same use of the mighty name, giving it such complements with reference to Himself as related Him, the all-sufficient One, to our needs. We have already seen how He said, "I am the bread of life" (John 6:35) to soul-hungry men. Now He says, "I am the light of the world" (8:12), to men groping in darkness.

It was the day after the Feast of Tabernacles. On the last day of the feast, two immense candelabra had cast a flood of light through the Temple court, but on this day following there was no such illumination. It was on that day, when the light of religious ritual was gone out, that Jesus cried, "I am the light of the world: he that followeth me shall not walk in darkness, but shall have the light of life" (8:12). Religion first, then philosophy, then science, then education has promised man light in his darkness, but with millenniums of these he is still groping. In none of these has the light of life been found. In the midst of the shattered lamps of human attempts to create light, Jesus stands forth, offering Himself as the true light, not as our paling lights which have only cast lurid glows and "lighted fools the way to dusty death," but the light which leads to life and heaven and God.

> I heard the voice of Jesus say,
>   "I am this dark world's Light;
> Look unto Me, thy morn shall rise,
>   And all thy day be bright."
> I looked to Jesus, and I found
>   In Him my Star, my Sun;
> And in that Light of life I'll walk,
>   Till traveling days are done.
>
>   HORATIUS BONAR

So have multitudes found, and so may you!

The study of the person of Christ in the blessed name has already shown us something of His work—to give light. In this chapter Jesus claims also to give liberty and life. Many boast of their freedom. The Jews did, despite their political subservience to Rome. The British sing lustily, "Britons never, never shall be slaves," while Americans boast of their free country. Yet how many Jews, Britons, and Americans are the victims of slavery worse than political, physical, or ecclesiastical! It is to men in the thraldom of sin that Jesus says, "If the Son shall make you free, ye shall be free indeed" (John 8:36).

> He breaks the power of canceled sin,
> He sets the prisoner free.
>
> Charles Wesley

Finally, what is man's supreme need and longing?

> 'Tis life, whereof our nerves are scant,
> 'Tis life, not death, for which we pant:
> More life, and fuller—that I want!

Jesus has the answer. "If a man keep My saying, he shall never die" (8:51, author's trans.). This He says to man already "dead in trespasses and sins" (Eph 2:1), to man borne down with a thousand reminders of his mortality. Eternal life He brings and offers free. "He that believeth on me hath everlasting life!" (John 6:47).

He went out into the darkness to bring us into the light; He allowed Himself to be bound that we might go free; He died that we might live. In face of all that, what think ye of Christ?

26

JESUS MAKES GOOD HIS CLAIM

JOHN 9:1-12

This incident presents four marked features of the works of God:

1. The priority of the divine glory (vv. 1-3)
2. The urgency of the divine mission (vv. 4-5)
3. The individualism of the divine method (vv. 6-7)
4. The sensationalism of the divine operation (vv. 8-11)

IT WAS NOT LONG till the statement of Christ, "I am the light of the world" (John 8:12), was met with a real challenge in living form—a man blind from birth. How will He meet the test? Not by qualifying His affirmation, but by reiterating it, and proceeding to confirm it by action.

The reactions of Jesus and of His disciples to the blind beggar were very different. Jesus looked upon him with active compassion, while the disciples regarded him with quizzical curiosity, as an exhibit in some philosophical or theological showcase. "Master, who did sin, this man, or his parents, that he was born blind?" (9:2).

They linked suffering with sin. So far so good. In the application of the fact, however, they were very wrong. Since suffering is related to sin, they argued, all suffering must be the direct consequence of some specific sin. The connection must always be very close, if not immediate. This man was a sufferer. He must be suffering for his own sin or that of his parents. Whether they were thinking about sin committed in a former life, or sin foreseen by God and therefore punished aforetime, we cannot say. At any rate, their error lay right here.

That all the suffering in this world flows from the common fountain of sin is undoubtedly true, and when we suffer, we suffer as members of a sinful race. But that all our sufferings are the results of our own sin, or of the sin of those immediately related to us, is not true. Job suffered as a member of a sinful race, but not for sin of his own committing. He is called in Scripture, "perfect and upright" (Job 1:1), and the whole thesis of the book bearing his name is to confute this very argument of the disciples, which was also that of Job's three friends. Here Jesus answers very directly, "Neither hath this man sinned, nor his parents: but that the works of God should be made manifest in him" (John 9:3). Our Lord was not imputing sinlessness to this man and his parents, but simply stating that their sin was not the reason for his blindness.

That raises another question. Does God have a right to make men suffer in order to demonstrate His works? Here is a doctor with great skill in bone setting. Would he have a right to inflict a fracture on his child in order to demonstrate his skill? By no means. But if the child has a broken arm, the skilled father would be within his rights, and would be forced by his duty, to inflict such pain as was necessary to the proper healing of the bone.

This is a broken world, and very much suffering is involved, not only as a direct result of the sin which has come in to afflict us, but also in the redemptive processes. God's own Son was given over to the sufferings of the cross for this purpose, and can we wonder if pain will be experienced by those who are the objects of the saving work? When the work is done, and we stand before God in the perfected likeness of His Son, we shall confess that it was well worthwhile. Suffering is purposeful, "for he doth not afflict willingly nor grieve the children of men" (Lam 3:33). If the glory of God is secured through the sufferings of men, it is not because God has launched an arbitrary program of self-exaltation. The priority of the divine glory is linked with righteousness, truth, and grace.

There was a great urgency in our Lord's mission. The Son of Man *must* be lifted up. "He *must needs* go through Samaria" (John 4:4, italics added). So here, "I *must* work the works of him that sent me, while it is day" (9:4, italics added). That sense of necessity and urgency our Lord would share with us. The Greek of this verse reads "*we* must" rather than "*I* must." The apostle Paul accepted the call, answering with that magnificent statement, "Necessity is laid upon

me; yea, woe is unto me, if I preach not the gospel!" (1 Cor 9:16).
Into this fellowship of necessity we, too, are called.

There are three elements in this urgency of service. The first is commission. Our Lord continually speaks of having been sent by the Father, and His great passion, His very meat, is to do the will of Him who sent Him. Always a commission, whether political or military or ecclesiastical, lays a burden of necessity on the commissioned. Are we accepting the "must" of our commission?

The need, too, emphasizes the urgency of the task. When Jesus said in the Temple courts, "I am the light of the world," it was a majestic statement, but when He repeated the words in the presence of the blind beggar, it must have been with a new ring in His voice, as if eager to pour light upon those darkened eyeballs.

The time element also adds urgency. "The night cometh, when no man can work" (John 9:4a). I remember the long twilights of the western highlands of Scotland, when one could sometimes read a newspaper in the light of the afterglow near midnight. Tropical nightfalls are not so. The darkness settles very quickly after sundown. The latter is usually the way night falls on our opportunities for Christian service. The youth we had intended to warn falls *suddenly* (so it would seem) into sin. Sickness and death *suddenly* take away those to whom we had hoped to witness someday. "The night cometh, when no man can work" (9:4b) as soon as the opportunity is passed. May God make us more urgent "while it is day!" (9:4).

One of our greatest preachers once told his people, if they had on their shelves manuals on how to lead men to Christ, to go home and burn them. While not supporting the exhortation, I appreciate his thought. There is a danger that we become book learned in holy things, and go out to apply indiscriminately the methods taught in the textbooks. Our Lord was a great individualist, and He treated men as individuals, not as pieces of machinery rolled off the assembly line. Other blind men were given sight, but not by the same method. When God makes a man, He breaks the mold. When God treats an individual, He scraps the method. We do not find our Lord using the same method twice, because He deals with men as men, not as "cases." He uses invariable and fixed principles, and applies these in an infinite variety of methods.

Notice, then, the principles underlying the methods here. We say Jesus made clay and put it on the sightless eyes. This is incidental. It is part of the method. What Jesus really did was to awaken faith in this man. Others came with the request that their eyes be opened, thus giving evidence of faith already quickened. The Lord undertook for this man unasked, but He must have cooperating faith. If the man could have seen this kingly, kindly Man before him, that might have stirred faith. That means of arousement being denied, Jesus gave him the touch of His hand, coupled with an act suggestive of healing. Then, we say, following the narrative, Jesus sent him to the pool of Siloam to wash his eyes. That again was the method, relatively unimportant as over against the all-important principle, the exercise of the faith which had been aroused. Here, then, are the invariable principles: faith must first be stirred, then called to action. The Christian worker must master the master principles, then seek the wisdom which is from above, even the leading of the Holy Spirit as to the variety of methods by which these principles are to be operated, for men are personalities, not bits of mechanism.

Some say that God's works are never sensational. That is not true. The divine operation is always sensational, and it was particularly so on this occasion. That excited questioning among the neighbors was indicative of the sensation the healing had stirred. Everybody knew the blind beggar. Therefore everybody saw the marvel of his salvation. Everybody was aroused by it, and started an inquiry. That is the sensationalism of the gospel. A young butcher in a northern Canadian city was converted. He boasted that everybody knew him. They knew him for the sinner that he was, and when he turned to Christ they knew him for the amazing change in his life. He used to give his testimony on the street corner thus: "All you folks know me. You know what a sinner I have been. Now you see for yourself what Jesus Christ has done for me." That was undeniable testimony, and many and earnest were the discussions all over town about what had happened to this drunken butcher. That is the sort of sensation that counts for something. Great sinners who meet a great Saviour cause a great stir, and others begin asking questions which lead to their salvation, too. May God give us days of true gospel sensationalism!

27

PERFECTED IN THE FIRES

JOHN 9:8-38

In this chapter we see how a series of testings was used to lead the man cured of his blindness into full spiritual sight:

1. The questioning of the curious neighbors (vv. 8-12)
2. The inquisition of the prejudiced Pharisees (vv. 13-17)
3. The desertion of the cowardly parents (vv. 18-23)
4. The taunts of the bullying Pharisees (vv. 24-33)
5. Excommunication leads to communion (vv. 34-38)

IT IS A LONG STEP from calling Jesus "a man . . . called Jesus" (John 9:11a) to worshiping Him as the Son of God. Yet that is the progress made by a man born blind and given sight by our Lord. A series of progressively severe testings was the providential means of this spiritual development. He was perfected in the fires.

Immediately upon being healed he faced the fires of neighborly curiosity. When he settled their questions and doubts as to his being the very blind beggar whom they had known those many years, they insisted on knowing the "how" of the marvelous healing. His reply was a simple, ungarnished, straightforward statement of the facts, with no attempt at explanation. "A man that is called Jesus made clay, and anointed mine eyes, and said unto me, Go to the pool of Siloam, and wash: and I went and washed, and I received sight" (9:11). The addition of any immaturely conceived theory relating to the event would have spoiled his testimony. He stuck to the facts of his experience. He did not expatiate on the wonder of the cure. He did not explain that he had received in an instant what an infant only acquired gradually—discrimination of objects, perspective, and such other powers. It was too soon for him to realize all that. The years would enable him to analyze the experience more fully. The simple testimony of young converts is always refreshing, but the years will bring, in addition to new and richer experiences, a fuller understanding of the first experience.

I am sure the good neighbors had no intention of casting their friend into a den of lions, but they certainly did when they dragged him excitedly to the Pharisees to show them the marvel. It must have been a shock to them and him alike when their rulers' first answer to the wonderful story was a condemnation of the One who had wrought the miracle, because He had done it on the Sabbath. The narrow bigotry of the Pharisees stood out in that moment as a horrible revelation to this man who had looked up to them as the leaders of his people. However, the condemnation was not unanimous, for some argued, "How can a man that is a sinner do such miracles?" (9:16). The apparent unreasoning prejudice of the one group drove the man into the camp of the more moderate, and started him wondering who and what this Performer of miracles could be. Now the wonder was more wonderful to him than to anybody else, because he was enjoying the blessing of it. So by the time the council asked him for his opinion of the One who had given him his sight, he was ready to go further, and to speak more positively, than any of them. "He is a prophet" (9:17*b*), he cried, as one who had reached a great conclusion.

He has progressed, but he still has a long way to go. More fire will further quicken his newly awakened spirit and illumine his expanding mind. The third test is a severe one. Surely the parents grieved all those years over the affliction of their child! And surely they would rejoice with him and stand with him in the hour of questioning. Instead, they turned cowards. That decree to excommunicate any who should confess Jesus properly frightened them, and rather than commit themselves to any statement which the Sanhedrin might interpret as a confession of Jesus as the Christ, they abandoned their newly restored son, leaving him to the "mercy" of the council. The fire burns fiercest at the center, and when the test enters the home relationship, it is severe and bitter.

Left by his neighbors, forsaken by his parents, disillusioned about the rulers of his people, the man now stood alone to face the bullying

taunts of the unscrupulous Sanhedrinists. Nobly he stood his ground.
They insisted on a condemnation of Jesus as a sinner. He would have
no part in their opinions and judgments, but stood solidly on the
facts of his experience. "One thing I know, that, whereas I was blind,
now I see" (9:25b). It is pretty hard to argue with a man who refuses
to budge from the facts of the case. The Scottish poet has said,

> Facts are chiels that winna ding,
> An' daurna be disputed.

Explanations of facts may be all awry, but that does not affect the
facts. It is not true scholarship that builds theories on theories, and
it is poor theology that rests on speculation. The apostle Paul was a
master of doctrine, but the gospel which he preached was a cluster of
facts: "that Christ died for our sins according to the scriptures; and
that he was buried, and that he rose again the third day according
to the scriptures: and that he was seen" (1 Cor 15:3-5).

The Pharisees, like lawyers cross-questioning a witness who stands
like a bulwark against them, tried to get a restatement from him, in
the hope that they would puncture the wall of facts. By this time he
had summoned amazing courage, and had lost all respect for his in-
quisitors, so he took a poke at them: "You are not deciding to become
His disciples too, are you?" (John 9:27, author's trans.). That is rich,
and they could only answer with taunts, ending with the statement
that they did not know where this Jesus came from. That proved the
text for a splendid sermon, which went thus: "We know where a man
comes from by the way he speaks and acts. If he gets his h's mixed up,
and uses 'jolly good' in every second sentence, and keeps his fork in
his left hand when eating, and has baggy trousers, and puts his shoes
outside his bedroom door for polishing—we know he comes from England. Now here is One who speaks heavenly language, walks with a
heavenly air, does heavenly deeds, including the opening of my blind
eyes, and you say you do not know where He comes from! And you
are supposed to be intelligent, spiritual leaders!" Thus the fires of
inquisition have brought the man to the conclusion that Jesus is come
from God, and that He is One in touch with God and with God's
power. The fifth test, the final, will bring him to perfect vision.

"And they cast him out" (9:34b). Excommunication was a severe blow for a Jew. It was degradation. If he had been a beggar before, he was worse than a beggar now; for whereas he enjoyed the sympathy of his fellow Jews till now, he could only have their scorn henceforth. He went out, doubtless with a heavy heart, but with a longing for God Himself such as he had never known. Then Jesus found him, not by chance, but deliberately. It was the first time he had seen his Benefactor, but he knew Him. There was only one such Man in all Jewry. He would sit at this Man's feet and learn of the God his soul yearned after. "Dost thou believe on the Son of God?" (9:35b). The man who a moment ago was "talking up" to the Pharisees with well-merited scorn now speaks in the humblest of tones—not cringing, but reverent and vibrant with desire. "Who is he, Lord, that I might believe on him?" (10:36). Here is a heart made ready in the fires for the revelation of God, and he has not long to wait. "Thou hast both seen him [beautiful reference to the recovering of sight, both physical and spiritual!], and it is he that talketh with thee" (10:37). Blessed be the day that gave him eyes to feast upon the Son of God! Blessed be the Son of God who would not only give sight to a blind beggar, but would call an excommunicated, disillusioned, deserted man into fellowship with Himself! "And he worshipped him" (10:38). Were the fires worthwhile?

> When through fiery trials thy pathway shall lie
> My grace, all-sufficient, shall be thy supply;
> The flame shall not hurt thee; I only design
> Thy dross to consume, and thy gold to refine.
>
> JOHN RIPON

28

THE GOOD SHEPHERD

JOHN 10:1-21

After a general view of the allegory, this chapter presents Jesus as:

1. The door (vv. 7-10), offering to the sheep
   a) Freedom
   b) Fodder
   c) Fullness

2. The Shepherd (vv. 11-18)
   a) Laying down His life for the sheep
   b) In intimate communion with the sheep
   c) Yearning over the "other" sheep

THE "GOOD SHEPHERD" sermon arose out of the healing of the man born blind, and really begins in the last verse of chapter nine, in answer to the question of certain Pharisees, "Are we blind also?" (John 9:40). The double "verily" introduces solemn truth, in this case presented in the form of an allegory from shepherd life. Not a detail in this graphic portrayal but would be quite familiar to the hearers—much more so than to us who are unacquainted with Eastern ways. The low-walled sheepfold harboring several flocks for the night, the door or opening with the porter squatting in it to keep watch, the marauder stealing over the wall to carry away a helpless lamb, the shepherd calling his sheep by name and so separating his own flock, the sheep deaf to every voice save that of their own shepherd, the trek to new pastures when all the sheep have been gathered, the sheep following the singsong voice of their shepherd as he leads the way: it is all there, simply but picturesquely drawn for us.

But if the Pharisees to whom the words were first addressed had the advantage over us in immediate acquaintance with the picture, we who have been suckled on the New Testament, who have sung almost from infancy, "Saviour, like a shepherd lead us," are miles ahead of them in understanding of the allegory. There may indeed be a few items to which we cannot attach, dogmatically at any rate, a spiritual content, but we dwell with delight on the thought of Christ our Shepherd calling us, leading us, folding us, securing us. We are thankful that the thieves and robbers cannot snatch from His unremitting care, and that our ears have been attuned to His voice so that strangers cannot beguile us with their chantings. The Pharisees knew none of that. They recognized the picture, but they did not understand the allegory. Therefore Jesus proceeded to an application, specifically in two directions, concerning the door and the shepherd.

In each of the two divisions of this matchless pronouncement, our Lord draws contrast between Himself and others. When speaking of Himself as the door of the sheep, He introduces the thieves and robbers who came before Him, false prophets and false messiahs who came in their own name, having no commission from God.

Again, Jesus contrasts Himself as the Good Shepherd with the hireling. There are three marks of the hireling: he is not the shepherd, the sheep are not his own, and he cares not for the sheep but for his own skin. It was a telling picture of the Pharisees whom our Lord was addressing. Let it not be so of us who are set as shepherds over the Lord's flock.

"I am the door" (10:9a), says our Lord. There are those who have become very liberal in their recognition of many ways of salvation, but the so-called "narrowness" of the Christian evangelist is but the "narrowness" of the Lord Himself, and that is "the narrowness of truth," as A. T. Robertson has said. "By me if any man enter in, he shall be saved" (10:9b). Even more dogmatically He stated the exclusiveness of the way of salvation later, saying to His disciples, "I am the way, the truth, and the life: no man cometh unto the Father but by me" (14:6). The apostles had good authority for declaring, "Neither is there salvation in any other: for there is none other name under heaven given among men whereby we must be saved" (Acts 4:12). Unless we proclaim "no other way," we are false teachers.

This salvation into which we enter by Christ is characterized by three rare benefits—freedom, fodder, fullness.

Freedom! He "shall go in and out" (John 10:9). With some people and in some places one feels himself under constant restraint. In the fold of Jesus there is none of that. One is "at home" there. And what a place in which to be at home! Better than kings' palaces! I like to think here in terms of the Temple or the tabernacle, where, having entered through the outer curtain, representing the Lord Jesus Himself, the New Testament saint is not confined to the outer court or courts, but is at liberty to press on without restraint into the holy place of illumination, nourishment, and worship, and even with all boldness into the holiest of all, the place of communion. Free, in the house of God! That is the portion of the child of God. "If the Son therefore shall make you free, ye shall be free indeed!" (8:36).

Fodder! "And shall find pasture" (10:9, ASV). Really it is the shepherd who finds the pasture for the sheep, but our Shepherd leads us to the pasture in such a way that it is like a discovery of our own. As you have grazed in the pastureland of Holy Scripture, have you not so "discovered" a choice morsel, and as you "chewed the cud" on it, have you not repeated, "He maketh me to lie down in green pastures" (Psalm 23:2)? The fatness of His house is the fodder of His flock.

Fullness! "I am come that they might have life, and that they might have it more abundantly" (John 10:10b). The life that He gives is in contrast to the havoc wreaked by the false christs who destroy men for their own advantage. The "more abundantly" is in keeping with our Lord's way of giving. A similar word is used by Paul when he tells us that "grace did much more abound" (Rom 5:20). There is an overflow in the life that Jesus gives. It is life with a surplus. The surplus is surely for the blessing of others.

Three very important things Jesus declares about His work as the Good Shepherd. First, He gives His life for the sheep. Because He *is* the Shepherd, because the sheep are His *own*, given Him by the Father from all eternity, because He *does* care for the sheep—all in contrast to the hireling—He lays down His own life in order to give life, surplus life, eternal life, to His sheep. Gunnarsson, the Danish author, gives a vivid and moving description of Benedikt, the Iceland shepherd, who made an annual journey into the mountains, after the fall roundup, just to find and save any sheep, whosesoever they might be, that had been missed. The hardships he endured, the risks he ran, the disappointments he suffered, and the unspeakable satisfactions he experienced in rescuing perishing sheep, are all told with peculiar pathos.

> But none of the ransomed ever knew
> How deep were the waters crossed,
> Nor how dark was the night that the Lord passed through
> Ere He found His sheep that was lost.

This laying down of His life was a sovereign act, yet it was an act of obedience. Both sovereignty and obedience were required to give His death its redemptive value. If He died the death of a helpless victim, how could He save helpless victims? At the same time "the obedience of Christ is the most important circumstance of His death," says Calvin, for it was in the obedience unto death that He satisfied divine righteousness.

A beautiful intimacy exists between the Good Shepherd and His sheep. The King James Version falls down on us here. The Greek says: "I am the Shepherd, the lovely one, and I know mine and mine know Me, even as the Father knows Me and I know the Father." Now doubtless there is an ineffable communion within the Godhead quite beyond our apprehension, but our Lord has entered into our humanity, and made us partakers of the divine nature, that that same kind of communion may mark our relationship with Him. We shall learn more about this "mystic, sweet communion" in the upper room discourses.

The Good Shepherd thinks about the "other sheep" (John 10:16a), who are not of the Jewish fold. He thinks of them, not sentimentally, but in terms of a great necessity. "Them also I must bring" (10:16b). That is why we Gentiles are "in" today. Do we share His passion for the "other sheep"? Some of them live next door to us. Some of them are in "the regions beyond." Does our Christianity overleap boundaries of denomination, nation, color, race? Many have shared my emotion at the grave of David Livingstone in Westminster Abbey, where, upon the slab is written his blessing upon those who would help to heal the open sore of Africa, and then this verse, "Other sheep I have, which are not of this fold: them also I must bring." It is one thing to have an emotion; it is another thing to be moved. Have we been moved for the "other sheep"?

29

I AND THE FATHER

JOHN 10:22-42

There are two main movements in this section:

1. Jesus affirms His deity in reply to the questioning of the Jews (vv. 24-30)
2. Jesus argues His claim in reply to the threatening of the Jews (vv. 31-38)

NEARLY THREE MONTHS passed. Another feast came around, the Feast of the Dedication, celebrating the purification of the Temple of Judas Maccabaeus after its defilement by Antiochus Epiphanes. Walking in Solomon's porch, Jesus was suddenly surrounded by a group of determined Jews. "How long do you lift up our soul?" (John 10:24, author's trans.), they asked impatiently. What they meant, of course, was "How long do you hold us in midair, in suspense?" Then, in a tone expressive of their purpose to have the matter settled once for all, they demanded an explicit statement as to His Christhood.

Jesus acceded to their demand to be explicit, but in a far bigger claim than their question implied. They asked whether He were the Messiah appointed to lead Israel out of Gentile bondage, into all the blessings of the Davidic covenant, as the preferred nation. Jesus came back with a clear claim to absolute and essential deity, culminating in the statement, "I and the Father are one" (10:30).

Our Lord's approach to that tremendous statement is marked with dignity and laden with precious truth for us. He began by declaring that He had already told them with great plainness who He was in something more than verbal affirmation. His works, wrought in His Father's name, were a demonstration more telling than a mere statement.

How, then, had the Jews failed to perceive the testimony of the works of Jesus? Not because the works were lacking in evidential value, but because of a native alienation of their hearts from Him. "Ye believe not, because ye are not of my sheep" (10:26). To this day the infidel boastfully demands proof, demonstration, of the Christian truth, while he goes on believing many things which have no foundation in evidence. Consider how the unbelieving world has swallowed the evolution pill whole, compounded of one hypothesis bearing up another. Yet the completely substantiated facts of Christianity are ignored. The reason for the rejection of Christ is not in the evidence, but in the heart. "Ye are not of my sheep."

The two distinguishing marks of Christ's sheep are that they recognize His voice, and they follow Him. They may be slow to hear and slow to follow, but they ultimately do it. H. V. Morton, in his splendid travel book, *In the Steps of the Master,* tells of a shepherd near Jericho who wanted to lead his flock of goats from one hillside to another. The goats were so intent on devouring some scrub that they failed to follow him. Noticing this, the goatherd called to them from the opposite hillside, in sounds scarcely human. The goats heard his voice, and bleated out their answer, but they did not follow. Then the man called out another sound, a kind of whinny, and one goat with a bell around its neck (apparently the leader of the herd) trotted over to him. The two disappeared behind a rock and remained there until the herd became conscious of the absence of both shepherd and leader. As they were thrown into a panic, the shepherd again uttered his laughing call, and the whole herd raced after him. Sometimes the Lord's sheep have to be put in a panic to make them follow Him, even after they hear; but whether readily or slowly, they hear and follow.

After characterizing His sheep, the Lord gave that word of assurance and security which has brought peace to so many of us: "and I give unto them eternal life; and they shall never perish, neither shall any [whether] man [angel or devil] pluck them out of my hand. My Father, which gave them me, is greater than all; and no man is able to pluck them out of my Father's hand" (10:28-29). "I defy the world," wrote Alexander Peden to the prisoners in Dunottar Castle, when Scotsmen were suffering for their faith, "I defy the world to steal one lamb out of Christ's flock unmissed." While Paul gives us this: "I am persuaded that neither death, nor life, nor angels, nor principalities, nor powers, nor things present, nor things to come, nor height, nor depth, nor any other creature, shall be able to separate us from the love of God, which is in Christ Jesus our Lord" (Rom 8:38-39).

All this to lead us up to the staggering declaration, "I and the Father are one!" It does not stagger *us* anymore, for we have so learned Christ, but it did stagger the Jews. Here was a man before them calmly laying claim to be of one substance with God—to be very God in His own nature! They asked Him to speak plainly, and He spoke more plainly than they reckoned on!

Their answer was stones. That is always easier than argument, though it never settles the matter. But at least the stones indicated that the Jews had understood, as they soon said in words, for when Jesus tauntingly asked them to specify the good work for which they were about to stone Him, they answered, "Not for a good work, but for the extremest form of blasphemy—making yourself very God!" (John 10:33, author's trans.).

In reply to their threatenings, and while they stood helpless to throw the stones they had picked up, Jesus offered two arguments to enforce His claim, one from the Scriptures and one from His works. The Scriptures, which cannot be broken, call them gods who were hearers of the Word of God. If mortal men were so dignified with the divine title, how much more should He, the sanctified and sent One, be allowed His claim to the unique title of "the Son of God" (10:36)? There is no modification of the claim here, only the appeal to Scripture was an effectual answer to the charge of blasphemy.

The second appeal was again to His works, which He declared to be the works of His Father. If these works did not carry the hallmark of divinity on them, then the Jews were free from responsibility to believe in Him, but if the works were manifestly the works of God, then, though they might not accept His naked affirmations, they were under obligation to accept the testimony of the works. The utter fairness as well as the logic of such argument must surely appeal to all.

Believing the works is the kindergarten of faith, but to what heights of spiritual understanding does it lead! It is not "that ye may know, and believe" (10:38), as the King James Version has it, but "that ye may come to know the mystery of the mutual indwelling of the Father and the Son, and then go on in an ever increasing knowledge of its wonderful fellowship," as we ourselves are caught up into it. Again we marvel that Jesus should utter such words to a group of hostile Jews thirsting for His blood; but He was speaking beyond them to you and me, who by grace have come to believe and know Him.

So again He had spoken plainly, and again the Jews understood Him. Though powerless to stone Him, they tried to apprehend Him, but the same paralysis seized them as He passed from them, and departed into Transjordania. There He had a happy experience. The sermons of the burdened John the Baptist still lived, and when the Jews of Perea saw and heard Jesus, they believed in Him, for they said, "All things that John spake concerning this man were true" (10:41, author's trans.).

In these two respects John the Baptist was a good model for all preachers, and we might well ask ourselves two questions. First, how long do our sermons live in the memories and hearts and lives of our people? Over fifty years ago I was preaching in Pitlochry in Scotland. I visited an old lady, past ninety-three, who had sat under the preaching of the godly Murray McCheyne when she was still young. How she talked about those days, and brought forth from her amazing memory whole paragraphs of his sermons preached those many years before! May God give our people good memories, and give us sermons worth their remembering, sermons translated into life!

And the second question: If the Lord Jesus should appear in person among us, would our people recognize Him from our sermons?

30

CHRIST UNVEILED IN THE PRESENCE OF HUMAN SORROW

JOHN 11:1-44

In this chapter we trace an unfolding of the character of Jesus in three distinct stages:

1. In Perea—a revelation to His disciples (vv. 1-15)
2. Outside Bethany—a revelation to the mourners (vv. 20-37)
3. Before the tomb—a revelation to all (vv. 38-44)

I AM WRITING THIS in Gatlinburg, Tennessee, in full view of the Great Smokies. Doubtless many a tourist has driven over the fine transmountain highway of Tennessee and North Carolina, and reported that he had seen the Smokies. But had he? The aspect of these mountains is continually changing. In a sense they themselves are constant, but every degree of shift of the sun, every cloud that forms above and around them, every alternation of atmospheric conditions, every turn of the seasons, changes the face of the mountains, brings out some new beauty, reveals some new glory. So every man is being continually revealed. Each new crisis means a new unveiling, showing some strength or some weakness, some charm or some defect, not known before.

The gospels portray our Lord for us, not by statements that He was strong, gracious, loving, kind, and so on, but by a wonderful cluster of incidents which constitute a progressive unfolding of His matchless character. Some of these are richer in revelation than others. Of all His earthly works recorded, none is more revelatory than this last of John's "signs," the raising of Lazarus.

134

Jesus was in Perea when He received news of His friend's sickness. He knew more than the messenger announced, namely, that since the messenger had left Bethany, Lazarus had died. In face of this great sorrow which visited the home most loved by Jesus, we may expect a rich unveiling of the Master. The first phase of that unveiling was before His departure for Bethany, and consists of a pronouncement, a postponement, and a proposal.

It was a startling pronouncement, especially in view of Christ's knowledge of the death of Lazarus. "This sickness is not unto death, but for the glory of God, that the Son of God might be glorified thereby" (John 11:4). We have already considered the priority of the divine glory in human suffering in the case of the man born blind. There the question was the root of the suffering, whether it sprang immediately from sin. Here it is a question of issue, whether the end will be death. Both answers are great negatives, with equally great positives following: in the former case, the works of God were to be manifested, while in this the glory of God is to be revealed. But as God will not be glorified at another's expense, we may be sure that the suffering out of which He obtains glory will be but the momentary travail out of which His children will gain the "far more exceeding and eternal weight of glory" (2 Cor 4:17) also. Remember, it was one of Jesus' best friends who had died. The sorrow was His, but He lived above the shadow of death, in the realm of the glory, just as I have seen the peaks of the big Smokies bathed in sunshine while their flanks were laden with clouds. Jesus knew that glory, not death, is the final issue. Can we live up there with Him?

The message of the sisters implied a request to come at once, but Jesus delayed for two days. The reason for the delay is as remarkable as the fact of it. "Now Jesus loved Martha, and her sister, and Lazarus ... therefore ... he abode two days still in the same place where he was" (John 11:5-6). We should have expected a very different "therefore." It was the delay of love. Lazarus was already dead when the messenger came to Jesus, so His going immediately would not have prevented the death; but it might have prevented the burial, and it certainly would have robbed the miracle of its full value, and His disciples and friends of the full weight of blessing intended for them in that great sign. The Lord did not allow the impatience of grief to run away with the patience of love. "Therefore will the LORD wait, that he may be gracious unto you" (Isa 30:18). Are we willing to wait for Him while He waits the fullness of time? Once again our Lord is not hurried by the panic of the moment, but waits the striking of the hour.

At last comes His proposal, "Let us go into Judea again" (John 11:7). That was just like saying, "Let us go back into the lion's den!" So it seemed to the disciples, and so they said. To Jesus, however, there was nothing foolhardy in going into the midst of His enemies when duty, that is, the Father's will, lay there. There was nothing of chance or risk in His action. He was walking in the full light of the will of God. Therefore, He was sure of His twelve hours, and He would not try to make them thirteen by avoiding danger. There is really only one safe place in the world—right in the center of the will of God. There "no weapon that is formed against thee shall prosper" (Isa 54:17), there you will live out all your days and accomplish all your ministry. That was the confidence of our Lord, and it may be yours, and mine.

It was at this point that Jesus indicated the purpose of His proposed visit to Judea—to awake Lazarus out of sleep. So death to Jesus was a sleep! He spoke as if He had already done combat with the monster and rendered it a powerless servant crouching at His feet. He actually called it names! Men have called it the "King of Terrors," and given it titles of dread and awe. Jesus called it "sleep," not frivolously or lightly, but sincerely, because He knew how He was about to abolish death, and bring life and immortality to light through the gospel. The disciples did not yet understand their Lord's new name for conquered death, so He was constrained to use their own term, saying, "Lazarus died" (John 11:14, author's trans.). Later they learned to use His term, and Paul learned it, too, and gave us that priceless gem of comfort, beginning, "I would not have you to be ignorant, brethren, concerning them which are asleep" (1 Thess 4:13), and again, "them also which sleep in Jesus will God bring with him" (4:14).

The Lord's delay must have been an added grief to Martha and Mary, for they had learned to lean on Him. When at last He came, then, He had to meet those women, weighed down not only with the grief of their bereavement, but with a questioning sorrow over His apparent neglect. How will He appear in the glare of such a trying situation? The sisters in turn said to Him, as they met Him just outside the village, "If thou hadst been here, my brother had not died" (John 11:21, 32). (Notice that they did not say, "If Thou hadst come when we sent Thee word," for evidently the death had occurred before the messenger reached Jesus.) The Lord's response, however, was very different in each case. He comforted Martha by giving her faith new heights to scale. He comforted Mary by adding His tears to her mourning.

Martha seems to have been in great conflict and confusion of spirit, as she had been before in a lesser crisis. Faith would make excursions toward Jesus and then retreat. She seemed to wax bold in saying, "I know, that even now, whatsoever thou wilt ask of God, God will give it thee" (11:22), but as soon as Jesus spoke of Lazarus rising again, she pushed it off to the last day. Hesitant faith takes refuge in the future tense. It was then that our Lord showed that resurrection and life are not found in an event but in a person, Himself. "I am the resurrection and the life: he that believeth in Me, even though he die, he shall live; and every one who liveth and believeth in Me shall not die, no, not to all eternity" (11:25-26, author's trans.). So our Lord seeks to make a revelation of Himself appropriate to the need. Martha needed something more than a theological hope. She needed a living hope centered in the person of the Lord Himself. If we have Him, we have all, and need not wait for "some far-off divine event to which the whole creation moves" for the realization of our heart's longing. He is here, our present bread, light, Shepherd, life. Blessed sorrow, which brings us Christ Himself!

When Mary came at the command of the Master, she greeted Him with Martha's words. They must have said that to each other many times since four days ago: "If only He had been here, our brother would not have died!" We are not told that Martha came weeping, or wailing, or accompanied by a group of mourners. She possibly was busy getting things done. Mary, on the other hand, is still seen as the sensitive soul, deeply moved. The sight of her grief as she fell at His feet strongly affected Jesus. "He groaned in the spirit" (11:33), we are told. A. T. Robertson says that the verb here means "to snort with anger like a horse." The element of anger was decidedly present. How could He be angry in the presence of such grief? Was it the sight of the professional mourners who so intruded on the sisters with their noisome, insincere wailing? Or was it not that He saw in this present grief a picture of all the havoc that sin had wrought in God's fair world? At any rate, He was not smug and complacent about human sorrow. He "agitated Himself" about it; and some of us who claim to be His followers need more of His anger and agitation in the face of the multiplied wrongs that are in the earth.

"Jesus wept" (11:35). That was His response to Mary's tears. Martha must have known what Jesus would do about it, and He revealed to her that what He was met the whole situation. Mary made no such demand on the Master, but simply cast herself and her grief at His feet, and He responded by mingling His tears with hers. To Mary, who had been at Jesus' feet before, His presence and sympathy were a complete answer.

> Is there anyone can help us, one who understands our hearts
>   When the thorns of life have pierced them till they bleed:
> One who sympathizes with us, and in wondrous love imparts
>   Just the very, very blessing that we need?
>
>   Yes, there's one, only one,
>   The blessed, blessed Jesus, He's the one.
>   When afflictions crush the soul,
>   And waves of trouble roll,
>   And you need a friend to help you, He's the one!

But why did He weep when He knew that in a few minutes He would call Lazarus forth, and "give . . . beauty for ashes, the oil of joy for mourning, the garment of praise for the spirit of heaviness" (Isa 61:3)? Because the sorrow was no less real for being of short duration. God knows that "our light affliction . . . is but for a moment" (2 Cor 4:17), but is He the less compassionate on that account?

The final stage of the revelation was before the tomb. Jesus issued three commands, the first and the last to those about Him, possibly the servants of Mary's household. No miracle was required to roll away the stone and to unwind the graveclothes, so He did not undertake these lesser tasks. God will make us do for ourselves all that we can do, but He will do all for us that we cannot do. It may be there is some Lazarus who cannot be raised from the dead until we roll away a stone—some sinner who cannot be saved until we remove some hindrance. Is there something in your life that is sealing another's eternal grave? There is many a living soul, too, still cumbered with the wrappings of the tomb, Christians dragging around the habits and ways of the old life—the old death, rather. "Loose him, and let him go" (John 11:44*b*). "Ye which are spiritual, restore such an one in the spirit of meekness" (Gal 6:1). We have a ministry to each other, to help free one another from the marks and trappings of former days when we were "dead in trespasses and sins" (Eph 2:1).

Before issuing His second command, that to Lazarus, and while the grave was open before Him, Jesus gave thanks to the Father, for He would have it known that He did not do this from Himself, but as God's sent One. The glory of the Father was uppermost in His mind continually. Never would He use a situation to exalt Himself independently of the Father, till at last He could say, "I have glorified thee on the earth: I have finished the work which thou gavest me to do" (John 17:4). Consider, then, how we sin when we use God's work as a means of self-glorification! In a time of revival a minister friend of mine confessed to his congregation that he had studied in all his ministry to exalt himself. Artistry, oratory, effect, all were there, and always he stamped a large portrait of the preacher on the minds of the hearers. He is not in a class by himself. May God make us all more like the humble Servant-Son!

"Lazarus, come forth!" (John 11:43). It was a specific command, as the call to salvation always is. Jesus expected Lazarus to hear Him, and He did, for Lazarus was "asleep" to Him, though "dead" to others. The command put to the test our Lord's statement to Martha, "I am the resurrection, and the life" (11:25), and the issue proved His claim true. That same voice calls today. If you hear you will live, and live forevermore. If you refuse to hear now, you will hear one day, and come forth to a resurrection, not of life, but of condemnation. "Hear, and your soul shall live!" (Isa 55:3).

31

APPOINTED UNTO DEATH

JOHN 11:45-57

This final chapter deals with:

1. The utter panic of the Sanhedrin (vv. 47-48)
2. The knavish speech of the high priest (vv. 49-50)
3. The saving purpose of God (vv. 51-52)

THE CHAPTER which has progressed so triumphantly ends in deep gloom. The "sign" of the raising of Lazarus was so convincing that the Pharisees and the chief priests were thrown into a panic lest the whole populace should go over to Jesus and acclaim Him as the Christ. They who had kept asking for a sign admitted to each other that He had given many signs, but the multiplied evidence only aggravated their hostility. They had done nothing, were doing nothing, could do nothing, to match the mighty works of the Galilean. Clearly their position in Israel was precarious. They were losing out with the people, and Jesus was winning. Suppose there should be a general movement at the next Passover toward Him, then the Sanhedrin, recognized by the Romans as the center of the limited Jewish autonomy, would be thrown out in the uprising, with the result that the Roman power would stamp out the last remnants of Jewish freedom and depose the Sanhedrin as incapable of keeping order. That was their fear, arising wholly out of their determined unbelief and their perverted idea of the Messianic mission.

As a confused discussion proceeded in the council, Caiaphas the high priest rose up and was given audience. His speech was brief enough, but it said everything. Scorn and subtlety marked it: scorn at the inability of his fellow Sanhedrinists to arrive at a most manifest conclusion, subtlety in proposing the death of Jesus as for the salvation of the nation rather than for the satisfaction of their own hate. He gave a supercrime the appearance of a most meritorious act, a regrettable but necessary sacrifice. Expediency was his argument, but national expediency rather than personal: and how often a policy which would be universally condemned in the personal sphere is hailed as virtuous in national affairs! From the beginning of this nation the rights of private property have been recognized, and the courts would protect an owner from a designing neighbor. But when Tsali and his band of Cherokees resisted transportation from their native Smokies to the far West, they were considered criminals and mutineers against a "righteous" government who wanted their territory, and it was deemed a most generous act to allow the last two thousand Indians to remain, at the price of the heads of Chief Tsali and his sons. Of course, later generations condemn such things of the past, while adding their own contributions to national crime. It is a universal condition, and it only requires a clever Caiaphas to garb the deed in virtuous garments to secure its perpetration.

The high priest had spoken. It was the *vox ex cathedra,* and "from that day . . . they took counsel *together* for to put him to death" (John 12:53, author's trans.). Note that word "together." Pharisees and Sadducees, who scorned each other's company, and came together in Sanhedrin bent on seeing that the other party obtained no advantage, were now seen tête-à-tête in little groups, forgetting their hatred of one another in their zeal to find a way of accomplishing the high priest's decree.

But while the high priest spoke only knavery so far as his own intent was concerned, he spoke better than he knew. Joseph said to his brethren, "As for you, ye thought evil against me; but God meant it unto good" (Gen 50:20). So with the speech of Caiaphas. It was wicked, devilish, but it was prophetic. God took those wicked lips, and made them speak words which the man's own heart intended for evil, but which really summed up the entire mission of Jesus. He came to save the people by dying for them. The death of Jesus, however, was to have a wider outreach than the words of Caiaphas implied. He spoke only of the Jewish nation. The divine intention embraced the world. "God so loved the world that he gave his only begotten Son, that whosoever believeth in him should not perish, but have everlasting life" (John 3:16).

What is the situation, then? The high priest has given the official word that Jesus must die. The Sanhedrin is holding constant meetings to consider ways and means. The proclamation has gone forth that anyone knowing the whereabouts of Jesus must report, so as to expedite the arrest. But over all that, the divine purpose of salvation through the death of the blessed Son makes the approaching tragedy the very goal of Christ's mission. That is His "hour," of which He has so often spoken. He retires from Jerusalem, not to run away from that hour, nor yet to delay it, but because it has not yet struck. He must die as the Passover Lamb, and when next He comes up to Jerusalem it will be to that Passover which the whole Christian church has since celebrated in the simple ritual of the bread and wine.

So "the Word was made flesh, and dwelt among us" (1:14), that He might "taste death for every man" (Heb 2:9), and "gather together in one the children of God that were scattered abroad" (John 11:52). Have we, then, some word of acclaim for Him?

> Thy saints proclaim Thee King, for in their hearts
> Thy title is engraven with a pen
> Dipped in the fountain of eternal love.

32

MARY AMONG THE IMMORTALS

JOHN 12:1-8

In this chapter we learn:

1. The secret of the Master's feet
   a) Mary at the Master's feet (v. 3)
   b) The beauty of the Master's feet (Isa 52:7)
   c) Blessing at the Master's feet (Matt 23:12)

2. The anointing of the Master's feet
   a) The element of sacrifice (v. 5)
   b) The element of understanding (v. 7)
   c) The element of diffusion (v. 3)

THE WOMAN who cheered the heart of Jesus in that fateful hour when He was entering the shadows of His passion is one of the notables of heaven. Her act of devotion, intrinsically beautiful, borrows added charm from its dark setting, being wrought at the very gate of the lions' den, at the door of the fiery furnace. There is more than one act, however, to make this woman immortal among immortals. She knew the secret of Jesus' feet.

The first time we are introduced to Mary in the gospels, we find her sitting at Jesus' feet, learning. Her excitable sister, Martha, bustling about preparations for dinner, would have her rebuked for her failure to help, but the Lord champions her right to "that good part" (Luke 10:42).

Mary next appears on the pages of the Holy Writ in the story of the raising of her brother from the dead. Here again she is at the feet of the Master. There is no word of Martha falling at Jesus' feet when she meets Him outside the village limits of Bethany. That is left to

Mary, and in this she gives evidence of a spirit of submission to the holy will of her Lord which seems to be lacking in her sister.

Now, the third and last time that Mary appears in gospel story, she is still at Jesus' feet. Martha, who would have made a choice president for a women's society, is still serving dinner, but again Mary forgets the material realm in a passion of worship. The whole history of this woman, then, can be summed up in three acts around the holy feet:

1. She sits at His feet as a disciple, learning.
2. She falls at His feet as a suppliant, submitting.
3. She kneels at His feet as a worshiper, adoring.

If we were to ask Mary her reason for being so much at Jesus' feet, I think she would give us two answers. First, she would tell us that His are the most beautiful that ever touched earth; and if pressed for an explanation of their exceeding loveliness, she would reply in the words of Isaiah. "How beautiful upon the mountains are the feet of him that bringeth good tidings, that publisheth peace; that bringeth good tidings of good, that publisheth salvation!" (Isa 52:7). And, indeed, those undefiled feet have walked, not only the dusty ways of Galilee, Samaria, and Judea, but the highways and byways and streets and lanes of our great sorrowing world, carrying cheer, healing, comfort, life, and salvation to the burdened, weary, and heavy-laden.

Her second answer would be: He is the beloved Master, and the place of the disciple is at His feet; He is Lord over all, and the place of the servant is at His feet; He is the blessed Saviour, and the place of the sinner is at His feet; He is my God, and the place of the worshiper is at His feet. The lower we go in the presence of the Lord Jesus, the higher we shall be exalted. Martha *served* before Him, Lazarus *sat* before Him, and Mary *bowed* before Him. Who is the highly commended one? Which of the three did Jesus place among the immortals, whose deed should be welded inseparably with the gospel story? It was of the one at His feet that He said, "Mary hath chosen that good part" (Luke 10:42). It was to the one at His feet that He granted the sweet communion of His tears. It was of the one at His feet that He said, "Wheresoever this gospel shall be preached throughout the whole world, this also that she hath done shall be spoken of for a memorial of her" (Matt 26:13, author's trans.). In this realm every stoop down is a step up.

> Thus looking within and around me, I ever renew—
> With that stoop of the soul which, in bending, upraises it too—
> The submission of man's nothing-perfect to God's all-complete,
> As by each new obeisance of spirit I CLIMB to His feet.

Mary's offering deserves attention. "A pound of ointment of spikenard, very costly," John says (12:3). This was no common olive oil, pressed from the olives which grew around Mary's home, but a rare Oriental product, fit for an emperor. Judas, shrewd businessman that he was, calculated the value of the ointment, apart from the alabaster cruse which contained it. Three hundred pence was his valuation, and Mark's account suggests that as a conservative estimate. Now at that time a penny was a regular day's wage for a laborer, and he worked twelve hours for his penny. Therefore approximately a year's wages was poured out in one moment of adoring worship on the feet of Jesus.

Such calculations are dangerous. They have a tendency to dull one's perceptions of higher values. So it was with Judas. He was so taken with the mathematics of the situation that he had no sensibilities for the finer elements. He had so accustomed himself to gauge things in terms of pennies and talents that spiritual values were unreal to him. His horizon had steadily narrowed till it was bounded by dollars and cents, and covetousness had cramped his soul so that he had no place left for love's high expressions and devotion's lavish sacrifice. "Waste!" he cried at sight of the flowing liquid nard. Then, to cover his greed, he very piously remembered the poor who might have benefited from the distribution of the three hundred pence, till the other disciples were clean carried away by his "good sense" and "philanthropic spirit." But the Spirit of inspiration unmasks the hypocrite most mercilessly: "This he said, not that he cared for the poor; but because he was a thief, and having the bag, WAS IN THE HABIT OF PILFERING what was put therein" (John 12:6, author's trans.).

The Lord's estimates are not according to market value. The poor widow's offering in the Temple was only half a cent, but it was more than all the lavish gifts of the wealthy, because it bore the hallmark of sacrifice: it was "all her living" (Mark 12:44). So Mary's offering was worth infinitely more than three hundred pence to Jesus, for it represented love's thought, love's preparations, love's self-forgetfulness.

> Measure thy life by loss, and not by gain;
> Not in the wine drunk, but in the wine poured out:
> For love's strength standeth in love's sacrifice.

Judas reckoned himself into a suicide's grave and a Christless eternity. Mary threw herself away in the lavish abandonment of love, and found a place among the nobility of the Kingdom of heaven. "He that . . . [saveth] his life shall lose it: and he that loseth his life for my sake shall find it" (Matt 10:39). So,

> Give what thou canst: high heaven rejects the lore
> Of nicely calculated less or more.

What if our all-out devotion to the Lord Jesus draws the criticism and the condemnation of men, even of fellow disciples? We shall have Jesus Himself for our Champion, our shield, and defense; and His word of commendation will more than repay all the misunderstandings of those about us.

We should not know, had Jesus not told us, that Mary had prepared that ointment for the day of His burial. Apparently she had taken in what the disciples consistently failed to grasp, despite the repeated declarations of the Lord, that He must go to the cross. She did not say, with Peter, "This be far from Thee, Lord" (Matt 16:22, author's trans.). She accepted His word, sorrowful though it was, and prepared for the dire event. Why, then, did she not keep the ointment until the actual burial? Was it a sudden impulse that seized her to anoint Him alive rather than dead? We might learn even from this not to keep back all the flowers until our friends are gone. But may there not be something more? He is the King, and this prophetess of love rises up to bestow on Him the anointing of the true Israel with truly royal ointment. If He rides into Jerusalem to thorns for a crown and a cross for a throne, He will at least not lack the anointing of love which will sweeten the rest of that bitter coronation.

One phrase we must not overlook in regard to this precious anointing. With the breaking of that sealed alabaster cruse and the pouring of its contents on the feet of the beloved Master, "the house was filled with the odour of the ointment" (John 12:3*b*). And that sweet odor has come down to us, undiminished by the years. Suppose Mary had not broken her cruse that day, nor poured out her precious ointment on the feet of Jesus. No perfume would have filled the house; it is likely that the preparation, like that of the other Mary, would never have reached the body of Jesus; and the fragrance of Mary's act of devotion would not be blessing our hearts today. Sealed ointment never fills a house with its odor. Streams of blessing flow with the breaking of alabaster cruses and the pouring out of the ointment. How was Morrison such a blessing to China, Carey to India, Judson to Burma, and Livingstone to Africa? They also broke their cruses at the feet of Jesus, and poured themselves out in loving sacrifice, so the house of China, of India, of Burma, of Africa was filled with the odor—and lo! it was a sweet savor of Christ. Yet all these are but diminutive reproductions of the great original, Jesus Himself, who "poured out his soul unto death" (Isa 53:12) for a lost world. Can we estimate all the sweetness that has come into this so needy world through the sacrifice of the Lord Jesus? We know in our own lives how His fragrance has chased the foulness. One day, when "the knowledge of the glory of the LORD shall cover the earth as the waters cover the sea" (Hab 2:14, author's trans.), shall it be fully said, "the house is filled with the odor of the ointment."

33

LITTLE GETHSEMANE

JOHN 12:20-33

In this chapter we shall see how the request of the Greeks brought
to our Lord's mind:

1. The law of the cross (vv. 23-26)
2. The horror of the cross (v. 27)
3. The fruit of the cross (vv. 31-32)

THE CONDUCT of our Lord was rather baffling that day. He rode into
Jerusalem amid the ovations and acclamations of a great host of
ardent admirers who acknowledged His kingship, hailed Him in the
name of the Lord, and called for His great salvation. With all that
He exhibited not the slightest trace of excitement; His equanimity
was undisturbed, as if He were on the quiet hillside alone with nature
and God. Yet the request of a few Greeks for an interview moved
Him to the depths of His soul, throwing Him into a paroxysm of
emotion second only to that experienced in Gethsemane. There must
surely be some profound significance in that seemingly trivial
incident.

The request of the Greeks was simple enough, perfectly legitimate,
and most courteously and respectfully submitted to Philip: "Sir, we
would see Jesus" (John 12:21*b*). Let us pause here a moment. These
words have something for us in themselves. I shall never forget the
first time their message came home to my own heart. I was but a lad,
and had been invited to preach in a Scottish church of some importance. The opportunity was one which meant much to an ambitious
youth, and I had determined to make the best of it. As I sat down in
the pulpit chair, my eye caught these words engraven on the minister's

side of the pulpit: "Sir, we would see Jesus." I bowed my head in shame and confession, and asked that the desire of the congregation should be fulfilled that day.

We can understand our Lord's reaction to the request of the Greeks only as we remember that in the days of His flesh He was a "minister of the circumcision" (Rom 15:8), sent to "the lost sheep of the house of Israel" (Matt 10:6). The wall of partition still stood between the Jews and the rest of the world, to be broken down by the cross of Christ. Jesus was quite conscious of the limitations of His mission on that side of the cross, and at least once expressed His divine impatience in regard to it: "I have a baptism to be baptized with," He cried, "and how am I straitened till it be accomplished" (Luke 12:50). This call of the Gentiles, then, flashed before our Lord's vision the glory of His larger mission, into which He must enter by way of the dark hour that was even now striking for Him. His first thought was of the glory beyond, in keeping with that word to the Hebrews, "who for the joy that was set before him endured the cross, despising the shame" (Heb 12:2). This "hour" had been in His mind and heart from the beginning of His ministry, and now it was upon Him, as the coming of the Greeks testified; but the purpose of the hour for a moment covered the horror of it. "The hour is come, IN ORDER THAT THE SON OF MAN MIGHT BE GLORIFIED" (John 12:23, author's trans.).

I recall the golden glory of the Ochil Hills in Scotland when the whin bushes broke out in blossom. But you must know that every whin blossom grew out of a hard, sharp thorn. So the glory of Christ, as the world's Redeemer, grew out of the sharp thorns of Calvary, the sorrows of that dreadful *hour,* when all God's waves and billows swept over Him. Tradition tells us that when General Wolfe was leading his army up the St. Lawrence River toward Quebec, every oar muffled, he read Gray's "Elegy in a Country Churchyard," and, coming to the line, "The paths of glory lead but to the grave," he said to the officers accompanying him, "I should rather be the writer of these lines than the conqueror of Quebec." Jesus has given us a far brighter philosophy than that. Man's glory ends in the grave, but with Christ, death, darkness, and the grave are first, accepted voluntarily, and then comes the glory; and it is everlasting.

From the glory beyond, Jesus' thought reverted to the necessity of the death that must intervene. "Except a grain of wheat fall into the ground and die, it abideth itself alone; but if it die, it bringeth forth much fruit" (John 12:24, author's trans.). The cross is the way of harvest, as it is the path of glory. Our Lord called upon nature to illustrate that great spiritual law, and indeed all nature testifies of it. You have seen an old dead log lying along the ground, and perhaps sighed for the end of an ancient king of the forest. Come back years later, and in the same place you may see a yellow birch standing on its peculiar stilts. What has happened? Yellow birch seeds never grow in the ground, but in the shallow soil of a decaying log. The young tree feeds on the rotting wood until it is able to send its roots around the outside of the log into the ground. The old log crumbles, but the new tree rises in strength on its dust. So Jesus said of Himself: out of His dying, multitudes should rise into life eternal. Redeemed men are the harvest of His suffering and death, not of His teaching and example.

"As he is, so are we" (1 John 4:17*b*). Living for self is the sure way of losing everything; dying to self is the path of life and blessing. Dr. Walter Wilson tells of a funeral service at which he presided, with only five people present. The five were the widow, a neighbor woman, the undertaker, the preacher, and the dead man. Dr. Wilson asked the widow why there were so few present at her husband's funeral. She replied, "My husband never cared for anybody but himself, never gave a nickel to a soul; this is the result. Nobody is sorry that he is dead." "He that loveth his life shall lose it" (12:25). And if a man can so lose everything in this world, how will he stand before God? On the other hand, all that wealth of dying and living seen in such men as William Booth and George Müller is carried up to glorify the life everlasting which is theirs in the presence of God.

"If any man serve me, let him follow me" (12:26). Now Jesus is speaking about going to the cross, so what He actually means here is that the only service He recognizes is the Calvary kind. Service that costs nothing counts for nothing; but service that costs will be abundantly compensated, first with the everlasting companionship of the King, then with special honor bestowed by the Father. So the law of the cross is just this: the cross is the gateway to glory, the imperative of harvest, the path of life, and the gauge of all service.

As our Lord spoke thus, first of His own cross as the way to His glory, and then of its application to the disciples, the lure of the glory beyond seemed to recede, and the horror of the great darkness fell on Him. Gethsemane, while a climax and a crisis, was not a solitary incident. Mark tells us of the consternation and amazement of the disciples as they noticed the appearance of their Master on their going up to Jerusalem, so that they fell behind, fearing to intrude on the struggle which His countenance betrayed. That the shadow of Calvary was upon Him then is evident from the fact that He immediately called them and began to tell them of the coming tragedy. So here, the coming of the Greeks, and His own declarations, brought the anguish to His soul. He entered into "little Gethsemane." Bishop Ryle has pointed out the remarkable parallel between the two experiences.

(a) "Now is my soul troubled"—corresponds with, "My soul is exceedingly sorrowful, even unto death."
(b) "Father, save Me from this hour"—parallels, "O My Father, if it be possible, let this cup pass from Me."
(c) "For this cause came I unto this hour"—is in keeping with, "If this cup may not pass away from Me except I drink it, Thy will be done."
(d) "Father, glorify Thy name"—is in accord with, "The cup which My Father hath given Me, shall I not drink it?"

The grief and the struggle are not so intense here as in Gethsemane, but the elements are the same. In either case we see that it was no light thing for our Lord to go out to the cross. Being very God did not make easy to Him what is hard to us. He was true man, and what you and I find grievous was painful to Him also. On the other hand, Jesus was no less a man than others, to shrink where others have gone unflinchingly forward. He was not less heroic than His martyrs who have faced the flame, the sword, the lion in His name. Then I learn this about the death to which He was going out—that it was not the common death of a man. He shrank, not from physical pain, but from the spiritual experience involved in that death; the sin of the world was rolling in upon Him, and He was going forth to taste for every man the bitterness of a lost soul. It was death with its sting full of poison that He must know. The curse of the ages must rest upon Him. Shut out from the Father's face, He must know the blackness of the pit, the horror of hell. That is what troubled His soul and threw Him into a conflict from which He emerged triumphant with the cry, "Father, glorify thy name!" (John 12:28). When my soul draws back in dread from the lesser cross which is mine, I am glad He knows and understands, and He gives grace to say also, "Thy will be done" (Matt 26:42), and, "Father, glorify thy name."

The darkness lifted from His soul, and our Lord began to dwell again on the glories beyond the cross, the triumphs which would emerge from this titanic struggle. First He spoke of a twofold judgment—of this world and its prince. This world, in crucifying the Lord of glory, fully and finally revealed its antagonism to God, His Law, His love, His truth. No further witness, no further demonstration is required. This world is judged by the cross of Christ. If the execution is stayed, it is only as the period between the passing of the death penalty on a murderer, and its carrying out; and in the meantime the grace of God is operating to gather the multitude of redeemed ones to Himself; for the blood which spells the final guilt of the world writes the pardon of believing sinners. The position of the world is that expressed apocalyptically in Revelation 7:3. "Hurt not the earth, neither the sea, nor the trees, till we have sealed the servants of our God in their foreheads."

With judgment passed upon the world goes a casting out of its prince, "the dragon, that old serpent, which is the Devil, and Satan" (Rev 20:2). "I beheld Satan as lightning fall from heaven" (Luke 10:18), declared Jesus on one occasion. That fall, however, did not bar him from access to God among the sons of God, as is evident from the story of Job. Instead of giving account of his own stewardship as "prince of this world" (John 12:31), he used his access to lay accusations against the people of God, so becoming known as "the accuser of our brethren" (Rev 12:10). The cross of Christ changed all that. His title as "prince of this world," which even our Lord did not challenge before His cross, is never acknowledged after it, while the blood of atonement bars him from the court of heaven. Instead of an accuser, "we have an advocate with the Father, Jesus Christ the righteous" (1 John 2:1), in remembrance of which the apostle Paul shouts triumphantly, "Who shall lay any thing to the charge of God's elect?" (Rom 8:33). The adversary will indeed accuse us to our faces, to discourage us, but he will not face the sprinkled blood in heaven, and even we may put him to flight with the word, "the blood of Jesus Christ his Son cleanseth us from all sin" (1 John 1:7b). To the same purpose is the great vision of the twelfth chapter of Revelation, where the dragon is foiled in his attempt to destroy the man child, who, after His conflict with the dragon, is caught up to the throne of God. "And there was war in heaven: Michael [the archangel, connected in Scripture with resurrection] and his angels fought against the dragon; and the dragon fought and his angels, and prevailed not; neither was their place found any more in heaven. And the great dragon was cast out, that old serpent, called the Devil, and Satan, which deceiveth the whole world: he was cast out into the earth, and his angels were cast out with him" (Rev 12:7-9). I am satisfied that Satan's access to heaven is ended, and that he is now engaged in persecuting the remnant of the seed, both Jewish and Gentile. The scepter is no longer his, but Christ's. The rightful Sovereign, however, has not yet been received into His realm, nor will He until He has, through judgments, swept the old prince now in the position of usurper, and all who follow him, out of the way. At the return of the Lord, Satan, already cast out of heaven and out of his princely office, will be cast out of the realm, into the bottomless pit, and still later into the lake of fire, whence he can never emerge to harass and deceive. All this casting out goes back to the cross. "Now shall the prince of this world be cast out" (John 12:31).

The Greeks sought to see Jesus, but they were a little premature. Still a few days were required for the breaking down of that "middle wall of partition" (Eph 2:14). Yet a few days they must occupy the place of "aliens from the commonwealth of Israel, and strangers from the covenants of promise" (Eph 2:12). But Jesus saw before Him the rending of the veil, the abolishing of the enmity, and the door of salvation opened to the Gentiles through His blood. How He longed to take those Greeks to His heart, but it was as if He said: "I am still straightened. Until My baptism of death, I am a Minister of the circumcision, sent unto the lost sheep of the house of Israel. But wait a few days only and I shall through death cast off these bonds, break down this wall, and open My hands to all." "I, if I be lifted up from the earth, will draw ALL men unto Myself!" (John 12:32, author's trans.). That remarkable cry means at least this—it takes in us of the Gentiles. And I know it to be true, for

> He drew ME, and I followed on,
> Charmed to confess that voice divine.

Have you felt the magnetic pull of this wonderful Man of Calvary? And have you come?

34

LAST CALL

JOHN 12:34-43

In this chapter the public ministry is brought to a close:

1. The Saviour sounds out a final invitation (vv. 34-36)
2. The apostle sums up the final count (vv. 37-43)

THE ACCLAIM of the crowds who surrounded our Lord on His brief journey from Bethany to Jerusalem did not represent the official attitude of the holy city toward Him. Once within the city gates, He quickly found Himself again in an atmosphere of antagonism and unbelief. "Christ crucified [is] unto the Jews a stumblingblock" (1 Cor 1:23), said the apostle Paul years later. It was that from the beginning. As soon as Jesus mentioned the "lifting up" of the Son of Man, the unbelief of the Jews rose to the attack. "We have heard out of the law that Christ abideth for ever," they declared, "and how sayest thou, The Son of man must be lifted up?" (John 12:34). It sounds very sincere, for the Old Testament is replete with foregleams of the abiding glory of the Messiah. But had they forgotten Psalm 22 and Isaiah 53 and Daniel 9 and Zechariah 13 and hosts of other Scriptures, all speaking of a suffering, broken, lifted-up, cut-off Messiah? There had been enough fulfillment of Scripture in the life and ministry of Jesus, enough likeness to the prophetic blueprint of the Messianic character, enough evidence of divine origin, to answer their question, "Who is this, the Son of man?" (12:31, author's trans.). Theirs was not the sincere questioning of the seeking soul, the inquiring of hearts ready to believe, but rather the caviling of determined unbelief. Therefore, our Lord, instead of answering their questions, pronounced a last warning and extended a last gracious invitation as the last act of His public ministry.

It was a faithful warning. Their light had come, the very light of life, and here they were, deliberately putting it away from them. There could be only one result—darkness, with confusion, uncertainty, and terror. "He that walketh in darkness knoweth not whither he goeth" (John 12:35b). No one sentence could more aptly describe the agelong experience of the Jews. For nineteen hundred years he has been the WANDERING JEW, driven from pillar to post, never sure of his dwelling place. With little intervals of comparative security he has had nearly two millenniums of bitterness. Why? Because he would have none of God's lovely Christ. The principle is an eternal one. All the chaos of nations today is attributable to the same cause. God's Christ has not been honored in the so-called Christian nations, till now a night of confusion and disaster has settled down on the world, and who knows the way out?

But the gracious Saviour would not withdraw Himself without making one last plea: "While ye have the light, believe on the light, that ye may become sons of light" (12:36a, ASV). Three relationships to the light are here indicated in the words *have, believe,* and *become*. It is not what a man *has* that spells salvation, but what he *is*. However much knowledge he may have, he sustains no saving relation to the light until he has become a son of light, and the link between *having* and *being* is *believing*. That is what changes the man, and makes him something other than he was. Reduce all this to personal terms, for the light is not something abstract, but a glorious Person, the Lord Jesus Christ. "Ye have the light." You have had knowledge of Him from infancy, when first you crooned, "Jesus loves me," at your mother's knee. All the information that you have accumulated concerning Him over the years will not of itself save you. The way to turn your knowledge into a means of salvation is to act upon it, and commit yourself to the Lord Jesus as your Saviour and Lord. You *have*; now *believe,* and you will *become*.

"These things spake Jesus, and departed, and did hide himself from them" (12:36b). That departing and that hiding were a final judgment on the persistent unbelief of the Jews. In that act our Lord abandoned them to their unbelief, to reap the awful and long harvest of it. It is a sad thing to see a man departing from God and trying to hide himself from God, as Adam did in the garden; it is infinitely sadder when God departs from a man, and hides Himself from him. It is true that

> While the candle holds to burn
> The vilest sinner may return,

but let that sinner disdain God's mercy, and he may find God very far away when he needs Him nigh, hiding His face when he would fain find Him. "Be not deceived; God is not mocked" (Gal 6:7). "Seek ye the LORD *while he may be found,* call ye upon him *while he is near*" (Isa 55:6, italics added).

The last scene in our Lord's public ministry shows the Jews still adamant in their unbelief. The apostle now comments on the situation. He believes that the recital of the signs which he has given us in his gospel is sufficient to induce faith in the Lord Jesus, and so bring life eternal. How much more should the Jews, seeing not only those narrated by the apostle but the many others omitted by him, have believed! But it was not so, and here is the inspired estimate of the situation: "They believed not. . . . Therefore they could not believe" (John 12:37-39). Unbelief has a terrible power to rob a man of the very faculty of faith. It is a law of nature that unused powers atrophy. It is so in the physical realm. We have seen pictures of "holy" men of India who have held their arms in set positions, uplifted or stretched out, until they have lost all power to use them. We know, too, that if we do not exercise our minds in listening to music or in the reading of poetry, we gradually lose our sense of appreciation of their beauty and harmony. Just so, every time a man says "no" to the call of faith he cripples his ability to believe, till at last he is of the number of whom it is written, "they could not believe" (John 12:36).

Because this is a law which God has established in every department of His universe, the operation of the law is put down as the work of God. That is why it is written that "the LORD hardened the heart of Pharaoh" (Exod 9:12). He did it by the sure operation of this very law. Similarly, it is written here as the further explanation of the Jewish leaders' inability to believe: "He hath blinded their eyes, and hardened their heart" (John 12:40). A man can no more fool this law than he can bluff God. When a person begins to lose feeling in the blizzard, he is in dire peril, and must be whipped to action if his life is to be saved. A man who has resisted the call of God until he is "past feeling" has gone a long way toward utter reprobacy, and needs some severe jolting, if perchance he may be aroused to his danger and exercise his last powers of faith.

Just as pitiable as those atrophied in their unbelief was another group whom the apostle describes—chief rulers among the Jews who were driven in all honesty to believe that Jesus was come from God, but who would not risk excommunication for Christ's sake, "for they loved the praise of men more than the praise of God" (12:43). They were convinced, but not persuaded, allowing momentary gain and reputation to rob them of all the blessing of following Christ. I have no doubt that there are great multitudes today who are fully convinced of the truth of the gospel, but who stand outside the circle of its blessing because of what it would cost them to confess the Saviour. They know that salvation is free, but they know equally well that it costs to be a disciple. Ungodly gain would have to be abandoned, restitution would have to be made, prestige would have to be sacrificed, promotion might have to be forfeited, the whole map of life would have to be altered.

There is a double answer to all such hesitators. First, "What shall it profit a man, if he shall gain the whole world, and lose his own soul?" (Mark 8:36). And second, "There is no man that hath left house, or brethren, or sisters, or father, or mother, or wife, or children, or lands, for my sake, and the gospel's, but he shall receive an hundredfold now in this time, houses, and brethren, and sisters, and mothers, and children, and lands, with persecutions; and in the world to come eternal life" (Mark 10:29-30). Those who "count the cost" so carefully would do well to work out this problem—"What will it cost me *not* to confess Christ?"

35

LOVE TO THE UTTERMOST

JOHN 13:1-17

In this chapter we consider:

1. The stoop of the Master (vv. 1-5)
2. The mutiny of the servant (vv. 6-10)
3. The application of the lesson (vv. 12-17)

THE GOSPEL STORIES are so consistently simple in their recitation that when we come to one introduced with such an elaboration of phrases, we are at first nonplussed. Three verses are occupied with the setting, which is partly inward, dealing with the high consciousness of our Lord, and partly outward, dealing with the circumstances of the hour.

Sensitive men are usually conscious of approaching crisis. Jesus, in addition to the intuition of the sensitive soul, had the prescience of divine illumination. He was at last entering into the hour for which He had come into the world. It was to be an hour of such darkness, such anguish, as no man before Him had known, but He was upheld by the realization that it was also the hour of return to the Father.

In that hour Jesus was supremely conscious of three things—His universal sovereignty, His heavenly origin, and His divine destiny. The infinities swept His soul. He was released for the moment from the straightenment of the flesh, and knew the awful dignity of supreme, eternal godhood.

The outward setting was very different. Before Him was spread the simple paschal meal, which spoke of the sacrifice He was about to make for a world's redemption. About Him were the chosen twelve, not one of whom could as yet enter into the mystery of His being and approaching passion. Beside Him was one of those twelve whose heart was even now the residence of Satan, and in whose mind were dark thoughts of betrayal. The mind of Jesus and the mind of Judas were in that hour as far distant as heaven is from hell.

In such a setting our Lord stooped to the menial act of washing the feet of His disciples. None of them had volunteered this courtesy, either for their Master or for their fellow disciples, so the Master did it for them. You would not expect men who habitually argued among themselves who should be accounted greatest in the Kingdom of God, to bemean themselves by washing one another's feet! Men who tried to put in their claims to prominent seats in the Kingdom would hardly be found doing slaves' work for the others. Small men trying to be big cannot afford to stoop. The truly great man is never bemeaned by doing the lowly task. But the action of our Lord was more than that of the great man who can afford to humble himself. It was in a moment of unusually keen realization of His divine nature, mission, destiny, and power that our blessed Saviour laid aside His outer robes, tied a towel around His loins, and, thus garbed in slave's livery, went through the process of washing the feet of those dull-minded, dull-hearted men, as carefully as He would have arranged new planetary systems. Will God wash men's feet? Will the holy God wash sinners' feet? He did. And He did it at a time when that would have seemed a very unnecessary detail in the eyes of any other man, when He might have been wholly absorbed with the dreadful hour which was come upon Him. What explanation can be given of such self-abasement, and at such a time? The Spirit of revelation writes the wonderful story under the title, "Love to the Uttermost."

The importance of the incident lies not only in the literal act, but in the symbolic significance of it. Our Lord was acting out a parable of that complete stoop of His, from the heights of glory to the depths of shame, for the redemptive cleansing of sinners. From the feast of heavenly communion He rose up to become the Servant of Jehovah and assume the task which involved so much abasement. The robes of eternal majesty were laid aside for the humble garb of human flesh.

> Hast thou not heard that my Lord Jesus died?
> Then let me tell thee a stranger story:
> The God of power, as He did ride

> In His majestic robes of glory,
> Resolved to light; and so one day
> He did descend, undressing all the way.
>
> The stars His tire of light and rings obtained,
> The cloud His bow, the fire His spear,
> The sky His azure mantle gained;
> And when they asked what He would wear,
> He smiled, and said as He did go,
> He had new clothes a-making here below.

Instead of a basin of water, He brought to this deeper cleansing a fountain of blood, His own precious blood poured out in the sacrifice of atonement. He had to stoop very low, low enough to wash the feet of the vilest sinner. So He shed His blood, not on the battlefield, as a soldier, but on the cross, as a malefactor.

> His blood can make the foulest clean;
> His blood availed for me.
>
> CHARLES WESLEY

When Peter enters, it is usually with a thud. Passionate, impulsive, unaccountable Peter: we all love him, even when he is most wrong. The feet washing could not go smoothly when he was there. It seemed to him utterly incredible, and completely out of place, that the One whom he believed to be the Christ, the Son of the living God, should do this for him. "Dost thou wash my feet?" (John 13:6), he exclaimed in protesting wonder. The emphasis is on the *thou* and the *my*, which come together in the Greek, throwing up the contrast in striking boldness. Christ's answer was a plea for present trust, in view of understanding which would come later. And Peter did understand "after these things" (21:1); after his fall and recovery, after the sufferings and death of the Master, after the resurrection triumph, after the forty days of wonderful reappearances, after the mighty baptism of the Holy Spirit at Pentecost.

The words of Jesus have wider scope than the original settings. "What I do thou knowest not now, but thou shalt understand after these things" (13:7, author's trans.), how many times these words have brought comfort and courage to the hearts of God's people in the cloudy and dark day!

Not now, but in the coming years,
It may be in the better land,
We'll read the meaning of our tears,
And there, sometime, we'll understand.

We'll know why clouds instead of sun
Were over many a cherished plan;
Why song has ceased when scarce begun;
'Tis there, sometime, we'll understand.

God knows the way, He holds the key,
He guides us with unerring hand;
Sometime with tearless eyes we'll see;
Yes, there, up there, we'll understand.

Even here we gain ever new understanding of His ways, and are able to look back and say, "He hath done all things well" (Mark 7:37).

Peter passed from question to assertion, rejecting the Lord's proposal to wait for understanding. And when Peter made an assertion, he used no uncertain terms: "Thou shalt certainly not wash my feet as long as the world stands!" (John 13:8, author's trans.). And we can picture him drawing his feet up within the folds of his robe, suiting the action to his words. When we remember that this act of our Lord's was a symbol and parable of the cross, we can see in Peter's bold refusal to have the Lord wash his feet another way of saying, "Be it far from Thee, Lord; this shall not be unto Thee." So once again, with all his good intentions, Peter was acting the part of Satan, seeking to divert Jesus from the way of the cross. The most fatal errors and the deepest wrongs may be packed in the wrappings of the best intentions.

See how the Lord turns our worst mistakes to good account. Out of Peter's well-meaning mutiny comes a deep, rich lesson. "If I wash thee not, thou hast no part with me" (13:8b). No communion without cleansing! When a little fellow comes in from playing in a fine, big mud puddle, "A' smoored wi' glaur," as the Scotsman would say, does his mother, all dressed for company, allow him, *in that condition*, to climb on her lap and hug her? No! She takes him first to the place of cleansing, and maybe there are some wry faces and woeful moans before he is in condition to be taken up in mother's arms. *Cleansing before communion!* Do you feel as if God is shutting you out when you go to prayer? Does He fail to speak to your heart when you read the Word? Does your service seem to go for nought, as if He were not accepting it? Most likely the secret is right here. Some sin, some disobedience, some negligence has blocked the channel of communion, and He is waiting for the confession which will open the way for forgiveness and cleansing, in order that you may again have part with Him in the fellowship of love and service. "If we confess our sins, he is faithful and just to forgive us our sins, and to cleanse us from all unrighteousness" (1 John 1:9).

Once again Peter's impulsive assertion gave place to equally impulsive prayer. If cleansing meant communion, and communion were contingent on cleansing, he would go in for all the cleansing that could be obtained. For Peter, with all his rashness and contradictions, really loved the Lord. "Lord, not my feet only, but also my hands and my head" (John 13:9). I don't blame Peter for that speech, for his hands and his head, as well as his feet, had got him into many a scrape. The trouble with Peter was that he made so many speeches, "not knowing what he said" (Luke 9:33), as on the mount of transfiguration. Yet how patiently Jesus dealt with him, answering what was really quite an impertinence with a wonderful lesson on the difference between the bath of regeneration and the repeated washings of sanctification. "He that is bathed" (John 13:10, ASV) has so been washed from all sin that he stands forever perfect and entirely clean before God, so far as judgment is concerned. Sin is no longer imputed to him, but the complete righteousness which Christ presented to God as the representative Man is forever put to his account. The fact remains, however, that sin does enter the daily life of the believer, and while it does not affect the believer's standing before God as Judge, it *does* affect his communion with God as Father. That first bath, wherein our sins were forever washed away, so that the court of heaven has no count standing against us forevermore, cannot be repeated, and does not need to be, for it cannot be annulled. But the daily walk must be brought under review, and everything removed that would hinder the full exercise and enjoyment of our privileges as sons of God. So, "if we walk in the light, as he is in the light . . . the blood of Jesus Christ His Son *keeps on cleansing* us from all sin" (1 John 1:7, author's trans.).

I do not believe that the Lord was establishing an ordinance in this place, as He did later in regard to the bread and wine. He acted out a parable of His own self-abasement for the saving of a lost world, and made it symbolic of the behavior of the saints toward one another. He gave us an example, not an institution. He showed us that to be like Him we must be servant of all. If literal feet washing falls in the way of our humbly serving after His pattern, then by all means we must literally wash feet. When Abigail was brought to David to become his wife, she fell before him, saying, "Let me be a servant to wash the feet of the servants of my lord" (1 Sam 25:41, author's trans.). There is a lot of pride and false dignity which must crumble before such a standard of Christian service. Dr. Holden tells of an occasion when the late bishop of Durham, Handley C. G. Moule, entertained him and others, including William Booth, the founder of the Salvation Army, in the bishop's palace. It had been a full day of conference, and they were all more or less weary. The bishop conducted the general, for whom the day had been specially strenuous, to the easy chair beside the blazing fire in the drawing room. Kneeling down before him, the godly bishop proceeded to unlace the old man's heavy boots, drew them off, and carried them away, then brought a pair of soft, comfortable slippers, again kneeling down to place them on the tired feet of his guest.

We all know that that is the way we ought to live and serve. Our Christian joy will come, not on the wings of such knowledge, but in the hand of obedience to it. "If ye know these things," said Jesus, using a construction which indicates that we do know; but when He added, "happy are ye if ye do them" (John 13:17), He did not suggest that we all *do*. Add obedience to krowledge, and blessed are ye!

36

THE TRAITOR

JOHN 13:18-30

In this chapter the betrayer of Christ stands before us:

1. The traitor cataloged (saint or fiend?)
2. The traitor announced (vv. 18-22)
3. The traitor identified (vv. 23-26)
4. The traitor dismissed (vv. 27-30)

SOME HAVE TRIED to exonerate Judas, in whole or in part, by attributing to him motives better than his act. Believing (his defenders contend) that Jesus was the Messiah, but impatient of His methods, he attempted to force the issue by placing Jesus in a situation where He must bestir Himself and claim His title. Not only secular writers have sought a justification of Judas, but some Christian leaders, including an Evangelical like Joseph Parker. In face of the epithets applied to the traitor by Jesus Himself—devil, son of perdition—I cannot countenance any such mitigation of blame.

Others have gone to the opposite extreme, and on the ground of these very epithets have concluded that there was something supernatural in Judas. Dr. G. Campbell Morgan writes: "I do not believe Judas was a man as other men. I believe he was a devil incarnate; I believe he was the son of perdition; and I believe that after his death, by his own hand, he went 'to his own place.' My own conviction has long been that Judas was raised up to do the darkest deed in human history, and that he was actually a devil incarnate." For my own part, I do not think these descriptions of Judas necessarily indicate a supernatural origin. A man can become a devil by selling himself to the devil; he can become a son of perdition by opening his heart to hell.

Hell was Judas's "own place," not because he natively came thence, but because he chose the way that leads thither.

Judas was a man with a native frailty, which was his undoing because he did not bring it to the Saviour for subduing. His weakness lay very close to his strength. He was a man of keen business sense, which nurtured a germ of covetousness until it became a passion dominating his whole outlook. The question arises, was Judas made bearer of the common purse because he was a good businessman? If the office was elective, that may have been so. But I think that our Lord had a voice in his appointment, and that He had this particular member of the band assigned to the task, not so much for his strength, as for his weakness. It is well known that medical men try to localize an infection in order to treat it the more effectively. Here, then, was an office, in which the infection of covetousness was localized, so that what looks at first sight like putting temptation in the way of this man was really an opportunity for him to face his sin. At this point victory must be won, or at this point all would be lost. The power of God was present to heal him, but he would not be healed, till the disease broke forth in an eruption of foulness whose stench remains to this day. The more he yielded to his sin in pilfering from the meager purse, the more he hated the sinless One against whom he was sinning, until at last he was willing to accept blood money in a plot of betrayal against his best and divine Friend. It has been well said that "Judas was the worst of men because he was false to the best of men." Never play with a weakness, lest it prove itself a powerful monster of destruction.

Who would have dreamed that when David cried out to God from his sickbed about the familiar friend who had turned traitor against him, he was really predicting the Saviour's betrayal by Judas? It was no fanciful interpreter who gave us that, but the Lord Himself saw the prophetic import in what would seem to have only local reference. David's betrayal, then, was a type of his divine Son's betrayal, and his complaint became a Scripture which must needs be fulfilled in the Messiah. Then, after all we can say about Judas's responsibility and guilt, and his opportunities for recovery, we learn the other side of the truth, the divine sovereignty side, that this reprobate man was chosen for this very purpose: "I know whom I have chosen . . . that the scripture may be fulfilled" (John 13:18). Paul's tremendous argument about Pharaoh in Romans 9 could be equally applied to Judas.

A great agitation shook Jesus as He announced the foul treachery about to be committed: "Verily, verily, I say unto you, that one of you shall betray me" (13:21*b*). Many a wound had He received at the hands of the Jews, and many more would He receive at both Jewish and Gentile hands, but *"one of you!"*

> This was the most unkindest cut of all;
> For when the noble Caesar saw him stab,
> Ingratitude, more strong than traitors' arms,
> Quite vanquished him: then burst his mighty heart.

Let Shakespeare sing for us the baseness of such ingratitude:

> Blow, blow, thou winter wind,
> Thou art not so unkind
> As man's ingratitude;
> Thy tooth is not so keen
> Because thou art not seen
> Although thy breath be rude.
>
> Freeze, freeze, thou bitter sky,
> Thou dost not bite so nigh
> As benefits forgot;
> Though thou the waters warp,
> Thy sting is not so sharp
> As friend remember'd not.

I think the Lord had a twofold object in refraining from an open identification of the traitor. For one thing, He knew that this heart-searching on the part of all the disciples would be a wholesome discipline in view of the coming test to their faith and loyalty. If we can be deceived into thinking that we cannot sin in this direction or that, Satan has gotten us well prepared for that very sin. Was it not so with Peter just a little later? A little more trembling for himself would have cast him more on the Lord for strength. But at least their awakening to the possibility of the sin of treachery in their own hearts was a wonderful fortifying of the disciples against it. Then, too, with all of His knowledge of what Judas was about to do, Jesus never relaxed

His gracious efforts to redeem that sold-out man. With the horrible crime already half committed, the gracious Lord would not confirm the traitor in his deed by openly pointing him out. Rather, He would give him every opportunity to abandon his evil project, approaching the subject in such a way that a heart still human would have revolted from the unspeakable crime. Yet it was meet that someone in the apostolic band should receive the intelligence, in order to bear witness to the perfection of our Lord's foreknowledge. Who should more appropriately receive it than John, the special intimate of the Master? And who should more appropriately signal John to ask than Peter?

The bosom of Jesus is a good place to learn secrets. You will receive joyful confidences there, and the Lord will trust you further by letting you into the more sorrowful secrets of His heart. When glad and prosperous days come to us, we call our friends and neighbors to rejoice with us; but when evil attends our way, we seek out our most intimate friends, who will enter into our griefs with us. Are we close enough to Jesus to share His burdens? Then, too, have you wondered why John did not jump up, when by the sign of the sop Jesus indicated to him that Judas was the guilty one, and denounce the traitor before the whole company of the disciples? Was it because he was so stunned, as if Judas were the very last that he would have suspected? Or was it that He was close enough to Jesus to have his passions subdued even in face of so appalling a discovery? The miracle of grace is surely operating in this "son of thunder" (see Mark 3:17) ! I am sure there would be fewer volcanic eruptions among the saints of God if we dwelt more deeply in the bosom of our Lord.

"After the sop Satan" (John 13:27a) . Strange association! That sop was more than a sign of identification to John. It was a mark of special honor and favor to him who received it; to Judas it was a last, powerful call back from the way of destruction which he was following, and a last tender invitation to a life of blessed, loving communion with the Lord. Surely there must have been a convulsion of emotion in the heart of Judas in that moment; till Satan, afraid that he was about to lose the instrument which he had so cunningly prepared for this very hour, entered into him a tidal wave of evil, destroying the last vestige of finer feeling in the already so hardened son of perdition.

The disciples must have felt the tenseness of the atmosphere as this spiritual battle was waging, although quite unacquainted with the nature of it. Jesus, completely Master of the situation, knew the very moment when Judas finally threw his whole being open to the entrance and domination of Satan. There was nothing further to do, save to separate that devil from the little company of His true apostles, and to commit him to his evil designs. Yet even the manner of the dismissal of Judas still left the way open for him to return in penitence, for only Jesus and Judas, of the whole group, knew the meaning of the ambiguous words, "What thou doest, do quickly" (13:27b). Even John, who had been let in on the secret of the traitor's identity, had no idea it was coming so soon, and doubtless shared the general thought that the exit of Judas at the command of Jesus had to do with his office of treasurer for the little company. So if he had even then turned back from his black purpose, he would have returned to an unsuspecting company.

"He then having received the sop went immediately out: *and it was night*" (13:30, italics added). That last phrase has caught the imagination of Bible readers ever since this record was given to the church. It suggests the pall of eternal darkness coming down upon this man who had sold himself to sell the Son of God. It was the outer darkness, a night that knows no dawning. The hour would come when Judas awoke to the awfulness of his deed, but his remorse would be met only by the sneers of the priests and the laughter of hell. It would be no awakening to the light of a new and better day, but a plunge deeper into the darkness as he, by his own hand, went "to his own place" (Acts 1:25b). Whoever goes out from the presence of Christ goes out into the night, but whoever abides with Him dwells in eternal day.

37

TABLE TALK

JOHN 13:23—14:23

In this chapter we find Christ answering some very pertinent questions:

1. John asks a question about the traitor (13:25)
2. Peter asks a question about death (13:36)
3. Thomas asks a question about the way (14:5)
4. Philip asks a question about the Father (14:8)
5. Jude asks a question about self-revelation (14:22)

THE APOSTLE JOHN does not relate the actual partaking of the Passover feast, nor the institution of the Lord's Supper. He does, however, give us some of the "table talk" during that period. From the washing of the disciples' feet to the departure from the upper room, the conversation was punctuated with questions, which not only indicated the vast topics which were exercising the minds of these men as the Lord sought to brace them for the coming tragedy, but opened up avenues of revelation in the replies of Jesus.

John asked his question at the instigation of Peter. "Lord, who is it?" (John 13:25), he queried, as he leaned on Jesus' bosom, his lips close to the Master's ear. It was not a question of base curiosity. Both Matthew and Mark tell us that the announcement of a traitor in the company elicited from all of the disciples the question, "Is it I?" They were taken with a great agitation at the news, and looked around about at each other to see whether any bore the stamp of guilt; but each one, sure it could be none of the others, sickened at the awful thought that it might be himself. For the moment, even Peter could not be sure of himself. There is something noble about this readiness on the part of these men to doubt themselves rather than suspect each other. It rather compensates in measure (if we may speak the language of men) for their childish wrangling for high seats in the Kingdom.

Receiving no enlightenment from the barrage of self-accusing questions, Peter, impatient of suspense, motioned to John to use his position of advantage to secure an answer. The bosom of Jesus is a good place to get answers to one's questions. There is an intimacy of fellowship and a wealth of enlightenment to be obtained there. When we were out on conducted hikes in the Smokies, it was by keeping close to our guides that we became acquainted with them, secured some good close-up pictures of the objects of demonstration, and had our questions answered with added information. How many hearts are full of questionings! But men beat their questions into weapons of defense against the approach of the Lord Jesus, instead of coming to Him who alone can answer them. Press into the inner circle, and, leaning on Jesus' breast, instead of being weighted down with a load of empty negatives, you will be led into all the truth. See how John not only had his question answered, but witnessed a new demonstration of the grace of the beloved Master in handing the traitor the token of friendship.

Peter's question was about the Lord's departure: "Whither goest thou?" (John 13:36). Jesus had told them repeatedly that He was going out to death, and to Peter, as to men generally before Christ "abolished death, and brought life and immortality to light" (2 Tim 1:10*b*, ASV), there was a great *Whither?* attached to death. The Old Testament revelation had punctured the blackness of death with a few gleams of hope and assurance, especially in Messianic passages, but on the whole death was still the unexplained mystery, "a land of darkness, as darkness itself" (Job 10:22), where the praises of the Lord were not known. Peter, then, was but asking the question of the multitudes "who through fear of death were all their lifetime subject to bondage" (Heb 2:15). "Whither goest Thou? Thou hast been saying Thou must die, but whither doth death lead?"

Jesus, as a master Teacher, did not always answer questions categorically. He carried His questioners along until their minds were capable of receiving the revelation. He did not immediately say, "I

am going to the Father." Before the end of the discourse He will say
so quite definitely, when He will have prepared them to receive it.
In the meantime He has something for Peter. Remember that to Peter
death is not yet "to be with Christ; which is far better" (Phil 1:23) —
it is still the great "Whither?" In face of that, his statement is the
more admirable: "Why cannot I follow thee now? I will lay down my
life for thy sake" (John 13:37). And he meant it too! Only he did not
know himself. He did not know how like he was to the Potomac Light
Infantry, which disbanded at the outbreak of the Civil War, and to
which one of its members proposed the toast, "The P.L.I., invincible
in peace, invisible in war." Jesus knew that Simon Barjona was not
yet the rock, and He answered, "not *die,* but *deny.*" Nevertheless
afterward, Cephas would emerge, to fulfill his vow and win the mar-
tyr's crown.

Thomas was not given to smooth words. He was rather blunt in
his expressions. His question was not only an interruption of the
Lord's discourse but a blatant contradiction. What Jesus had said
about the Father's house and the many mansions should have answered Peter's "Whither?" to a discerning mind, but Thomas was
still "dull o' the uptak'," as the Scots saying is. So when Jesus said,
"Whither I go, ye know the way" (14:4, ASV), he rather rudely inter-
jected, "We don't even know where you are going! How then do we
know the way?" (v. 5, author's trans.). Jesus answered both questions
in His reply, while making a yet bigger revelation. The Father, even
God, is the destination: not His only, but the goal of all creation. But
how may men come to God? Not by a ritual, not by a creed, not by
an institution, not by an ethic, but by a Person: "I am the way . . . no
man cometh unto the Father, *but by me*" (14:6, italics added). An
amazing statement for One persistently speaking about His approaching death! That death, then, would not mean the closing of the way,
but the opening of it. It is "a new and living way . . . consecrated for
us, through the veil, that is to say, *his flesh*" (Heb 10:20, italics
added).

Not only is there no coming to God apart from the Lord Jesus;
there is no knowing God apart from Him. "I am the truth" (John
14:6), He says —"the full outshining of His glory, and the exact image
of His substance" (Heb 1:3, author's trans.). "And the life" (John

14:6) —for as there is no way to God nor knowledge of God apart from Christ, so there is no relation possible with God except in Him. "This is the record, that God hath given to us eternal life, and this life is *in his Son*" (1 John 5:11, italics added). "This is the true God, and eternal life" (1 John 5:21).

"Shew us the Father" (John 14:8), exclaimed Philip, with considerable emotion, as of one giving utterance to the deepest hunger of his soul. Jesus had followed up His claim to be "the truth," in whom alone God could be known, with the further statement, "If you had come into experimental knowledge of Me so as to know Me truly, you should have perceived my Father also: and from now you are coming to know Him and have so seen Him that you have the vision of Him continually before you" (14:9, author's trans.). That was exactly what Philip, true seeker after God, was longing for, not yet knowing that in Jesus he had found. His request, "Shew us the Father," was an unbaring of his deepest soul and the echo of many a God-seeking heart. It was this very quest that kept him following Jesus. He believed that Jesus, if anyone, could lead him and his fellow seekers into this knowledge, but he had expected Jesus to reveal the Father *apart from Himself*. That was his great error, which kept him blinded to the true glory of his Lord all the three years of their walking together. Our Lord's answer to Philip's request, then, was a reproof of his blindness and a correction of his error, as well as a wonderful declaration of the perfect oneness of the Godhead. Jesus is Himself the answer to man's search for God. "He that hath seen me hath seen the Father" (14:9*b*). The "light of the knowledge of the glory of God" shines "in the face of Jesus Christ" (2 Cor 4:6). So now we paraphrase and correct Philip's prayer by crying, "Lord Jesus, shew me Thy face, and I am satisfied." Christ Himself is the revelation of the Father. Do not be looking for anything beyond Him or apart from Him.

Finally we have Jude's question, arising out of the Lord's promise of self-manifestation to those who loved Him. "What is come to pass," asks this thoughtful disciple, "that Thou art about to manifest Thyself to us, and not to the world?" (John 14:22, author's trans.). Jude had been expecting a world manifestation, in keeping with the common Messianic conceptions. He now clearly recognized that the Lord was planning a different kind of program. His question is suggestive of a

new order of things, a new dispensation, in which the revelation of
Christ would be made, not to the world at large, but to an election.
For answer, Jesus indicates the form of that manifestation, that it is to
be by means of an indwelling of Father and Son in the believer. Is the
world to be deprived, then, of the revelation of Christ? No! But it
is to come to the world through these God-indwelt channels.

> Channels only, blessed Master!
> But with all Thy wondrous power
> Flowing through us,
> Thou canst use us,
> Every day, and every hour.

See, then, what things were occupying the minds of these men: a
searching out of sin, the "afterwards" of death, the way to God, the
vision of God, and the testimony of Christ. So after all we may say
about their dullness and slowness, we have to admit that they grappled
with big questions. Those, too, were the early days of the gospel. How
much progress have we made after two millenniums of gospel enlightenment? Do we think big thoughts? Is our table talk about big
things?

38

A FRUITFUL VINE

JOHN 15:1-8

In this chapter we consider

1. The vine and its branches (vv. 1, 5)
2. The fruit and its increase (vv. 2, 3, 8)
3. The fruit-bearing and its law (vv. 4-5)

JESUS DID NOT SAY, "I am the root, ye are the branches." Jesus *did* say, "I am the vine, ye are the branches" (John 15:5). The vine includes the root, the stock, the branches, the tendrils, the leaves, and the fruit. He is the whole: and here is the wonder of the statement—we are part of Him! Blessed identification! This is in keeping with 1 Corinthians 12:12 (italics added) : "For as the body is one, and hath many members, and all the members of that one body, being many, are one body: *so also is Christ.*" Christ is the whole body, and we are part of Him. The very title, Christ, embraces the Lord Himself, and His people, in this wonderful unity.

Both figures teach us that one life is common to the Lord and to all believers. As the same life functions in the windings of the stock, the spreading of the branches, the clinging of the tendrils, the unfolding of the buds, and the maturing of the clusters, so the same life, which is Christ, expresses itself in us according to our several appointments. Just as, in the unity of the Body, our Lord reserves to Himself the office and functions of the Head, so in the unity of the vine He reserves the office and functions of the root. We are the branches. We cannot assume or claim a position in the vine more fundamental than He declares. Now the branches, while sharing the one life common to the whole vine, are dependent for that life on the root which distributes to all the parts. In other words, the branches are not the seat of the life, but the root is. So "God hath given to us eternal life, and this life is *in his Son*" (1 John 5:11, italics added). Hence our utter and continual dependence on Christ for the supply of life, and therefore for everything that life signifies—victory, communion, power. Although stated in another connection, that word of the apostle is true here: "Thou bearest not the root, but the root thee" (Rom 11:18).

The end of a vine is not to spread branches, but to bear fruit. What part of the vine bears the clusters? Certainly not the root, but the branches. So it is in that part of Christ which is you and me that the fruit is to be brought forth. The Lord will supply the life, the nourishment, the energy, but in us the fruit is to be displayed. The glory of a vine is its fruit. It is a wonderful and solemn thought that the Lord is depending on us for the display of His glory. We read that He is coming "to be glorified in his saints" (2 Thess 1:10). But may He not have a little glory in us now? I hope so.

Before going further we ought to inquire, What is this fruit which we are to bear as branches of the vine? And, speaking negatively first, it is not "church work." We must surely affirm in all honesty that much activity going by that name is not fruit, but fungus. Fungus is a parasite, and so is much church work, being not only foreign to the true purpose of the church, but actually killing the church and its testimony. Then, too, much legitimate and necessary activity may be fungus because it springs from pride and selfishness and ambition rather than from the spirit of life in Christ Jesus. The searchlight of the Holy Spirit will reveal the true nature of all our activities, if we allow Him to search. Dr. Torrey has told of the leading soprano in his choir in Chicago, who, being searched by the fire of the Holy Spirit, confessed that she had till that time sung only for her own gratification and not for the glory of God; and a minister acquaintance of mine made a similar confession regarding his preaching. Fruit or fungus?

Primarily and chiefly, the fruit which we are called to bear is character. The apostle Paul calls it "the fruit of the Spirit" (Gal 5:22), and is it not the "supply of the Spirit" (Phil 1:19) that produces the fruit? Here, then, is the cluster: "love, joy, peace, longsuffering, gentleness, goodness, faithfulness, meekness, self-control" (Gal 5:22-23, ASV). It is the ninefold excellency of our Lord Jesus, and that is to appear in us. If you say it is impossible, then deny the possibility of apples growing on an apple tree. "I am the vine" (John 15:5). If the fruit of the vine is "love, joy, peace, longsuffering, gentleness, goodness, faithfulness, meekness, self-control," then such is the fruit of the branches. And please remember that it is not a matter of one branch bearing love and another bearing joy and so on, any more than we have trees growing apples on one branch and cherries on another. The same fruit grows on every branch, and that a cluster of nine excellencies, which are the very image of Christ.

Then with the fruit of character comes the fruit of service. The same Spirit who works in us these graces of Christ will also reach out through us to bless others in Christlike ministry. "He that believeth in me, as the Scripture hath said, out of his inner man shall flow rivers of living water. This spake He of the Spirit, which they that believe on Him should receive" (John 7:38-39, author's trans.). The nature of that ministry will be determined by the Holy Spirit. Some will be specially fruitful in soul-winning, some in instruction, some in comfort, some in practical helpfulness. All will be to the glory of God. It will be fruit, not fungus. One may not always know the extent of his own fruitfulness in service. A peach tree does not count its own peaches. It just grows them, and the Master counts them.

As has often been pointed out, three degrees of fruit-bearing are hinted in this passage, in the terms fruit, more fruit, and much fruit: in keeping with the thirtyfold, sixtyfold, and hundredfold of our Lord's parable of the sower and the four soils. Here the operation of the Husbandman comes in. God had a vine, Israel by name, which He transplanted from Egypt to Canaan and gave it great care; but it turned out to be a "degenerate plant" to Him. In His Son He has found the "true vine" and of this He is very jealous, saying, "I the LORD do keep it; I will water it every moment: lest any hurt it, I will keep it night and day" (Isa 27:3). Spurious growths that bear no fruit He will ruthlessly cut away. Fruit-bearing branches He will prune for increased bearing, until He is glorified in the much fruit; for always it is the keeper of a tree, not the tree itself, that receives the award and the glory. And did you notice that the Word of the Lord is the "cathartic" used on the branches? Don't shrink from the medicine, though it be sharp at times. "It's gude for what ails ye!"

It is recorded that on the great day when Buffalo expected the fulfillment of its hopes and the fruit of its labors in bringing electrical power from Niagara Falls, there was no illumination in response to the throwing of the great switch. Consternation reigned, and the experts, brought from all parts of the country, failed to find the trouble. Lord Kelvin, brought all the way from Glasgow, discovered an apparently slight oversight. Pointing it out, he declared that at this point they were disobeying the laws of electricity; let them obey nature's law in this particular, and they should have light. They repaired the breach, obeyed the law, and Buffalo was flooded with new light.

Would we bear fruit, in character and service? There is a law of fruit-bearing which must be obeyed, and, when obeyed, will surely bring results. "Abide in me, and I in you. As the branch cannot bear fruit of itself, except it abide in the vine; no more can ye, except ye abide in me" (John 15:4). What is the law of fruit-bearing? Abiding!

Dr. Bieber of Philadelphia gave me this illustration at the dinner table when we were at a Bible conference together. Archbishop Ussher, the noted Bible chronologist, was greatly afflicted with gout in his old age, so that his activities were few. He had himself seated in an east window in the morning, where he enjoyed the brightness of the rising sun. Toward noon he was moved to a window with southern exposure, where the warm rays of the midday sun cheered him. As afternoon wore on he watched the decline of the sun and the glory of its setting. He was abiding in the sun. Do we thus bask in the presence of our blessed Lord, allowing the rays of His love and of His Spirit to penetrate our inmost soul? I think we might well say that abiding in Christ is the practice of the presence of Christ. It is union and communion. And that is the law of fruit-bearing.

Did you ever see a grape branch "trying hard" to bear fruit? No! It just abides in the vine, and the fruit forms and ripens in obedience to that law. Neither will trying hard to be like Christ produce the fruit of holiness and of acceptable service. "He that abideth in me, and I in him, the same bringeth forth much fruit: for without me ye can do nothing" (John 15:5). A fruit-bearing branch receives all from the root and gives all in the fruit; so does a fruit-bearing Christian.

Abide in Thee, in that deep love of Thine,
My Jesus, Lord, Thou Lamb of God divine;
Down, closely down, as living branch with tree,
I would abide, my Lord, my Christ, in Thee.

Abide in Thee, nor doubt, nor self, nor sin,
Can e'er prevail with Thy blest life within;
Joined to Thyself, communing deep, my soul
Knows nought besides its motions to control.

Abide in Thee, 'tis thus alone I know
The secrets of Thy mind e'en while below;
All joy and peace, and knowledge of Thy Word,
All power and fruit, and service for the Lord.

39

THE COMFORTER

JOHN 14:15-18, 25-27; 15:22-27; 16:7-15

In this chapter we are shown the different ministries of the promised Comforter:

1. The Comforter, Messenger of communion (14:15-18)
2. The Comforter, Messenger of peace (14:25-27)
3. The Comforter, Messenger of witness (15:22-27)
4. The Comforter, Messenger of conviction (16:7-11)
5. The Comforter, Messenger of revelation (16:12-15)

IT WAS A SAD GROUP that huddled about Jesus in the upper room that night. He had become dearer to them than life itself, and they were now faced with the dismal prospect of His departure. They could not quite take it all in, but His talk about betrayal and denial and mockery and crucifixion was bringing down upon them a pall of gloom, a sickening sense of desolation.

Having told them the worst, Jesus now undertook to comfort them. "Let not your heart be troubled" (John 14:1), He exclaimed. That is easily said, but had He a cure for their troubled hearts? Jesus never bids us "cheer up" without giving good cause for cheer. First, He exhorted His failing disciples to unflinching faith in Him, as in God, whatever tragedies they might see Him passing through. He then told them of the Father's house whither He was going, and of the many dwellings among which He would prepare a place for their eternal abode. With that He gave them the thrilling promise of His return for them, when they would be reunited with Him forever.

Blessed consolations! But none of these words canceled the fact of His leaving them, and they could not rise above the desolation of the little or long time between. This world would now be very empty for them. No loves, no friendships would ever fill the place of His presence. They already felt themselves groping along as orphans in a world that had nothing to offer them. Then it was that Jesus said, "I will not leave you orphaned: I come to you!" And this time He was not speaking of His "second coming," but was interpreting the meaning of the preceding promise, "I will pray the Father, and he shall give you another Comforter, that he may abide with you for ever; even the Spirit of truth; whom the world cannot receive, because it seeth him not, neither knoweth him: but ye know him; for he dwelleth with you, and shall be in you" (John 14:16-17).

So that is what Jesus was to them—Comforter! Called alongside for their help, He had been their constant Companion, Counselor, and Guide, yet in such a way that they were not unmanned and weakened, but consistently strengthened and fortified. Now, despite their sense of helplessness in face of His departure, they were actually far more fitted for life than before they had met Him. Yet the kind of life He would have them live was still too much for them, and always would be. They would always require the mighty help which He alone could give them: yes, and a help beyond what He ever could give in the present relationships. It was expedient for them that He should go, not that He might leave them alone, but that He might come to them in a new way, with help equal to the need. And the answer was—the other Comforter, the gift of the Father at the high request of the Son, a presence never withdrawn, dwelling within, so one with Jesus that He might be called the Lord's "other self." By His abiding, their fellowship with the beloved Lord would be more real, more complete, more enduring. Instead of being lost to them, He would be "closer . . . than breathing, and nearer than hands or feet." So the Comforter, the Spirit of truth, is the divine Messenger of communion.

There are some people whose presence inspires confidence and ministers peace. John McNeil, the Scottish evangelist, tells us that when a young man, he had to walk seven miles of dark, lonely road from Greenock to Inverkip when he went home at the end of each week. Although he was a rugged lad, and naturally courageous, there was something eerie about that road, and the many tales of robberies and assaults in the glen did not tend to allay his fears. One specially dark Saturday night, about two miles from home, he was startled with a sudden call out of the blackness of night before him: "Is that you, Johnnie?" It was his father's strong voice, and, after the first shock of the unexpected, fear vanished, and he walked the remaining miles with his father, freed from all panic of the way.

I think that is how the disciples felt about the presence of Jesus. How often had His words filled their distraught hearts with peace, and His presence quieted their panic! But words have a way of fading from the memory and losing their first power when the speaker's voice is stilled. Jesus had plainly told them that He was sending them forth "as sheep in the midst of wolves" (Matt 10:16). How would they fare in the storms ahead without His quieting presence and cheering voice? How could they battle down their fears and carry a peaceful heart without Him? Right there He answered their thoughts: "Peace I leave with you, my peace I give unto you: not as the world giveth, give I unto you. Let not your heart be troubled, neither let it be afraid" (John 14:27).

But how? His way of giving peace was not the world's way, which is always a temporary expedient. He was to purchase this promised peace with His own blood, and then bestow it in the sending of His other Self, the Comforter, who would keep these assuring words of the Master alive in the hearts of His people, and speak words of like power for every occasion. "The Comforter, the Holy Ghost, whom the Father will send in my name, he shall teach you all things, and bring all things to your remembrance, whatsoever I have said unto you. Peace!" (14:26-27a). So the Comforter, the Holy Ghost, is the divine Messenger of peace.

"They hated me" (15:18, author's trans.), says Jesus, echoing the words of the psalmist for a brief summing up of the effects of His ministry, especially on the ruling classes of Jewry. They hated Him whom all heaven loved. They hated Him who brought heaven's love to men. They hated Him to death who loved unto death. In hating Him, they gave final evidence of their hatred of God whom they professed to love.

Why did they hate Him? They hated Him for His words, and for His works. The words He spoke to them took away their last excuse for sin. No longer could they veil their sin under any pretext of ignorance. They could not cut corners on the Law after this Prophet of Galilee's exposition of it. There could be no more trimming of the letter nor disregard of the spirit. Nor could they longer hide their hypocrisies under a cloak of sanctimonious superiority. He had torn the mask from their evil faces, had uncovered the rottenness of the hidden sepulchers, and had set the rulers of Jewry in a light which made publicans and sinners appear like saints beside them. Before His burning words they must either repent unto salvation or steel themselves in hate to their own destruction. As a class they followed the latter course.

The works of Jesus stirred their hate as much as His words. They were mighty works which they were unable to match. They were beneficent works which stirred their jealousy. They were redemptive works which they attributed to evil powers. The more completely the works evidenced His coming from God, the more deliberately they accused Him of league with Beelzebub. In their determined hate of the Son whom they would not acknowledge, they threw all fear of God to the winds and hated the Father also. His proffered gift to them was love and light and life. They returned to Him as their free gift hate, intense and bitter.

So Jesus went out wrapped in the shroud of human hate, calumny, and shame, and the few disciples were being left behind to represent Him; that meant being "despised and rejected of men" (Isa 53:3) as He was, and it looked like a hopeless task to reverse the world's judgment of malice. The Master had an answer to that situation also. There would be witness borne to Him in the days following the deep humiliation—honorable witness, potent witness, divine witness: so that the few disciples who went forth, while treated as the offscourings of the earth, would be in high and holy company, would have Almighty support in their witness. "When the Comforter is come, whom I will send unto you from the Father, even the Spirit of truth, which proceedeth from the Father, he shall testify of me: and ye also shall bear witness" (John 15:26-27a). Blessed partnership! So the Comforter is the divine Messenger of witness.

The testimony of Jesus Christ carries a threefold pronouncement most repugnant to the natural man. That pronouncement is concerning sin, righteousness, and judgment.

Sin is thought of in terms of murder, adultery, theft, drunkenness, lying, and the whole catalog of vices. Who would ever think of putting unbelief at the head of the list? Some might indeed regard a rank atheist as a sinner. (He used to be thought of as unfit for decent society; now he is quite respectable!) But a rejection of Christianity, especially in its more orthodox expression, is quite a mark of intellec tual superiority, an indication of commendable broad-mindedness, indeed the criterion of the truly modern man. Yet the sin of unbelief in Christ not only tops the list, but includes all the others, so that when that is removed, all are taken away. Not that faith carries virtue to cancel all sin, but faith lays hold of the great cancellation wrought on the cross. A Christian woman was asked, rather bitterly, if she thought deathbed repentance did away with the sin of a whole life. "No," she replied, "but Calvary does." Christ's work of sin-bearing has put men in a new relation to sin, belief or unbelief being the great determinant. Believe, and the score is settled; believe not, and the count remains.

Righteousness, according to man, is a matter of his own exertions, and men will defend their own righteousness to the last ditch, despite God's declaration that "all our righteousnesses are as filthy rags" (Isa 64:6). Righteousness has been thought of under three aspects—the righteousness that God is, the righteousness that God demands, and the righteousness that God bestows. We have no question about the infinite perfection of the righteousness which God is. The difficulty arises in the matter of the righteousness which God demands. Many define that in terms of man's best, and in that error perish. God has not two standards of righteousness—an absolute one for Himself, and a comparative one for man. His demands must tally with what He is. When He makes known His demands, it is first in a perfect law, and then in a perfect interpretation and living demonstration of that law. Jesus Christ has shown us both the righteousness that God is, and the righteousness that God demands. The ascension of Christ to the Father's right hand is the great assurance that God has accepted the righteousness which He as Son of Man offered, so that when we proclaim righteousness to men, it must be in terms of the perfections of Christ. Can we attain to that righteousness? Thank God! The message of righteousness includes this, that God bestows giftwise that perfect and accepted righteousness on us sinners, who could by no means attain to it by our own efforts.

Every man, in his folly, demands judgment in his own right, on his own merit. A day of judgment is generally acceded, when God will weigh men's good deeds over against their evil deeds, and vice-versa, and mete out to all accordingly. The Christian teaching is of a different order. This whole world is involved in judgment with its prince, the devil. In speaking of His cross, Jesus said, "Now is the judgment of this world: now shall the prince of this world be cast out" (John 12:31). Every man is included in that judgment, and is "condemned already" (3:18) until he renounces his allegiance to the rebellious prince, and seeks the shelter of the atoning blood. "He that heareth My words, and believeth Him that sent Me, hath eternal life, and cometh not into judgment, but is passed out of death into life" (5:24, author's trans.).

How will men ever believe such a testimony at our lips? They won't! It will require higher testimony than ours, though our lips may be used. That is why, in commissioning His disciples to deliver this testimony, Christ promised that the burden of convincing men should fall on a witness of higher rank. "It is expedient for you that I go away: for if I go not away, the Comforter will not come unto you; but if I depart, I will send him unto you. And when he is come, he will reprove the world of sin, and of righteousness, and of judgment" (John 16:7-8). So, then, the Comforter is also the divine Messenger of conviction.

Even the Almighty cannot teach us beyond our capacity. For three years these men had walked with the truth. Great was their privilege to be under the tutorage of the peerless Teacher, and mighty strides they had taken, both in truth learned and in capacity to learn. The very questions they were asking on this occasion showed that, while they had yet far to go, these were men of expanded soul. When our Lord spoke of them to the Father in the great communion chapter, it was with sincere pleasure, indicating that they had grasped some profound truths. But with all that, they were yet limited, and for all the intimate walk of the three years, there were yet vistas of truth into which the Master could not lead them because of their inability to receive it. There was wanting a certain maturity, without which the further revelation would confound rather than enlighten. "I have yet many things to say unto you, but ye cannot bear them now" (16:12). There is a danger, in these days of multiplied Bible conferences, for some to be exposed to teaching beyond their ability to receive, until, instead of profiting them, it cloys and frustrates healthy development. The truth becomes so much intellectual luxury, not a life-fashioning power. The principle of the graded lessons needs to be applied to stages of spiritual growth as much as to years of age.

Development is sometimes sudden. A child will seem to become adolescent almost overnight. Again, an awkward adolescent, irresponsible, very much in his own way, will suddenly find himself, and take on poise, self-confidence, alertness, responsibility, to the amazement of his friends. Frequently such sudden maturing is connected with some event or series of events which strikes at the root of the youth's soul—the death of his father, the call of his country, the vision of God, the entrance of love. Older people also will experience a belated maturing in relation to incidents of profound import.

So it was to be with the disciples of our Lord. The great Teacher had brought them a long way, but vast reaches of soul required opening for the reception of yet grander revelation, and only events of revolutionary character would accomplish that. They must walk through the valley of the shadow of death in the crucifixion of their beloved Master; they must taste the thrill of resurrection triumph in His rising; they must know the reality of communion with One risen from the dead, walking in the power of an endless life; and finally they must realize the insurge of God into their souls by the mighty baptism of the Holy Spirit. The few days covering those events would dwarf all the progress of the years preceding. These men would spring into spiritual manhood, full sonship, glorious maturity, till their hitherto questioning, uncertain minds would grapple confidently with truths bigger than the universe, purposes broader than history, visions higher than the heavens. For the Comforter would come to them as the Spirit of truth, to guide them into all the truth.

"What is truth?" asked Pilate, thinking perhaps that it was some sort of undiscoverable metaphysic, while the truth stood before him, a blessed, divine Person. The Holy Spirit makes no such mistake. If He is to lead us into all the truth, His theme will be Jesus, Jesus only. "He shall receive of mine, and shall shew it unto you" (John 16:14). Whether it be bringing to remembrance, or showing things to come, it will be always Jesus. Of such final import is the revelation He brings, that even the Holy Spirit will not speak from Himself, will not act apart from the high counsels of the triune Godhead: and in all He speaks and reveals, He will faithfully glorify the Son, the Lord Jesus, that every eye may be turned to Him, every knee bowed to Him, every tongue confess Him. If it be so with the Holy Spirit, what about us? Do we wait for our ministry? Do we make Jesus our constant theme? Do we turn the lamp of glory always on His face? So the Comforter is the divine Messenger of revelation.

Gather up the fragments, that nothing be lost. "I will send you another Comforter" (see John 15:26). And He turns out to be the Messenger of communion, of peace, of witness, of conviction, and of revelation. Do you see, then, how we need the blessed Paraclete in every department and aspect of our Christian life? If we would walk with Jesus, we must have the Holy Spirit to make His presence real to us. If we would know the peace which passeth all understanding, it must be breathed upon our hearts by the Holy Spirit. If we would faithfully and effectively witness for our Lord, and turn the shame of His cross into His glory, we must know the leading partnership of the Holy Spirit. If we would see men bow in submission to the truth of sin, righteousness, and judgment, we must depend upon the deep, convicting work of the Holy Spirit. If we would come to maturity of knowledge and understanding of the things of the Lord, we must allow the Holy Spirit to illumine our hearts and to turn light upon the face of Jesus for us.

> Our blest Redeemer, ere He breathed His tender, last farewell,
> A Guide, a Comforter bequeath'd with us to dwell.

> He came in semblance of a dove, with shelt'ring wings outspread,
> The holy balm of peace and love on earth to shed.

He came in tongues of living flame, to teach, convince, subdue;
All-powerful as the wind He came—as viewless too.

And every virtue we possess, and every victory won,
And every thought of holiness, are His alone.

Spirit of purity and grace, our weakness pitying see;
Oh, make our hearts Thy dwelling-place, and worthier Thee.

40

IN THE WORLD

JOHN 15:18-27

In this chapter we see the Christian in his relation to a world which lies in the wicked one:

1. The world's attitude to the Christian—hate (vv. 18-25)
2. The Christian's answer to the world—witness (vv. 26-27)

WHAT IS THIS "WORLD" which is consistently regarded in all Scripture as wholly inimical to God and His people, and concerning which so many exhortations are given that we should have no dealings with it, no love for it, no part in it? Is it the world of creation, which, despite the eclipse and the curse which have fallen on it through the sin of man, yet praises and magnifies the divine Creator? It cannot be that. Is it the dance, the theater, the tavern, the house of harlots, and all other institutions related to what we call "worldly pleasure"? No, it is not that. These may be part of the establishment of the world, but they are not the essence of it. The world is a kingdom, utterly antagonistic to the Kingdom of God. It is a spiritual kingdom, as the Kingdom of God is. It is controlled by God's great adversary, the devil, who rules through a highly organized hierachy of "principalities, dominions, and powers" (see Rom 8:38). The sphere of this kingdom is this world of ours, and its subjects are the human race—all who have not, through faith in the Lord Jesus Christ, been translated out of its darkness into the Kingdom of God's dear Son.

"The world hateth you" (John 15:19), said our Lord to His followers, having in mind, no doubt, the unseen rulers of this kingdom of darkness, but with special reference to its subjects, unregenerate men. All three synoptists record our Lord's saying to His disciples,

"Ye shall be hated of *all men* for my name's sake" (Matt 10:22, italics added). This hatred will not always take the form of personal animosity. Its essence is rather an attitude of unbelief, and often enough the worldling will rather admire the high ideals of the Christian while "regretting" his religious bigotry; or he will consider the believer a likable chap "if he were not so narrow," and so on. In war, how many who have no personal quarrels with each other, who may indeed be fast friends in personal relation, find themselves in the opposing ranks, and are bound to hate each other even to death! "Marvel not, my brethren, if the world hate you" (1 John 3:13), says the apostle John, echoing the words of His Master after years of experience of their truth. The world can do nothing else than hate us, even if men's personal feeling toward us be quite cordial.

Christ gives us two reasons for the world's hate. "If ye were of the world, the world would love his own: but because ye are not of the world . . . therefore the world hateth you" (John 15:19). Aliens must always be prepared to meet a degree of prejudice. When a foreign child comes into a school, there is at first a lively interest shown in him; and if he were only a passing visitor, all would be well. But it is not long before some child in the school has lit on some opprobrious nickname for the little stranger, and soon he is the butt of a deal of ridicule, the target of a lot of devilment, whom all and sundry regard as their rightful prey. That is the way of the world. The Christian is an alien, whose ways are not the world's ways, whose standards are not the world's standards, whose outlook is not the world's outlook: therefore "the world hateth you."

The second reason for the world's hate goes even deeper. "But I have chosen you out of the world, therefore the world hateth you" (John 15:19b). It is the fact that we used to be one of the world and have been withdrawn from it that makes the enmity more pronounced. Jews have no special antagonism against a Christian, provided he is a Gentile. But let a Jew become a Christian, and the hatred boils over. At an annual meeting of the Chicago Hebrew Mission I met a Hebrew Christian who, when first he announced his acceptance of Christ in his own home, received such a blow on the ear from his uncle and guardian that he has been totally deaf in that ear ever since. That uncle would not have thought of dealing that blow to a Gentile Christian. The special enmity is against those who have been called out from unbelieving Jewry. It is the same in heathendom. And since we all began as children of this world, this world will hate us when Christ calls us out from its ranks.

We are in good company in enduring the world's hatred. Our Lord says, "If the world hate you, ye know that it hated me before it hated you" (John 15:18). The servant must not expect better treatment at the hands of the enemy than the Lord Himself received. If the world had nothing better than a cross for Jesus, it will not have a royal carriage for His followers; if only thorns for Him, there will not be garlands for us. Four centuries before Christ, the great philosopher, Plato, expressed a belief which proved to be prophetic. "I am of opinion," he said, "that the truly righteous man, if he were to appear in the world, would be scourged, would be thrown into fetters, would be hanged." He came, and it so happened to Him. But, someone says, the attitude of the world is very different from what it was when Jesus was here on earth. The world has learned His worth, and if He were to come back now, He would be received with mighty ovations, and heralded as the world's Saviour and Sovereign! But would He? A woman was expressing that opinion at a large social function in London on one occasion, and, turning to rugged Thomas Carlyle, who was present, for confirmation of her view, she received the frank reply, "No, madam, if Christ came to London today they would take Him to Newgate and hang Him." I believe Carlyle was right. And Christ would receive no better treatment in New York or Chicago or Los Angeles. Jesus Christ would make such an exposure of the sin which goes unchecked all around us, even as He tore the mask off the Pharisees of that other day, that He would not long be endured. We are in enemy territory; let us not expect the treatment of friends. Only let us see to it that the world's hatred of us is really "for Christ's sake" (2 Cor 12:10), and not on account of anything hateful in us and unworthy of the gracious Lord whom we represent.

What is to be our answer to the world's hatred? Witness. That is the answer of love, even if it increase the hatred. The ethics of the medical association expect a doctor who has discovered a means of relief for human ills to make it known. Manufacturers' secrets do not hold in that sphere. There are times also when manufacturers are called upon to tell their jealously guarded secrets for the common weal. In his book *The Mirrors of Downing Street,* the anonymous writer, who calls himself "A Gentleman With a Duster," describes the occasion during the First World War when David Lloyd George called together the manufacturers of Britain in Whitehall to persuade them to pool their trade secrets in the interests of a greater supply of better munitions of war. There was much unwillingness, as these businessmen tried to show that such a proposition was beyond reason. Finally Mr. Lloyd George leaned forward, and in a quiet but dramatic tone which produced a deep hush, said: "Gentlemen, have you forgotten that your sons, at this very moment, are being killed— killed in hundreds of thousands? They are being killed by German guns for want of British guns. Your sons, your brothers—boys at the dawn of manhood!—they are being wiped out of life in thousands! Gentlemen, give me guns. Don't think of your trade secrets. Think of your children. Help them! Give me those guns." The secrets were laid out on the table, and the victory supply of munitions was forthcoming. Shall we then withhold from those who are perishing, going down into eternal ruin, our secret of life and salvation, which is the testimony of Christ? What if the world hate us on account of that very testimony! Was it not for a world that hated Him that God gave His beloved Son to the cross? Did He not love us when we were enemies and aliens in our minds by wicked works? Then shall not we also bear that witness which alone can make friends of many who are this day still enemies?

As the Lord indicated the reason for the world's hatred of us, so He gives a reason for our witness to the world. "Ye also . . . bear witness, because ye have been with me from the beginning" (John 15:27). The apostolic witness must be from the lips of those who had accompanied the Lord from the beginning of His ministry right to the time of His resurrection. *All* witness must be from those who have been with Him. The privilege of having met this glorious Lord, of having been with Him, of having heard His voice speaking peace to our own souls, lays upon us a sacred obligation to go out and tell others. Having found Him to be so otherwise than we thought in the days of our enmity, we must go to those who are still enemies and tell them: "You do not know this Jesus, or you would not so treat Him.

He is the fairest among ten thousand, He is altogether lovely. His love is sweeter than honey, and stronger than death. He loved me, and gave Himself for me." And even if the arrows of a thousand foes are raining around us, must we not call to those who are hurling them: "Come and see Him for yourselves, He will pardon, as He pardoned me. Come and see! Come and see!"

As we have the fellowship of the Son of God in the world's hate toward us, so also we have the fellowship of the Spirit of God in our witness to the world. See what the Lord says: "When the Comforter is come . . . he shall bear witness of me: and ye also bear witness" (John 15:26-27a, ASV). Here is divine help in ministry as well as divine companionship in suffering. Later the Lord gave the promise to His apostles this way: "Ye shall receive power, the Holy Spirit coming upon you; and ye shall be witnesses unto Me, in Jerusalem, in all Judaea and Samaria, and unto the uttermost part of the earth" (Acts 1:8, author's trans.). The commission carried full equipment, full provision. Have we, then, begun to discharge our commission of love to a world that hates us and our Saviour? Oh for an anointing love with which to fulfill the task!

Let me close with the words of the missionary chant:

> Ye Christian heralds, go proclaim
> Salvation through Emmanuel's name;
> To distant climes the tidings bear,
> And plant the Rose of Sharon there.
>
> God shield you with a wall of fire,
> With flaming zeal your hearts inspire,
> Bid raging winds their fury cease,
> And hush the tempests into peace.
>
> And when our labours all are o'er,
> Then we shall meet to part no more;
> Meet with the blood-bought throng, to fall
> And crown our Jesus Lord of all.

41

A LITTLE WHILE

John 16:16-24

In this passage our Lord tells His disciples what things lie beyond their brief separation:

1. A new kind of vision beyond the little while (vv. 16-19)
2. A new degree of joy beyond the little while (vv. 20-22)
3. A new order of prayer beyond the little while (vv. 23-24)

IN OUR SOUTHERN TRIP last summer we were too late to see the gorgeous spectacle of the rhododendrons in bloom in the Smokies, and the magnificence of the azalea trails in the deep South. We did, however, see the great cotton fields ripe, the multiplied snowballs nestling on their plants. Had we been there early enough for the rhododendrons and the azaleas, we should have missed the cotton. Even so, we were too early for the orange and pecan harvests. All this is just to the effect that we cannot see everything at once.

It is so in regard to an understanding of the Bible, which is like the Bellingrath Gardens, where there is a succession of budding, blooming, and ripening. It may be that some Scriptures have produced their ripe fruit for us, so that they are our continual meat and drink. Others have begun to yield up some of their sweetness and to unfold some of their beauties. Others again may be as unopened buds, which will burst for us tomorrow or next year, while there may be some century plants which will not bloom for us in this life. Ours to enjoy all the yield of beauty, fragrance, and nourishment afforded us, and to continue making regular excursions through the whole garden to see "if the vine flourish, whether the tender grape appear, and the pomegranates bud forth" (Song of Sol 7:12).

Some of the prophecies were "sealed up to the time of the end" (Dan 12:9, author's trans.), so that the prophets themselves were not always given to know "what, and what manner of time the Spirit of Christ which was in them did signify" (1 Pet 1:11). The apostle Peter found some things hard to be understood" (2 Pet 3:16) in the inspired writings of his fellow apostle Paul. It is not surprising, then, that our Lord spoke some words beyond the apprehension of His disciples, as in the instance before us, when His statement about "a little while . . . and again, a little while" (John 16:16) baffled them as much as if He had spoken in a foreign tongue, until they said bluntly to each other, "We don't know what He is saying" (see v. 18). Some Bible passages may be like that to us.

"A little while, and ye shall not see me: and again, a little while, and ye shall see me" (16:16). That was the bud which those anxious men could not pry open, and Jesus did not hasten its opening for them. The progress of events and the illumination of the Spirit would give them understanding of it afterward; and we, looking to the same Holy Spirit, and in the light of the text and historical developments, may enter largely into the truth of the passage.

Two words are used in the Greek which the King James Version translates "see." The American Standard Version brings out the fact that there is a distinction by rendering, "A little while, and ye behold me no more; and again a little while, and ye shall see me." That does not, however, convey much distinction in sense, which is just the weakness of our English tongue in comparison with the Greek, where fine shades of meaning can be so clearly indicated. Here, then, it is not just a matter of the Lord being withdrawn from view and shortly coming back into view. The disciples, after "the little while between" were to see Him in a very different way from their accustomed manner of looking on Him. Now for three years they had been regarding Jesus, critically, searchingly, trying to get at the root of His amazing personality. They had been richly rewarded, but were still full of questionings. He was about to go from their sight, still largely unexplained, only partly understood. But He would shortly fill their vision, and they would see Him with satisfied enlightenment. Westcott has it thus: "The vision of wondering contemplation, in which they observed little by little the outward manifestation of the Lord, was changed and transfigured into sight in which they seized at once intuitively all that Christ was."

When was this new, transfigured vision to be theirs? First guess would be, at His resurrection. But that word, "Because I go unto my Father," which the disciples echoed after Christ, indicates that it was His absence with the Father, not a return to them in bodily form, that was to secure the larger vision. It was after His ascension to the Father's right hand that He sent the Holy Spirit in that mighty Pentecostal effusion, and it was then that the eyes of the disciples received a new kind of sight to behold the Lord in a majesty and glory into which they could not penetrate while He was with them in the flesh or even in resurrection triumph. Still today the Holy Spirit gives to the newborn babe in Christ an understanding of his Saviour far beyond the results of many years' inquiry on the part of the unconverted.

Jesus did not tell the perplexed disciples all this. The interpretation of His enigmatical statement He left for the days of fulfillment, but for their support in the trying meantime He gave them a rapturous promise. "Verily, verily, I say unto you, That ye shall weep and lament, but the world shall rejoice: and ye shall be sorrowful, but your sorrow shall be turned into joy" (John 16:20). The Lord still gives promises where we seek explanations. We say, "Lord, what does all this mean that is come upon me?" And He answers, "I will never leave thee, nor forsake thee" (Heb 13:5b). We ask, "Why? How long?" He replies, "When thou passest through the waters, I will be with thee" (Isa 43:2). The explanations all come later, with the unfolding of time, or "it may be in the better land." The remarkable thing is, that His promise is of far more value to us than an explanation. We do not think so at the moment, but we soon learn it.

It was a day of sorrow for the disciples when Jesus was led off to the cross. The darkness over all the land but answered to the eclipse in their own hearts. But what was the promise of the Lord? "Your sorrow shall be turned into joy" (John 16:20). The joy, be it noted, was not to be a mere sequence, but a consequence of the sorrow. There was a sequence of joy that blessed third morning when the Lord burst forth from the tomb and showed Himself to His amazed followers. "Then were the disciples glad, when they saw the Lord" (John 20:20). The joy which came as a *consequence* of the sorrow, however, was that which flashed upon them by revelation of the Holy Spirit as He set the death of Christ before them in the light of the Old Testament preparations and of the Lord's own words brought to remembrance. Then "out of the eater came forth meat, and out of the strong came forth sweetness" (Judg 14:14). The cross which had for a little time been their shame, their despair, their unutterable grief, became their glory, their bliss beyond compare, as they contemplated its redemptive values, its atoning power, its limitless triumphs. Till that apostle "born out of due season" (1 Cor 15:8, author's trans.) held it aloft with a shout of defiant joy, "God forbid that I should glory, save in the cross of our Lord Jesus Christ" (Gal 6:14).

Is it not so with our lesser sorrows? He does not simply bring us through to joys unrelated to our griefs, as a mother gives a candy bar to a child that has been hurt. He makes our sorrow produce for us manifold blessing, so that our joy is the harvest of our affliction. Who among us cannot point back to dark days with profound thanksgiving because of the "treasures of darkness" which we gleaned as the spoils of our hard experience? Every mother knows the travail out of which has come the joy of nestling her child in her bosom.

This joy of renewed and transfigured fellowship was to be an abiding joy, so deposited in the heart that it could not be snatched away. No treasures deposited in the strongest bank vaults are so well guarded as the joy of the one in communion with Christ. I know this is contrary to the conception of the average man faced with the question of salvation. The attitude of many who accept Christ as a lesser evil than going to hell is well stated by a Mr. Garriock of Glasgow, Scotland: "Here goes for a miserable life and heaven at the end." Jesus said, "Your heart shall rejoice, and your joy no man taketh from you" (John 16:22). Which are you going to believe? I know what I have found!

The "little while" meant a new vision of the Lord, and the promise of abiding joy. It also meant the introduction of a comprehensive provision for all life's needs. Till now the disciples had been full of questionings. The "new order" would do away with that condition, bringing in its place a settled confidence and assurance. "In that day ye shall ask me no question" (16:23*a*, ASV). They would have the divine Messenger of witness in their own hearts giving the assuring witness both of Christ and of their relation to Him. Instead of questionings, then, they would come to God with definite requests, receiving equally definite answers. Both the asking and the receiving would be on a new basis—"in my name" (16:23*b*). Out of this new form of communion would spring the fullness of their joy. I think it will help us to tabulate the wonderful content of these last two verses of our passage:

1. The new confidence: "ye shall ask me nothing [no questions]."
2. The new practice: "ye shall ask [make request of] the Father."
3. The new basis: "in my name."
4. The new certainty: "He will give . . . ye shall receive."
5. The new comprehensiveness: "whatsoever ye shall ask."
6. The new result: "that your joy may be fulfilled" (v. 24, author's trans.).

Does it work? Try it, and see! In almost every testimony meeting in our church, several will give thanks "for definite answers to prayer," ranging from jobs to conversions, from healing of the sick to restoring of backsliders. And the joy!

So the "little while" was full of promise to the disciples, and into all that it meant to them we have entered. We also have another "little while" declared to us in Hebrews 10:37, which spells our blessed hope. "Yet a little while, and he that shall come will come, and will not tarry." Here the "little while" is doubly emphasized, and ought to read "yet a very, very little while." If the blessings beyond the first "little while" were great, what shall we say of the glories beyond this other near horizon? No wonder the last prayer of the Bible is "Even so, come, Lord Jesus!" (Rev 22:20).

> A little while, and we shall be
>   Where sin can never dwell;
> A little while, and we shall live
>   Where songs of triumph swell.
>
> A little while, and we shall hear
>   Our Saviour's whisper, "Come!"
> And we shall ever dwell with Him
>   In our eternal home.

A little while, and we shall see
Our Saviour face to face,
And we shall sing, through endless days,
The wonders of His grace.

42

THE SON ASKS TO BE GLORIFIED

John 17:1-5

In this chapter, after viewing the high-priestly prayer as a whole, we consider:

1. Christ's appropriate request for glory
2. Christ's previous right to glory
3. Christ's demonstrated fitness for glory

IT IS UNIVERSALLY FELT that in some wonderful sense the seventeenth chapter of John's gospel is the sanctum sanctorum of Holy Scripture. Here our Lord overleaps the cross, and permits us to hear Him commune with the Father as from the other side of the rent veil. In such a place any attempt at analysis seems almost irreverent, yet it is only as we understand the progress of this holy communion that we shall be able to appreciate its high value in the sphere of revelation. We approach, not to dissect, but to worship. Holy Spirit, take now of the things of Christ, and reveal them unto us!

This chapter is generally spoken of as a prayer; and in a manner, that is true, yet there is something so lofty, so entirely beyond what constitutes prayer for us, that I prefer to designate it *communion*. The words "I pray" indeed occur three times in our English version, but even there the Greek word so translated is one never used of man praying to God. It is the verb which signifies either interrogation, or making request *on the plane of an equal*. So in this prayer, as it is called, our Lord does not *petition* the Father, but stands on the ground of divine equality presenting august desires which meet with immediate response in that relation of perfect oneness within the Godhead.

The communion of this chapter, then, flows in three distinct movements. The first five verses deal with the Lord Himself, in a high request for glorification. Verses 6-19 have special regard to the apostolic band, while in the remainder of the chapter the whole church is in view. The first of these movements will occupy us in the present study.

How near was heaven to the soul of Jesus!—as near as the name "Father." Six times in the chapter our Lord so addresses God. It is not a God afar off whom this Prophet of Galilee is painfully endeavoring to discover: but One with whom the Son is walking in immediate, intimate communion, in perfect oneness of understanding, purpose, and will. The occasion of the present intercourse, moreover, is not something distant and uncertain, but an event, long anticipated, now arrived: "the hour is come" (John 17:1).

The hour! It had been appointed before ever the world came into being. The whole divine purpose had centered in it, all history had been converging upon it. "The hour" was a byword between the Father and the Son, and the Son had tried to add it to the primary vocabulary of His few innermost friends. "The hour is come!"—with all its darkness and anguish and humiliation. In face of it, what is the request of the equal but obedient Son? "Deliver Thy Son?" No! "Sustain Thy Son?" No! But, "Glorify Thy Son!"

Such a request would be altogether inappropriate and irrelevant on our lips, in any circumstances. We come to the same Father, and present petitions, saying, "Give us, forgive us, lead us, deliver us," and we mention glory only to ascribe it to Him—"for thine is the kingdom, and the power, and the glory" (Matt 6:13). See how the prayer which our Lord taught us to pray carries a confession of utter dependence, casting us as suppliants upon the grace of God. "Give us," for we are poor, and must draw upon Thy wealth. "Forgive us," for we are sinful, and must beseech Thy mercy. "Lead us," for we are foolish sheep, and must look to Thy wisdom. "Deliver us," for we are helpless, and must lean on Thy strength. That is the only appropriate way for sinners to pray. When Samuel the prophet rebuked Saul the king for his failure to carry out the injunctions of God in regard to Amalek, the king replied, "I have sinned: yet honour me now, I pray thee" (1 Sam 15:30). That was the prayer of a reprobate, and we do not wonder that he plunged deeper and deeper into shame and darkness until he hastened his own death on Mount Gilboa. David, the man after God's own heart, did not speak of his own honor in the day his sin was reproved. Listen to him! "Have mercy upon me, O God, according to thy lovingkindness: according unto the multitude of thy tender mercies blot out my transgressions. Wash me throughly from mine iniquity, and cleanse me from my sin. For I acknowledge my transgressions: and my sin is ever before me. Against thee, thee only, have I sinned, and done this evil in thy sight" (Psalm 51:1-4). And that is the man whom God established and highly honored, making him the royal father of the Messiah. Only one has a right to talk to God about glory—the equal and eternal Son, who, having accomplished His redemptive humiliation, now says, "Glorify thy Son" (John 17:1).

The request is enlarged upon and illuminated in the fifth verse: "And now, O Father, glorify thou me with thine own self with the glory which I had with thee before the world was." Now we know what glorification Jesus was asking—a return to what He had known, not only before His incarnation, but before the world was brought into being. When the provinces of Alsace and Lorraine were returned to France after the war of 1914-18, it was on the ground of previous right, that territory having been wrested from France by Germany in 1871. So our Lord asks for glory which is His by previous right, which He voluntarily laid down to undertake the task of redemption as the Servant of Jehovah. See in what amazing terms He speaks here: preexistence, eternal preexistence, a place of honor by the Father's side in that eternal preexistence, and a glory of being, shared without division in the equal Godhead. Now He is asking that that very glory should crown and enwrap His humanity, for He speaks as the Son of Man. Did you know that humanity has been glorified with the very glory of God, in the person of our blessed and all-glorious Lord, Jesus Christ?

Glory is in safe hands when it is bestowed upon Christ. He will not turn it to wrong purposes. He has a holy aim in seeking it: "Glorify thy Son, that thy Son . . . may glorify thee." So the end in view is not His own glory, but that of the Father, and He asks it for Himself because He will thus be able to turn more glory upon the Father. When the Father's glory was to be served by the Son's humiliation, the Son was fully willing for that, so He came to earth and accomplished the work entrusted to Him by the Father, not seeking the least alleviation of the shame and suffering involved, that the Father might be glorified. And now that the Father's glory would be served by the glorifying of the Son, He sought that, and He carries the glory as faithfully as He meekly bore the shame. Wonderful, wonderful Son of the Father!

Our Lord has demonstrated His fitness to carry glory by the use He made of authority. I gather He had asked this "authority over all flesh" (17:2, ASV), even as He was now asking to be glorified. Authority is dangerous in the wrong hands, and too much authority is dangerous in any merely human hands. That is why we cherish the democratic way. It makes a safe (or at least a safer) distribution of authority. The President of the United States of America has definite checks on his authority. The constitution, the cabinet, the senate, the house of representatives, all put limits upon his authority. The queen of England is even more limited in her authority, constitutional monarchy having developed into a definite democracy. Democracy may be slow and cumbersome in the crisis, but history gives ample evidence of the dangers of dictatorship. Even the total authority of the state is repudiated by us in our "government of the people, by the people, and for the people."

Here is One in whose hands universal authority is safe. He used it for life, not for death; for salvation, not for destruction. "Thou gavest him authority over all flesh, that whatsoever thou hast given him, to them, he should give eternal life" (17:2, ASV margin). This power over all flesh might indeed have been used in judgment, for all judgment is committed to the Son in that authority, but "God sent not his Son into the world to condemn the world; but that the world through him might be saved" (John 3:17).

Abraham Lincoln made beneficent use of his authority, when he refused to sign warrants for the shooting of soldiers guilty of misdemeanors, to the distraction of his generals, who were fearful of discipline already bad enough. "Don't ask me to do it," the President would say. "There are enough tears in our homes already, and I am not going to add to them," and with that he would sign pardons. So Christ used His authority to give life, but it meant laying down His own. Every penitent sinner who comes to Him, weighed down with the chains of judgment, He receives as a precious gift from His Father, and bestows the gift of life upon him. Jesus is in the business of signing pardons, and He writes them out in His own blood. So "the blood of Jesus Christ his Son cleanseth us from all sin" (1 John 1:7). Have you come for your pardon?

The One who has so used the universal authority laid on Him is well worthy of everlasting glory. "Wherefore God also hath highly exalted him, and given him a name which is above every name: that at the name of Jesus every knee should bow . . . and that every tongue should confess that Jesus Christ is Lord, *to the glory of God the Father*" (Phil 2:9-11, italics added). Every honor heaped upon the beloved Son will redound to the glory of the Father, throughout all ages. When universal sway has been acknowledged to Christ, He will turn it over to the Father and Himself be subject to the Father, "that God may be all in all" (1 Cor 15:28).

> All hail the power of Jesus' name!
> Let angels prostrate fall;
> Bring forth the royal diadem,
> And crown Him Lord of all!
>
> EDWARD PERRONET

43

KEPT!

JOHN 17:9-15

In this chapter we examine the divine method in securing the saints:

1. Kept by personal guardianship (v. 12)
2. Kept in the divine name (vv. 11-12)
3. Kept from the evil one (v. 15)

LORD, TEACH US TO PRAY" (Luke 11:1), said one of the disciples to Jesus after they had been listening to Him at prayer. And, indeed, one way that He taught them to pray was by allowing them to listen in as He prayed. I heard once of a pianist who wished to take lessons from the great Paderewski. He was accepted as a pupil, but all the lesson he ever received was the privilege of listening and watching as the master practiced. Here, in the true Lord's Prayer, we enter the listening post, and here, if we have any capacity for learning, we shall acquire some rich lessons in the art of prayer.

Our Lord's requests, in the large remaining section of the chapter, center first around the little group of apostles, and then widen to the whole company of believers to the end of the age. Not with the intention that certain blessings should be confined to the few about Him in that hour, and the other requests apply to all. When Jesus said, "Neither pray I for these alone, but for them also which shall believe on me through their word" (John 17:20), He was making over to all believers all that came before and after.

The actual requests are four:

The preservation of the saints (vv. 11-15)
The consecration of the saints (vv. 16-19)
The unification of the saints (vv. 20-23)
The glorification of the saints (v. 24)

"These are in the world . . . Holy Father, keep them in thy name
which thou hast given me" (John 17:11, ASV). No mother ever
prayed for her boy on the battlefield, nor wife for her fisherman husband in the storm, more passionately or tenderly than our Lord for
His own whom He sent into the world. "In the world." To Jesus that
meant "sheep in the midst of wolves" (Matt 10:16), constant, subtle
danger at the hands of unscrupulous, watchful, cruel foes. He had
known the shock of their onslaughts on His own person, and had
watched their dastardly attempts on His disciples. He was ever more
than a match for them, so that not only had He, Himself, passed un-
scathed through the battle, but had brought off His little band intact
and unhurt; the only one having fallen to the enemy being the traitor,
the fifth columnist, the Quisling of the group, who perished because
he was "the son of perdition" (John 17:12) from the beginning. Now
the Lord's confidence in the Father's keeping fully matches His yearning over His followers. There is pathos in the prayer, but no fear.
And when you have to see your children, in all immaturity and inex-
perience of their youth, leave your kindly, wholesome discipline to
face the world, remember that the same holy Father is able to preserve
them in purity and faith, as He did those early disciples.

Our Lord tells us the manner of His preservation of His own, but
unfortunately this does not come out in the King James Version. The
twelfth verse should read thus: "While I was with them, I *kept* them
in thy name which thou hast given me: and I *guarded* them, and not
one . . . [from among] them perished" (17:12, ASV, italics added).
He preserved them by being their personal Guardian. We can be
sure that the holy Father's method will be no less personal, and no less
effective. Several years ago, while in Kentucky, my wife and I were
taken to see that famous horse, Man o' War. He probably was the
most valuable horse in the country at that time. The Baptist deacon
who was his keeper was loud in his praises. Among other items of
information he gave us this, that never for a minute, night or day, was

this horse without a human eye upon him. Will not the holy Father, then, watch His children to preserve them? "The eyes of the LORD are upon the righteous" (Psalm 34:15) ; "I will guide thee with mine eye upon thee" (Psalm 32:8, author's trans.) . It is that which is implied in the very word used in our text. Bishop Moule says, "The Greek verb beautifully suggests the 'preservation' which comes through faithful and attentive 'watching.' The Lord asks for a care which means that eyes of love are upon His disciples, and that the unwearied action of the hands guided by these eyes is around them."

> Safe in Jehovah's keeping, held by His mighty arm:
> God is Himself my refuge, a present help from harm.

"Keep them in thy name which thou hast given me" (John 17:11*b*, ASV) is the reading favored by most manuscripts. It is a phrase which challenges attention, and is certainly worthy of study. "Thy name which thou hast given me" (17:12, ASV) . What is that name? God revealed His name to Moses as "I am." That is the ineffable name, God's memorial forever. We call it *Jehovah* (although we have no certainty of the exact spelling or the pronunciation) , or *Lord*. Jesus came and applied the name, *I am,* to Himself, as we have seen, filling out the sense to bring it into relation with our needs. He allowed Himself to be called *Lord* in connection with the designation *God*, as when Thomas said, "My Lord and my God" (20:28) . Later we are told that "God hath made that same Jesus, whom ye have crucified, both *Lord* and Christ" (Acts 2:36, italics added) . Again, the apostle Paul follows up the declaration of the self-emptying of Christ with this: "Wherefore God also hath highly exalted Him, and given Him *the name* above every name, that in the name of Jesus (belonging to Jesus) every knee should bow . . . that every tongue should confess that Jesus Christ is *Lord*" (Phil 2:9-11, author's trans.) . God the Father has given to His Son Jesus Christ His own ineffable name, Jehovah, Lord, great "I am." The New Testament designation is *Lord*. We are exhorted that whatsoever we do, in word or deed, we are to do it "in the name of the Lord Jesus" (Col 3:17) . The name of the Lord is the sphere of all our life and action. The name stands for all that Jesus is to us as Lord, so that to be in the name is to be in Him as Lord. The Lord's prayer is just this, then, that we be kept in

Him; and in keeping with the prayer is the exhortation to us, "Abide in me" (John 15:4). "The name of the LORD is a strong tower: the righteous runneth into it, and is safe" (Prov 18:10).

There is yet another item in this prayer for the preservation of the saints. "I pray not that thou shouldest take them out of the world, but that thou shouldest keep them from the evil [one]" (John 17:15). Immediate translation to heaven would be the easy way to keep us, but it would lack three very important elements in the divine purpose: we ourselves should lose the benefits of the discipline involved in serving Christ in face of a world's opposition; the world would be robbed of the living testimony of sinners transformed by the grace of God; and God would not have the most suitable instruments for His witness to the world—sinners saved by grace. We must be left here, "in the world" (17:11) but "not of the world" (17:16) to accomplish our mission to the world. The Middle Ages found very many withdrawing from the stream of ordinary life into the solitudes of mountains and deserts in an effort to avoid contamination and to give themselves wholly to God. The whole monastic movement was contrary to the spirit of our Lord's high-priestly prayer.

> We need not bid, for cloistered cell,
> Our neighbour and the world farewell.
> The daily round, the common task
> Will furnish all we need to ask:—
> Room to deny ourselves, a road
> To lead us daily nearer God!

The divine method of preservation is not isolation from the diseased world, for we are the Great Physician's attendants to carry the sin cure to the sick all around us. Physicians and nurses cannot be isolated from the contagion of disease, but they are inoculated with antitoxins in order to keep them from it. We are "strengthened with might by his Spirit in the inner man" (Eph 3:16) against the attacks of sin, and so secured from the domination of the evil one. "This is the victory that overcometh the world, even our faith" (1 John 5:4), not our retirement.

44

SANCTIFIED!

JOHN 17:16-19

In this chapter a twofold sanctification emerges:

1. Sanctification in regard to relation (vv. 16-17)
2. Sanctification in regard to mission (vv. 18-19)

SANCTIFICATION is primarily objective, having to do with relationship, but we cannot escape the subjective implications of it. A holy thing is simply an article set apart for specific uses, particularly religious uses. No change in the character of the object is contemplated. When we come to a person, however, consecration to religious pursuits very definitely involves the man himself. The "holy" men of impure religions, which present degraded conceptions of God, are like the deities they represent, unclean and vile. A man who is set apart for the true God, who walks in communion with Him, and is devoted to His will, cannot but become more godlike in character. The distinction between holiness as separation to God and holiness as conformity to the character of God appears rather in thought than in practice. Sanctification is the divine action by which holiness is accomplished, whether the forming of the new relation or the fashioning of the new character.

There is a remarkable symmetry in this sanctification passage of our Lord's high-priestly prayer. In verses 16 and 18 He indicates analogous positions which He and we occupy in regard to the world. These positions are made a reason for sanctification. In the first instance the sphere of this sanctification is the truth, the Word of God; in the second the basis is the self-sanctification of Christ. Here we have indeed a poem, if not in literary form, at least in structure of thought. We might tabulate it thus:

209

Relation to the world—not of it.
  Sanctification required by that relation.
    The sphere of this sanctification—the truth.
  Mission in the world—divinely sent.
    Sanctification required by that mission.
      The basis—the self-sanctification of Christ.

Let us clearly grasp, first of all, our position in this world as Christians. "As he is, so are we in this world" (1 John 4:17). Listen to the Lord Himself, not so much instructing us concerning what our attitude ought to be, as communing with the Father regarding what our position actually is. "They are not of the world, even as I am not of the world" (John 17:16). We do not belong here, because we did not originate here. Do you protest that we did spring from this world, and God changed our relation to it when He saved us? You forget that God did not take up the "old man" and improve him until he was no longer of this world. God gave us a birth from above, so that the "new man" is of heavenly extraction, the "old man" being out of the reckoning, done to death by the cross of Christ. We who are "new creatures in Christ Jesus" have no more spiritual affinity to this world than has our Lord. We may trace our lineage back to the *Mayflower* or the Norman conquest historically, but that is only "after the flesh." Our spiritual genealogy flows from another source. Like our Lord, we are "from above."

That fact is the rationale of the prayer for sanctification. Being a people apart, Christ prays that we may be what we are, in every expression and department of life. Suppose you were to visit the British embassy in Washington, what would you find? A people living under another flag, the Union Jack: a people of British extraction and origin, speaking with a British accent, following British customs, celebrating British holidays, interested in British affairs, rendering obedience to the British sovereign. They are not part of the American people. They are "sanctified," set apart, for British purposes, and their whole manner of life is in keeping with their position "in America but not of America." So sanctification, in the practical sense, is ever increasing conformity to the character of God, our heavenly Father, as He has revealed Himself on this earthly scene in the person of the beloved Son. This is not a negative thing—not merely the avoidance of certain indulgences which we happen to place in the category of worldliness. The members of the aforementioned embassy do not live their lives on the basis of studious avoidance of all things they might brand "American." They have brought their life with them from across the sea. They live with their eyes positively on London rather than negatively on Washington. Sanctification is just like that. Having our life from God, we live according to Him, more and more as we know Him better. The "don'ts" of the Christian life will not be much of a puzzle if our eyes are on the perfect pattern, "looking unto Jesus the author and finisher of our faith" (Heb 12:2).

Sanctification operates in the sphere of "the truth," and, Jesus adds, "Thy word is truth" (John 17:17*b*). It is as we walk through the lengths and breadths of divine revelation that we become in every part more and more divorced from worldly ties, more and more bound to the holy purpose and sweet will of God. Yet I hasten to say that the Word of God, the very truth itself, will not per se effect this sanctification of necessity. The other day a friend was telling me of a strange character who frequented the Jerry McAuley Mission on Water Street, New York, for a long time. He was nicknamed "Chapter and Verse," because of his almost uncanny mastery of Scripture references. His habit was to slouch down in a front seat, where he seemed to be in a daze. But let anyone, in sermon or testimony, misquote a Scripture, or give a wrong reference, and he was on his feet with "chapter and verse" and correct rendering. Yet that man gave no indication, to the day of his death, of any saving relation with Christ, much less of a sanctified walk. The Word does not sanctify, willy-nilly, but as we "let the word of Christ dwell in . . . [us] richly in all wisdom" (Col 3:16), as we "receive with meekness the engrafted word" (James 1:21), that whole vast range of spiritual truth becomes the mold into which our lives are poured, until, this present evil world having no more foothold, we are wholly set apart for God in practice as in the divine purpose, and the likeness of God shines out.

The second strophe of this beautiful thought poem begins with another aspect of our relation to the world, which also we hold in common with our Lord. "As thou didst send me into the world, even so sent I them into the world" (John 17:18, ASV). Here is divine mission—apostleship! We have no difficulty in conceding the divine mission of our Lord. We rejoice in the redemptive purpose of His coming into the world,

> Sent by the Father from on high,
> Our life to live, our death to die.

We readily acknowledge the divine mission of those who are universally called the apostles, sent forth as first heralds of the gospel, with special authority and grace for the establishing of the church. We shall even yield a recognition of divine mission to such men as Luther and Wesley and Carey and Morrison, who mightily affected the stream of history, or opened new continents to the gospel. But we find it harder to grant the dignity of divine mission, of apostleship if you please, to common ordinary Christians like ourselves. Yet that is implied in this statement of our Lord, who has in mind not only the original apostolic group, but "them also that believe on me through their word" (John 17:20, ASV). Our mission may not be spectacular, romantic, or dramatic, but it is divine. We are in this world by royal appointment, as ambassadors of the Kingdom of God, to declare and to manifest Christ.

If every Christian could have the sense of mission quickened in his heart, what a revival would sweep the world! Dr. Moulton, the great Greek scholar, carried this thought with him through life, applying it wherever he went. His brother, who wrote his biography, said concerning a holiday trip to India, "the entire visit to India was not a tour, but a mission." That phrase, "not a tour, but a mission," so gripped Dr. J. H. Jowett, a prince among preachers, that he preached one of his most powerful sermons on it; and indeed it is worth taking up as a measuring rod for our lives.

Our Lord's mission called for total sanctification, which in Him had no element of purification from sin, for "in him is no sin" (1 John 3:5). The sense here, then, is that aspect of sanctification which we often call consecration. There is no question of the measure of our Lord's consecration—it was complete, and it was continuous. "For their sakes I continuously consecrate Myself" (John 17:19, author's trans.). There is a twofold meaning in that "for their sakes." His consecration was in a task which was to benefit us in salvation; and

His perfect consecration was to be the pattern and inspiration of ours, even as He adds, "that they also might be sanctified in truth." To what extent, I wonder, have His prayer and pattern borne fruit in us? A nation committed to all-out war calls for the complete consecration of all its resources of manpower, wealth, and industry. Does the mission of salvation call for a less consecration? "I beseech you therefore, brethren, by the mercies of God, that ye present your bodies a living sacrifice, holy, acceptable unto God, which is your reasonable service" (Rom 12:1). Following the type of the Hebrew servant, let us make ourselves His by glad choice.

> My Master, lead me to Thy door;
> Pierce this now willing ear once more;
> Thy bonds are freedom; let me stay
> With Thee, to toil, endure, obey.
>
> Yes, ear and hand, and thought and will,
> Use all in Thy dear slavery still;
> Self's weary liberties I cast
> Beneath Thy feet; there keep them fast.
>
> Tread them down still; and then, I know,
> These hands shall with Thy gifts o'erflow:
> And pierced ears shall hear the tone
> Which tells me Thou and I are one.

45

UNIFIED!

JOHN 17:20-23

In this chapter, after considering artificial attempts to promote unity, we examine the divine reality:

1. The nature of the church's unity
2. The measure of the church's unity
3. Christ's contribution to the church's unity
4. The perfecting of the church's unity
5. The discovery of the church's unity
6. The testimony of the church's unity

ONE CANNOT FAIL, surely, to sense the urgency and the peculiar pathos of this request in the high-priestly prayer. No doubt the pathos of it appears more strikingly over against the multiplied divisions of Christendom today, and we are bound to be taken with a sense of shame as the words reach us in the confusion of our religious strife: "That they all may be one" (John 17:21a). Our first thought is that here is a prayer which has not been answered—not yet: but must await the consummation, when the church's travail will give place to her triumph. So we sing, with mingled shame and hope:

Though with a scornful wonder men see her sore opprest,
By schisms rent asunder, by heresies distrest;
Yet saints their watch are keeping, their cry goes up, "How long?"
And soon the night of weeping shall be the morn of song.

Meantime, we do the best we can to patch things up, and try to give the impression of a unity which we know does not exist.

Enforced uniformity is one method which has been often tried to secure the unity of the saints. The only good that such attempts have accomplished has been to challenge the hero in our great defenders of liberty of conscience. What country, having a Christian history at all, cannot produce men to stand beside Krummacher of Elberfeld in Germany, who, on receiving the emperor's orders to adopt the uniform order in his church, returned answer: "Tell his Majesty that as his most humble servant I am at all times ready to lay my head upon the block at his command; but when his Imperial Majesty makes himself lord over the Gospel, I despise his Imperial Majesty"?

Church union has in recent times been attempted to counteract and heal the multiplied divisions of the years. In this there has been a semblance at least of voluntariness, but there have been decided weaknesses both in principle and in results. It is significant that the outstanding divisions of the church have developed out of great revivals. There would have been no Protestant division if the Catholic church had accepted the Protestant revival. There would have been no Wesleyan break if the Church of England had accepted the evangelical revival. There would have been no Salvation Army as a separatist movement if the Methodists had accepted the Booth awakening. If we could have church union flowing from revival, it would accomplish a great purpose, but thus far it seems like an attempt to deal with results without attention to causes, to treat symptoms without a diagnosis of the disease. The apostle Paul laid the divisions in the Corinthian church to carnality. Church union which is not built on a mighty revival of spirituality is only a veneer of unity, carrying the seeds of contention into its new order. More than one attempt at church union has been marked by a trail of bitterness, injustices, and lawsuits, painful to contemplate.

These remarks are not intended to suggest opposition to church union in principle. The visible unity of the church would surely be a triumph without equal in all her history, but to be valid it must represent a return to the Word of God as the sole basis of both faith and practice. It would require a high degree of sanctification to make the necessary sacrifices of sectarian tradition, to determine the common faith from among the accumulated rubble of the centuries, and to preserve freedom of inquiry and interpretation within the bounds of that common faith. How long it would last is the question. A far greater measure of sanctity throughout the church might sustain such a union. That, or complete deadness might—until some Martin Luther arose!

But has the prayer of our Lord really gone unanswered? Are our sects without number an indication that the Father has, so far at least, failed to grant His beloved Son's request? Is the ecclesiastical unity for which men are striving, some by enforced unity and some by voluntary union, the thing for which Jesus prayed? And does God need our strong exertions to help Him to bring about the great desire of the Saviour's heart? There is only one answer to all these questions: a categorical *no!* The oneness which our Lord asked is of such a kind that it is not affected by the shattering of Christendom into ten thousand fragments. It is a divine operation, in which human action plays no part, and which diversities of background, tradition, outlook, custom, form, or prejudice cannot touch.

Catch the undertone of our Lord's request: "that they all may be one; as thou, Father, art in me, and I in thee, that they also may be one in us" (John 17:21). It is a vital, dynamic oneness, realized in a living relation with the Godhead which Christ defines in the simple yet profound phrase, "in us," and which corresponds to the relation within the Godhead indicated in the words, "as thou, Father, art in me, and I in thee." This is not the unity of a pile of bricks, but that of a body with its living members, or a vine with its living branches. "As the body is one, and hath many members, and all the members . . . being many, are one body: *so also is Christ*" (1 Cor 12:12, italics added). That is the Pauline figure, while our Lord Himself gives the other, "I am the vine, ye are the branches" (John 15:5). As a common life pervades the one body with its many members, and the one vine with its many branches, so we are one with God in Christ by the one Spirit. "By one Spirit . . . [were] we all baptized into one body" (1 Cor 12:13).

Listen again to the nature and measure of the unity requested by the Lord for His people: "that they may be one, *even as we are one*." How are the Father and Son one? In some pact, agreement, or alliance? No! But in spirit, nature, and essence. It is just as vain for men to strive after such a unity as for a sinner to strive after a righteousness that will make him acceptable to a holy God. The one is as

much a miracle and gift of God as the other. If "all our righteousnesses are as filthy rags" (Isa 64:6), all our attempts at union are mere
confusion. On the other hand, as we have been made "the righteousness of God in him [Christ]" (2 Cor 5:21), so we are caught up into a
blessed oneness in Christ, joined together, not by the mortar of human
inventions, but by the "one Spirit" of the holy Trinity.

See the wonderful contribution which our Lord makes toward the
answer of His own prayer: "the glory which thou gavest me I have
given them; that they may be one, even as we are one" (John 17:22).
So eager is the beloved Son for this unity of His people that He will
turn the special gift of His Father into the furtherance of it. What is
this particular glory of which He speaks as being the Father's gift to
Him? It must surely be the impartation of the divine nature—His
from all eternity—to His humanity. That glory He shares with us, till
we, men in whom the pristine stamp of God's image has been marred
to obliteration by sin, are made "partakers of the divine nature"
(2 Pet 1:4). That is a gift and a miracle, pulling us together far more
deeply and essentially than any mere conformity or outward association. The outward diversities cannot touch this!

The perfecting of this oneness is accomplished in a triple relation
of Father, Son, and saints: "I in them, and thou in me, that they may
be perfected into one" (John 17:23, ASV). The position of my hand
in the body makes it one with all the members and with the head; but
the life of the head in my hand causes it to function in coordination
with the rest of the body, so realizing and perfecting the union. So
our being in God (the Father and the Son) determines the oneness;
God (the Father and the Son) in us perfects it, in its operation,
realization, and demonstration.

It becomes apparent then, that the unity for which Christ prayed
is rather to be *discovered* by His people than *created, experienced*
rather than *brought to pass.* This discovery will not be made by a
large percentage of professing Christians, members of churches but
not members of Christ. It will be discovered by those in whom the
Holy Spirit has wrought the miracle of regeneration, and in measure
as the Holy Spirit has been allowed to fashion the life. It will be discovered in the teaching of Holy Scripture, as the Spirit sheds light on
the sacred page; it will be realized in the fellowship of the saints, as

the same Holy Spirit makes us sweetly conscious of the blessed kinship in Christ. This is one of the chief delights of Christian experience. To meet a fellow Christian is a vastly richer joy than to meet a fellow Scot, unless the Scot be also Christian. The man in Christ may be of a different race, a different color, a different temperament; there may be nothing in him by nature that would attract me to him; but before I am long with him I know that we belong to each other by ties closer than blood. I am conscious of this oneness before ever I know to what denomination the brother belongs, and, whether I am gratified or disappointed when I receive that information, the sense of oneness is not thereby affected. I think of a certain adherent of the "close brethren" walking arm in arm with a prominent Church of England bishop around conference grounds, in closest friendship and communion. What has happened? They have discovered the oneness of the Spirit.

So, then, the unity of the saints is an accomplished fact, a present truth, fulfilled by divine operation apart from human endeavor; a rare gem waiting discovery, not a product to be manufactured. This does not mean that there is nothing for us to do about it. Like many other evangelical truths, this becomes effective and operative with discovery. Along with the discovery comes the exhortation, "Endeavouring to keep the unity of the Spirit in the bond of peace" (Eph 4:3). The knowledge of a unity divinely wrought, purchased at so great a cost, so deeply cherished by the Lord, will set us to a jealous guarding of its experience in all our relationships with our brethren, until the world looks on in wonderment, exclaiming as they did in the days of old, "Behold, how these Christians love one another!" Then, whether there be one church government or many, whether there be uniformity or diversity of worship, the manifest unity of the Spirit will mightily convince men that Jesus Christ was sent from God with the blessed message of eternal love to lost men.

46

THE ARREST

JOHN 18:1-11

In this chapter we perceive three movements in the incident under review:

1. The impudent intrusion of Judas (vv. 1-3)
2. The sovereign surrender of Jesus (vv. 4-9)
3. The bungling blow of Peter (vv. 10-11)

OUTWARDLY this crossing of the Brook Cedron into the olive garden was a familiar act, for the garden was a favored retreat, where Jesus oft refreshed Himself and His disciples, away from the noise of the city and the burden of ministry. It was replete with memories sacred beyond utterance, for here hearts had been opened, confidences exchanged, lessons learned. Was it here that they heard Him pray as none other ever prayed, till one, speaking for all, besought Him, "Lord, teach us to pray"? Why must the place hallowed by such communion bear the blight of that foul deed of treachery? Enough that its olive branches should droop at sound of the Master's groanings, and its earth open her bosom to receive the drops of His sweat. Holy ground! Where my Lord won aforetime the battle of Calvary.

> Into the woods my Master went,
> Clean forspent, forspent.
> Into the woods my Master came,
> Forspent with love and shame:
> But the olives they were not blind to Him;
> The little gray leaves were kind to Him;
> The thorn-tree had a mind to Him,
> When into the woods He came.

Out of the woods my Master went,
And He was well content.
Out of the woods my Master came,
Content with death and shame.
When Death and Shame would woo Him last,
From under the trees they drew Him last:
'Twas on a tree they slew Him last.
When out of the woods He came.

SIDNEY LANIER*

The shame met Him at the very exit of that wooded arbor. "Judas
... knew the place" (John 18:2), and, devil that he was, shrank not
from invading its sacred precincts and disturbing its holy fellowship
with his treachery and violence.

Jesus scorned the traitor's act of identification and presented Himself. Even when Christ has shown Himself in strength in His people,
He has made men and women tremble. Mary, Queen of Scots, said
that she feared the prayers of John Knox more than all the armies
of England. The very passing of Charles G. Finney brought many
to their knees with a cry for mercy. Need we be surprised, then, that
when our Lord identified Himself under the all-glorious name, "I
Am," and His personality streamed forth in a glory and a majesty
hitherto concealed from the vulgar eye, all strength fled from His
enemies, as, in a first panic, they "went backward, and fell to the
ground" (18:6)? How easily could He have left them to their panic
and confusion, and so frustrated the whole plot! But this was their
"hour, and the power of darkness" (Luke 22:53), so, even as the angel
strengthened prostrated Daniel, Jesus recalled the floundering men to
their task, and sovereignly gave Himself into their hands; while He as
sovereignly commanded the immunity of His disciples, thus demon-
strating the security of those who trust in Him. If He could so assure
the safety of His helpless sheep in the hour of His own arrest, there
can be no doubt of His ability to preserve His weakest ones now,
ascended and glorified as He is. "He is able also to save them to the
uttermost that come unto God by him, seeing he ever liveth to make
intercession for them" (Heb 7:25). So He will be able to say in the

---

*"A Ballad of Trees and the Master," by Sidney Lanier, used by permission of The
Macmillan Company.

great day of the gathering together, as truly as in the shadows of Gethsemane, "Of them which Thou hast given Me I lost not one" (John
18:9, author's trans.).

Peter was better at casting a net than wielding a sword. He apparently tried to use his weapon like an ax, but unfortunately (or
fortunately) he had not taken lessons from Robert Bruce, who before
Bannockburn, as every Scottish boy knows, met the assault of the
English knight, Henry De Bohun, with a blow which for aim and
strength has never been rivaled. I remember to this day the exact
words in which the tale was recorded in my first or second reader:
"Then as the horse went swiftly past, Bruce rose in his saddle, lifted
his axe, and gave the rider such a mighty blow, that it struck through
his steel helmet and killed him." Peter had not been trained in that
school, and, with all his valiant determination to make good his boasts
of a few hours before, he struck a very bungling blow. He learned
later that the sword is for piercing hearts, not for cutting off ears, and
at Pentecost he proved himself a valiant swordsman, till all around
him "they were pricked in their heart, and said unto Peter and to the
rest of the apostles, Men and brethren, what shall we do?" (Acts
2:37). That day about three thousand fell at the feet of Jesus before
Peter's stalwart sword thrusts.

Are we skilled in the use of the sword, the Word of God? I am
afraid the Lord still has to follow some of us about, replacing ears
that we have chopped off. "He that hath ears to hear, let him hear"
(Matt 11:15), saith the Lord. How can they hear if we lop off their
ears? For that is just what we shall do if we go out in the energy and
impulse of the flesh and hew indiscriminately about us. If, on the
other hand, we allow the Holy Spirit to teach us the use of the Word,
it will prove to be His own sword, "living and active . . . piercing to
the dividing asunder of soul and spirit, and of the joints and marrow
. . . a critic of the thoughts and intents of the heart" (Heb 4:12, author's trans.).

Peter's chief error on this occasion was the repeated attempt to hold
Jesus from the cross. It seemed as if Satan were bent on using Peter
to thrust this temptation before the Lord. At Caesarea Philippi the
well-meaning but ill-learned disciple blatantly rebuked the Lord for
even talking about such a thing as going to the cross. In the upper

room he mutinied against the Saviour's lovely symbol of His stoop to the cross. Now he makes his foolish attempt to hinder the actual progress to the cross by attacking the band who had come to arrest the Master. Once again our Lord, straight from the triumphs of Gethsemane, scorns the temptation, and writes up a new motto for all His followers, "The cup which my Father hath given me, shall I not drink it?" (John 18:11). Never will the Father give you and me a cup half so bitter as that which He put to the lips of His well-beloved Son. The cup for us may contain a few drops of gall at times, but His was all wormwood.

> Death and the curse *were* in our cup;
>   O Christ, 'twas full for Thee!
> But Thou hast drained the last dark drop;
>   'Tis empty now for me:
> That bitter cup—love drank it up;
>   Now blessing's draught for me!

47

THE JEWISH TRIAL

JOHN 18:12-14, 19-24

In this chapter we examine the ecclesiastical trial of our Lord from three angles:

1. The political situation
2. The juridical analysis
3. The practical application

JESUS UNDERWENT two trials: one Jewish, one Roman; one ecclesiastical, one civil. The Romans allowed the Jews a certain measure of self-government, but had taken from them the *jus gladii*. A prisoner condemned to death by the Jewish authorities was therefore carried before the Roman governor, who had authority to confirm or revoke the sentence. The question may be raised why this procedure was followed in the case of Jesus, and not in the case of Stephen. It is likely that at the time of Stephen's trial the procurator was not in Jerusalem, in which case the Jewish leaders would not scruple to proceed without his authority. They would scarcely dare to ignore him, however, when he was right in their city. It is doubtful, moreover, if they would have risked the fury of the Passover crowds. The policy of the chief priests seems to have been to turn Jesus over to the strong hand of Rome as quickly as possible, for up to the last they feared the people, among whom Jesus had multitudes of admirers and friends, as the "triumphal entry" demonstrated.

It is a question whether what John gives us is the informal hearing before Annas or part of the trial before Caiaphas. The answer seems to hinge on verse 24. The Greek would read, "Annas, therefore, sent Him bound unto Caiaphas," rather than, "Now Annas had sent him bound unto Caiaphas," as the King James Version gives it. That is, the Greek would seem to make the action consecutive in the context, while the King James translation throws it back. The problem, however, is not quite so simple as that, so while scholars like Edersheim and Meyer stand on one side and scholars like Westcott and Ryle on the other, the question is not likely to be settled. My own inclination is to give the Greek of verse 24 its natural meaning, and allow that John, writing last of the evangelists, omits that phase of the trial under Caiaphas which the other three include, and gives the questioning before Annas which the others ignore.

The place of Annas is an interesting light on the conditions in Israel at this time. He had been brought from Alexandria thirty years before by Herod the Great and had been elevated to the pontificate, an office which he held for nearly nine years, being succeeded by five of his own sons, a son-in-law (Caiaphas), and a grandson. All the time therefore that the house of Annas was in the ascendency in Israel, Annas himself enjoyed all the prestige and authority of the high office without its responsibility. Some think that he continued as president of the Sanhedrin during this whole period. However that may be, he was the power behind the office, and his sentence determined the course of official action. This seems to be the reason for that preliminary hearing before him.

Caiaphas had already expressed his purpose to bring Jesus to death on the ground of expediency, and we can be very sure that Annas, whose notorious Temple-marketing Jesus had so roundly attacked, was of the same mind in the matter. But some semblance of legal procedure had to be invented. Lord Shaw, in his illuminating little work on the trial of Jesus Christ, draws a comparison of situation from Henry VI. Queen Margaret is made to say:

> This Gloster should be quickly rid the world
> To rid us from the fear we have of him,

to which the subtle Cardinal Beaufort replies:

> That he should die is worthy policy:
> But yet we want a colour for his death.
> 'Tis meet he be condemned by course of law.

The hearing recounted by John, whether before Annas or Caiaphas, was to discover such a "course of law" as would give "colour for His death." We shall not be surprised if fine scruples were ignored. The fact is, every principle of jurisprudence was thrown to the winds in the fixed determination of these ministers of "justice" to bring Jesus to death.

Up to the time of the arrest, the rulers of Israel had nothing on which to base a charge against Jesus, for all their attempts to entangle Him in His speech. They therefore resorted to the expedient of seeking to incriminate Him under cross-questioning, and that in a trial for life, which this decidedly was. Such a procedure was grossly contrary to Hebrew law, and Taylor-Innes calls it "the last violation of formal justice."

The high priest's interrogation about Jesus' disciples and doctrine not only was totally illegal, but hinted a secrecy and intrigue which played no part in Christ's ministry. Men usually suspect others of what they themselves practice. The whole Annas tribe was adept at scheming, notoriously so. Our Lord resented and denied the insinuation of secrecy, and couched His denial in a form which threw the charge back where it belonged. "*I* [emphatic] ever taught in the synagogue, and in the temple, whither the Jews always resort; and in secret have *I* said nothing" (John 18:20, italics added). His further answer unmasked the hypocrisy and illegality of the proceedings, reminding the high priest that he had no right to formulate a charge in a trial for life from anything He might answer in the course of the questioning, but was bound to base accusations on the testimony of accredited witnesses. "And," said Jesus in effect, "there is no lack of witnesses as to what I have been teaching" (see 18:21). That high priest was never more properly set down where he belonged than by the fearless, unmasking, yet courteous answer of our Lord.

Even the subordinate who guarded the prisoner recognized the effectiveness of the answer, and, minion that he was, struck Jesus, an act contrary to law, but calculated to win the approval of the so taken-down pontifex. Jesus was soon to fulfill the words of Isaiah: "He is brought as a lamb to the slaughter, and as a sheep before her shearers is dumb, so he openeth not his mouth" (Isa 53:7). Before that, He must testify of the corruptness of the whole procedure upon which the Jewish rulers were embarking, and rebuke the prejudice which marked the very beginnings of the trial. He reminded His smiter that bullying never settled anything, much less a case of law. It was up to the court to indicate any flaw in His argument; and in neither case had a guard any right to assault a man not only uncondemned, but even unaccused.

Thus the Lord Jesus received something less than justice at the hands of man, that we might receive something more than justice at the hands of God. If Christ had received justice from man, He should have been exalted to the highest seat of worship and dominion; if we received justice from God we should be sunk to the pit of eternal woe. In accepting the injustice at man's hands, Jesus received in His own bosom, from God's hands, the justice due to us; so now we receive, on the basis of justice accomplished, not justice, but mercy, grace, love, pardon, life, with "all spiritual blessings in heavenly places in Christ" (Eph 1:3). Ask justice of your fellowman if your cause be good, but ask not justice of God if you be wise; mercy is what a sinner needs, and thank God it is justly given through the holy expediency of God "that one man should die for the people" (John 18:14*b*).

So far we have been a bit more technical in this study than is our wont, but let us return to the questioning of Annas for another emphasis of a more practical nature. "The high priest *then* asked Jesus of his disciples" (18:19, italics added). That "then" comes right after the account of Peter's first denial of the Lord and his joining the enemies of Christ around their fire. I take it that Annas (or Caiaphas, if it were he) was quite ignorant of the episode of the denial, so his question was not related to it. The Holy Spirit has related the two for us, however, by emphasizing the sequence. When did the high priest question Jesus about His disciples? Right after one of the chief of them had cravenly denied Him and joined the company of His persecutors. Looking back a little further, we might say also that it was just after another of them had foully betrayed Him, and the rest had fled as for their very lives. Well might the scornful ecclesiastic inquire concerning the disciples, now conspicuous by their absence. Jesus did not reply to that question. Was He ashamed?

The world still inquires about His disciples, and it is amazing how unbelievers will single out the most unfavorable examples as types, and by them judge Christ and all pertaining to Him. Unjust? Yes! But we cannot alter it. Our best answer is to see to it that we at any rate shall be such disciples as will close the mouths of the critics. The day came when the same priestly group looked on these very same disciples, and "took knowledge of them, that they had been with Jesus" (Acts 4:13*b*). There could be no doubt about them after Pentecost. The marks of Jesus were on them; their identity was unmistakable. If we are living in the power of Pentecost, none will be able to question our discipleship, and the Lord will not have to blush for us.

Now it is a good thing to inquire into the teaching of Jesus. We only wish there were more of an inquiring spirit abroad. The spirit and motive of the inquiry, however, will determine its success. There was little chance of the Jewish high priest coming into an understanding of the teaching of our Lord that day. His purpose to incriminate Jesus was an impassable barrier to enlightenment. Only he is in the way of knowing the truth who is inquiring with a view to doing the will of God. That is a law of the Spirit, enumerated by the Lord Himself: "If any man willeth to do his [God's] will, he shall know of the teaching" (John 7:17, ASV). Inquiry into the teaching of Christ demands humility of spirit, and obedience of heart. Only after Saul of Tarsus said, "Lord, what wilt thou have me do?" (Acts 9:6), did he become the enlightened apostle. The best way to know more is to do what you know. That is the way of mechanics, and it is the way of Christ. "Teach me," we cry, but the great Teacher is silent until we add, "to do thy will!" (Psalm 143:10).

<h1 style="text-align:center">48</h1>

THE FALL OF PETER

JOHN 18:15-18, 25-27

In this chapter we trace:

1. Peter's steps up to the precipice
   a) Peter's boast (13:37)
   b) Peter's sleep (Mark 14:37-38)
   c) Peter's rashness (v. 10)
2. Peter's hurtle over the precipice
   a) The place of danger (vv. 15-16)
   b) The attitude of compromise (vv. 18, 25)
   c) The avalanche of denial (vv. 25-27)

IT CAN'T HAPPEN HERE!" So we boasted, when we ought to have been arming; and our enemies encouraged our blind security, for it suited their purpose well. The men of Laish, we read, were "a people that were at quiet and secure" (Judg 18:27), and in their assurance the Danites came upon them suddenly and dispossessed them. So it was with Peter, boastful in his self-sufficiency. "Though all forsake Thee, yet will not I! I am ready to go with Thee, both into prison, and to death! If I should die with Thee, I will not deny Thee in any wise! I will lay down my life for Thy sake!" Thus spake Peter, instead of giving humble, earnest heed to the loving warnings of His Lord, and arming Himself against the hour of temptation by much seeking after the Lord's strength. "When I am weak, then am I strong" (2 Cor 12:10), declared Paul, conscious of his own deficiencies but armed with "the whole armour of God" (Eph 6:11). Peter stands as a lasting witness to the converse proposition, "When I am strong, then am I weak." "Let him that thinketh he standeth take heed lest he fall" (1 Cor 10:12).

Self-sufficiency is a strong deterrent from prayer, and at the same time an effective soporific. It is not surprising that boasting Peter, and the others who backed up his assurance, slept when they ought to have been praying. The Master craved their fellowship in the hour of His agony in the garden, and when He found them in callous, unsympathizing slumber, He addressed His sorrowful rebuke chiefly to Peter, then added, with the suggestion that self-interest should keep them awake if high duty could not, "Watch and pray, that ye enter not into temptation" (Matt 26:41). But again they slept until the Master allowed them to go on sleeping. If they would not learn by His warnings, they must learn the harder way. Oh Peter, if thou hadst beaten thyself into watchfulness and prayer that night, the cock would have proclaimed thy triumph instead of thy shame. If thou hadst not left thy Lord to weep and sweat and pray alone in the olive shadows, thou wouldst not have slunk out a lone, defeated, weeping man with the first streaks of a mocking dawn.

But are we not condemning ourselves wherein we reprove Peter? Is there any value in marking his fault unless we take heed and correct our own manifold failures by a return to "watching unto prayer"? One who rushes out to the duties of the day, prayerless, is unprepared, and easy prey for the roaring lion who "walketh about, seeking whom he may devour" (1 Pet 5:8). Do not be surprised that the enemy's dart finds you vulnerable if you have not taken time to buckle on your armor.

Peter did indeed attempt to make good his boast by drawing sword against the enemies of his Lord. It was, however, a poor blow, which in itself dampened his ardent spirit. His wounded pride was still further hurt by the Lord's rebuke. Instead of being the hero, he had to submit to having the Lord cover his and the other disciples' retreat. That triple humiliation, but especially the rebuke to his well-meant sally, left him dazed, flattened, till it was a very different Peter who "followed him afar off" (Matt 26:58) from the Peter who boasted of superior loyalty and courage.

Many a young servant of Christ has drawn his sword with eager zeal to fight for his Master, mistakenly thinking that his Master needed defending, while he was predestined to take the world by storm. When I was a student in Glasgow, I was invited (coveted honor among us students!) to preach in a church in Greenock, whose pastor was noted for his piety and scholarship. What an opportunity to make short shrift of the enemies of Christ! I chose for my Malchus the giant of spiritism, and whetted my claymore for the desperate assault. For a good round hour, sir, these stolid Scottish Baptists listened in "dumb" amazement. It was a foregone conclusion that my Malchus would at least flee Scotland, if not be driven to the bottomless pit. But (would you believe it?) that board of deacons did not meet in extraordinary session to request that my manuscript be given honorable place among the records of their church; not a newspaper in the country reported my knockout blow to spiritism; not a publisher invited me to consider terms of publication! In fact, I never heard that a single séance was canceled. I failed even to cut off the *tip* of Malchus's ear. I know just how Peter felt when the Lord added rebuke to the humiliation of his failure. He was in poor shape to meet the fiery testings in the court of the high priest's palace. So boastful, sleepy, prayerless, bungling Peter stumbled on to yet more woeful failure.

Some Christians are safe where others are in mortal peril. The palace of the high priest held no danger, apparently, for John. His acquaintance with the priestly household probably gave him immunity from questioning. The ease of his carriage did not draw the attention that Peter's embarrassment did. He knew where and how to dispose himself advantageously and safely. He did not think of all that when he used his good offices to obtain admission for Peter, who was immediately taken with a feeling of strangeness which he could not hide. From his first entrance into the court he was exposed to a barrage of temptation from which John was quite exempt. Some of us may be able to go places and do things without harm, or even danger, to ourselves, while those same places and pursuits may be full of peril to other Christians. Many a John, in the enjoyment of his own immunity, has introduced a Peter to his spiritual downfall. The answer is not that the other fellow should not be such a weakling, but, "we then that are strong ought to bear the infirmities of the weak, and not to please ourselves" (Rom 15:1).

Peter, once in the place of danger, actually courted temptation; not intentionally, but with the idea, probably, that the best way to escape suspicion was to mingle with the crowd as easily as his convulsed emotions allowed. The fact is that he acted his denial of Christ before he spoke it. Nothing lowers Christian morale so much as keeping company with the world *on its level.* That is what Peter did. He warmed himself at the fire of Christ's enemies, partaking of their comfort and cheer. On that basis he had nothing for them. He could only compromise his position and hope that he would not be challenged. I suppose even then he did not suspect himself of denying the Lord if he were put to it, yet the tacit denial of his position was preparing his lips for the vocal denial so soon to come.

A child of God shows up badly in the lurid glare of the world's fire, and usually ends up badly. You remember how Samson played with Philistian fire and was burned by it. He showed up badly—as a heathen woman's playboy; and ended up badly—grinding blindly at the mill of his and God's enemies. It is better for us to dwell in the light of the Lord's countenance. Then we shall flash back some rays of His glory, and all our path will be "as the dawning light, that shineth more and more unto the perfect day" (Prov 4:18, ASV).

Perhaps you have seen a rock loosened from a mountainside, and as it hurtled down the slope it gathered more with it, till, before it reached the bed beneath, it was a veritable avalanche. Such is the action of sin. That first blunt denial of his acquaintance with Christ loosened the rock which took on avalanche proportions before Peter hit bottom, cursing and swearing, till anyone who knew Jesus would have said, "Certainly this man does not belong to Jesus, for no disciple of His would ever take on like that!" So it was a triple denial in kind as well as in number—the tacit denial of his compromised position, the categorical denial of his own statement, and the demonstrated denial of his foul language.

It is a sad story, written for our warning, but repeated very, very often, because the warning goes unheeded. But "there is hope of a tree, if it be cut down, that it will sprout again, and that the tender branch thereof will not cease" (Job 14:7). Judas went out into the night, but Peter went forth to bedew with his tears of sorrow and repentance the dawning of a new and better day. The cock indeed proclaimed the fallen apostle's guilt, but the heart of Peter carried an echo of promised restoration, and the vision of a look of recall from his beloved Master which surged his soul with a passion of penitence

and saved him from the traitor's despair. Although it is not John, but
Luke, who tells us about that look of Jesus, yet it played such a part in
Peter's recovery, that I introduce it here, with Mrs. Browning's interpretation, for the encouragement of others who may have shared the
apostle's sin, but who may also, after they have been converted,
strengthen their brethren.

> I think that look of Christ might seem to say—
> "Thou Peter! art thou then a common stone
> Which I at last must break my heart upon,
> For all God's charge to his high angels may
> Guard my foot better? Did I yesterday
> Wash *thy* feet, my beloved, that they should run
> Quick to deny me 'neath the morning sun?
> And do thy kisses, like the rest, betray?
> The cock crows coldly. — Go, and manifest
> A late contrition, but no bootless fear!
> For when thy final need is dreariest,
> Thou shalt not be denied, as I am here;
> My voice to God and angels shall attest,
> Because *I know* this man, *let him be clear.*"

49

THE FIRST PHASE OF THE CIVIL TRIAL

JOHN 18:28-40

In this chapter we trace the opening acts of the trial before
Pilate:

1. Pilate insists on a full inquiry (vv. 28-32)
2. Pilate asks a leading question (vv. 33-35)
3. Pilate listens to a wonderful statement (vv. 36-37)
4. Pilate fails in a high decision (v.38)
5. Pilate offers a fatal option (vv. 39-40)

BLIND GUIDES, which strain at a gnat, and swallow a camel!" (Matt
23:24). So had Jesus described the leaders of Jewry, and they gave a
prize demonstration of the accuracy of Christ's words on this occasion.
They were very punctilious about entering the praetorium—that
monument of Gentile domination!—lest they should defile themselves
on the eve of the Passover. But their consciences were quite capable
of stretching to embrace the squalor of inequity and illegality which
they had already perpetrated, and the game of craft and browbeating
which they were about to play on the Roman judge.

The first move was to secure the Roman confirmation of their sentence of death without the delay of an inquiry. Pilate, however, was
in no mood to deal so easily with them. If they were not prepared for
a complete investigation of the case, they would have to execute judgment within the limits of their privileges. As these did not include
the right to inflict the death penalty, they were forced to yield up their
prisoner for examination by the representative of Roman justice. So
Jesus and Pilate came face to face.

Two interviews took place between the prisoner and the judge.

The first revolved around the question of the kingship of Jesus, the second around His divine origin.

"Art *thou* the king of the Jews?" (John 18:33, italics added) , asked Pilate. The emphatic "thou" suggests some surprise. Jesus was not the kind of man that had been wont to stir Jewish insurrections. He had not the appearance of a daredevil leader of rebellion. On the other hand He looked every inch a king. Dignity, mastery, and strength were written in every feature, so that Pilate scarcely knew whether to form his words into a question or an exclamation.

Our Lord's answer was a counter-question which threw Pilate on the defensive. "Is this your own judgment of Me, or are you echoing another's statement?" (18:34, author's trans.) . Jesus was not answering a charge at all; He was pressing for a personal judgment on His claims. He still does that. When you who have been brought up on the gospel call Him Lord, He demands that you express your own judgment, your own faith, your own allegiance. You must not say "Lord" in thoughtless parroting of the language of your mother's faith, your family's religion, or your church's doctrine, but must make Christ your own by personal acceptance, and know Him in personal experience. The English harrier is one dog which takes nothing for granted. When the leader of the pack discovers a line, he throws up his head and gives tongue, to proclaim to all and sundry that he is on the track of a hare. The rest of the pack do not bound after the leader, taking his signal for their cue. Every one goes to the spot, and, assured of the line for himself, throws his legs into the pursuit and his tongue into the concert. Here is one place to be like a hound and not like a sheep. Believest *thou?*

It was not the fate of Jesus, but that of Pilate, which was being determined in that hour. Therefore our Lord talked freely and earnestly, not with any thought of securing Himself, but to give the soul before Him his supreme opportunity of salvation. His topic, in keeping with the charge brought against Him, and Pilate's leading question, was "My Kingdom." It was a Kingdom, He declared, which did not have its origin in this world—it was supramundane. Its purpose, then, could not be to bring one part of this world into subjection to another part, but to effect the sway of heavenly things over the hearts of men. Such a kingdom would not be established by force of arms, nor would its King resort to carnal weapons for His own security. Truth was His mighty implement of conquest, and His purpose in coming into the world was to lift up that glorious banner. He exercised His kingship in a work of witnessing, so that all whose hearts had been fired with the holy passion of truth would recognize in Him and in His words the treasure for which they had longed, and turn to Him as the needle of the compass to the magnetic north.

Thus once again did Jesus direct the interview into a personal crisis for His judge. Steadily had He developed His pincer movement around this man's soul, until, ere he realized it, Pilate was set to judge himself, and declare by his action whether or not he were a child of the truth. The Roman had sat down to judge this strange prisoner, and suddenly found himself challenged to become His subject in the Kingdom of truth. It was a moment of high decision.

Sir Walter Scott depicts one of the most dramatic moments of decision in all literature, when he has his vacillating hero, Captain Waverley, presented to Bonnie Prince Charlie, the charming representative of the ancient house of Stuart, who made such a romantic but futile attempt to regain the English crown for his deposed family in 1745. When the young soldier stood before the prince, the Stuart sympathy of every generation of Waverleys surged through his veins, till it seemed as if Waverley and Stuart belonged to each other and he was drawn irresistibly to the royal Pretender as to his rightful prince. Every other allegiance faded in that moment of decision.

There was no such affinity between Pilate and Jesus, no passion of truth in the Roman to rush out in recognition of the King of truth. He was a stranger to that high realm, and with the snap question, "What is truth?" (John 18:38a), he broke away, to plunge into an orgy of inequity and injustice, with the pillory of everlasting infamy as his reward. So does every man who turns away from Christ build the scaffold of his own doom.

"I find in him no fault" (18:38b). It was the word of acquittal, and ought to have brought the proceedings to a close, with the release of the prisoner. The false judge had his own game to play, however, and he was willing to make justice and innocence pawns in his game. It was to his advantage to win the favor of Jewry if he could, and he thought that by playing off Jesus against a notorious prisoner he might secure the release of Jesus by their own choice, and everybody be happy. Whatever his hope for the issue, it was a perversion of justice shocking beyond expression. Hence his irrelevant "but." "I find in him no fault. . . . But!" That "but" represented the self-interest which severed Pilate from the Saviour, and spelled his doom. "But me no buts," cries an impatient character of the dramatist Fielding. What is the "but" that hinders you from accepting the faultless Christ? Whatever it be, blot it out, and soon you will change Pilate's "I find in him no fault at all," into your own "I find in Him my all in all!"

It is amazing how men will prefer any sort of evil before Jesus Christ. A few weeks ago I heard a young man from the Ukraine relate his spiritual history. At one period he became so disgusted with the hypocrisies of the clergy that he threw all religion overboard and became, or professed to become, an atheist. All the time he was in that state of mind, and actively propagating his unbelief, there was no great opposition from his "orthodox" relatives, nor even from the church from which he had apostatized. When he came to a personal acquaintance with Jesus Christ, however, and began to profess simple faith in Him, parents, friends, and church turned on him like a pack of wolves. They tried restrictions, starvation, beatings, and many other forms of persecution, till at last he found a way of escape to free America. Religious as they were, they preferred atheism to Christ. "Not this man, but Barabbas! Now Barabbas was a robber" (John 18:40). Every Barabbas is just that. Whoever or whatever is preferred before the Lord Jesus will leave the soul bereft of life and hope and peace and virtue. It was a fatal choice which the Jewish nation made. Be sure you make a better. Christ for me!

50

SUFFERED UNDER PONTIUS PILATE

JOHN 19:1-16

In this chapter we follow Pilate's rapid descent to infamy:

1. Pilate subjects an acquitted Man to scourging (vv. 1-3)
2. Pilate appeals to the pity of the crowd (vv. 4-6)
3. Pilate reopens the trial on a new count (vv. 7-11)
4. Pilate capitulates before a veiled threat (vv. 12-16)

PILATE'S TRICK POLITICS had failed in face of the determined enmity of the leaders of Jewry against Jesus, and he was now in a most awkward and compromised situation. He had slackened the rope of justice and found some ugly knots tied in it. He was bound to respect the choice which he himself had offered to the Jews, but what would he do with the Man whom he had properly acquitted? He slid further down the decline of iniquitous procedure, subjected the acquitted Man to the scourge, and himself stood by as the Roman legionnaires carried out their mock coronation to the accompaniment of base assault. A fair counterpart of this deed of Pilate was enacted in Germany in our own day, when heroic Pastor Martin Niemoller, completely vindicated by the People's Tribunal, and about to proceed to his home, which had been decorated for a festive welcome, was rearrested on the personal order of Adolph Hitler, and thrown into a concentration camp. So if Hitler liked the company of Pilate, Niemoller could rejoice in the fellowship of his Lord's sufferings.

Granted that Pilate was trying to secure the release of Jesus, he had nevertheless committed, up to this point, two horrible travesties of justice. In his dilemma he attempted a play on the emotional tides of the crowd, seeking to stir pity for their victim, whom he had subjected to the scourge as a sop to their rage. "Behold the man!" (John 19:5*b*), he cried, as Jesus walked in, wearing the garland of thorns and the purple robe, His face streaked with streams of blood from the piercing thorns. Herein Pilate was making two fatal blunders. For one thing, this was not a case for pity on the part of the prosecutors, but for justice on the part of the judge. Then, too, he little recked the depth of hatred that called for the death of Jesus, hatred that had room for neither justice nor pity.

But Pilate was right in one thing. When he said, "Behold the man!" he wrote a title over the brow of Jesus which is His everlasting glory. Shakespeare makes Mark Antony say of the dead Brutus:

> His life was gentle, and the elements
> So mix'd in him, that Nature might stand up
> And say to all the world, "This was a man!"

Pilate's word goes far beyond that. "Behold the man!" He has no peer. Beside Him we are all less than men. His utter perfections, seen now in the crucible of suffering, flash forth the very image of God, while we stand before Him convinced and condemned of all the sin which has made humanity the broken earthenware that it is. Alas for us men, that in our own tarnishing we lost the true sense of the lovely, till for us "He hath no form nor comeliness; and when we shall see him, there is no beauty that we should desire him" (Isa 53:2). "Crucify him, crucify him" (John 19:6*a*). In these words the very discord of hell burst upon our world, and not until that chorus changes to "Crown Him! Crown Him!" will harmony be known. The cowardly judge capitulated in words which shiver all sense of justice: "Take ye him, and crucify him: for I find no fault in him" (19:6*b*). First, acquittal with abasement; second, acquittal with scourging; and now, acquittal with crucifixion!

"Ye have a *custom*" (18:39, italics added), said Pilate, and the Jews had turned it to their advantage against Jesus. Now, to strengthen the case for crucifixion, they called another weapon into service. "We have a *law*, and by our law he ought to die, because he made himself the Son of God" (19:7, italics added). See how those crafty men had procured the decree of death before ever bringing forward the real charge. Now Pilate had not altogether lost his conscience. He knew that he was not meting out Roman justice. Moreover, he saw that his trickery was no match for Jewish cunning. He could not play their game against them. At every turn in the attempt he had been worsted, until he found himself in the horrible plight of a Roman judge committing an innocent Man to the death penalty. It would have delighted him to tear the flesh of every Jew before him out of very chagrin, and the only mitigation of his situation was that Jesus was a Jew whom he could regard as the scapegoat for his rage.

When, however, he heard that word about Jesus claiming to be the Son of God, all his superstitious nature was stirred, and fear added poignancy to his chagrin. This was not the effect which the Jews anticipated. What they intended for a capping of their triumph threatened it, as Pilate, by returning to the judgment hall with Jesus, indicated that the trial was reopened. Will the judge do any better this time? He was like the many who "turn over a new leaf," only to soil it as they did every one before. Unless, by a personal acceptance of Christ, he had become a new creature, he was already far too deeply in the mire to pull himself out; and little did he know how well the Jews had discovered the vulnerable points in his armor, or what sharp arrows they had in their quiver. What a picture of the sinner making his feeble efforts to shake off his sin, only to find himself more and more shackled!

"Whence art thou?" (John 19:9), asked Pilate in great agitation. It was now a question of origin. In the former interview, Jesus had given ready response to his questionings, but the triple injustice had shown the man's craven insincerity, so the Saviour now held His peace, letting the proud Roman stew for a while in his own terror. Pilate could not understand this prisoner who would not act the part of a prisoner. He was conscious of a growing discomfort, being as much troubled by this remarkable Man's silence as by His words. To bolster his fast-ebbing dignity, Pilate reminded Jesus that he had the power of life and death over Him. That man talking of power! Where was his power when he played down to the Jews by offering them their choice between a condemned criminal and a faultless Man? Where was his power when he yielded to the rabble cry for blood and subjected Jesus to the rod? Where was his power when he capitulated with, "He is not guilty, but crucify Him"?

What an answer of scorn Jesus might have given him! But instead He made one more attempt to save His would-be judge from complete moral collapse. First He reminded this Roman that the authority he held was a sacred trust from heaven, not simply an honorable post which was the gift of the Roman emperor. He was called to exercise the power of his office in righteousness and judgment, as one accountable to God, not to Caesar only. There was enough religion in Pilate to know the truth and realize the challenge of this, and he must have felt some shame at the squalor of judicial crime in which he was now involved. However, Jesus' words were a certain mitigation of Pilate's deeds, carrying this further sense: Pilate was in authority by divine decree for this very thing, for it required a man of his quality (or lack of quality) to fall in with the Jewish demands, and so carry out the purpose of God in the sacrifice of "the Lamb slain from the foundation of the world" (Rev 13:8). So while Pilate was answerable for all his criminal injustice, he was not as guilty as the instigators of the death plot, the Jewish leaders who were bending the frail reed to their will. There is something pathetically compassionate in these last recorded words of our Lord to Pilate.

The procurator's last attempt to release Jesus exposed him to the Jews' poisoned weapon. "If thou let this Man go, thou art not a *Friend of the Caesar!*" (John 19:12, author's trans.). Ambitious Pilate coveted that honorable title, and read in the words of the Jews a threat to send such a report to Rome as would blast forever his hopes of attaining it. His collapse was final. He chose to be a friend of the Caesar rather than a friend of the Christ. He rejected the One who would have given him eternal life, and, in a base effort to save himself, lost all. Whatever truth may be gleaned from the various traditions which try to trace Pilate's after years, it is manifest that they were years of eclipse and tragedy, while his superscription is written for all generations in that damaging phrase of the Apostles' Creed, "suffered under Pontius Pilate."

> What will *you* do with Jesus?
> Neutral you cannot be!
> Some day your heart will be asking—
> "What will He do with me?"

51

ON TO CALVARY!

JOHN 19:16-24

In this chapter we follow our Lord to the place of sacrifice, and see several remarkable incidents:

1. The place—geographical and spiritual (vv. 16-18)
2. The cross—bearing and sharing (v. 17)
3. The title—not a crime advertisement (vv. 19-22)
4. The garments—the best robe for sinners (vv. 23-24)

HENRY VAN DYKE, in the account of his visit to the Holy Land, tells how he dutifully went from shrine to shrine around the spot which tradition has hallowed as the place of the crucifixion of our Lord. Despite his sympathy with the multiplied acts of devotion witnessed there, it was with a sense of relief that he sought the open, clear air, and climbed the lofty bell tower of the German Church of the Redeemer. From that vantage point he looked around, and his eyes lit upon a little rocky hill to the north, just beyond the city gate, and bearing the contour of a skull. Everything about this knoll, known now as Gordon's Calvary, seemed to secure for it the distinction so long claimed for the enshrined and enclosed spot in the Chapel of the Crucifixion. Just as he was so thinking, a man climbed on to the roof of the Greek "Centre of the World," ascended the dome by a ladder, and illuminated the great cross for the night. The writer adds: "Wherever the crucifixion took place, it was surely in the open air, beneath the wide sky, and the cross that stood on Golgotha has become the light at the centre of the world's night."

"The place called Calvary" is to us not so much a geographical location as a point in experience. It stands at the center of our spiritual

241

globe, and means none the less to us if we have been denied the privilege of touching the silver star that marks the traditional crevice or of gazing at the gaunt outlines of that skull-shaped hill. No doubt a sight of the geographical spot will call the historical fact to mind very vividly, but it will require more than a sight-seeing tour to bring the spiritual reality home to our hearts. The Holy Spirit brings Calvary right where we are, so that we need no pilgrimage over lands and seas to behold with raptured vision the sight of a Saviour bearing our sins in His own body on the tree, until we sing with Bunyan's Pilgrim:

> Thus far did I come, laden with my sin,
> Nor could ought ease the grief that I was in
> Till I came hither: what a place is this!
> Must here be the beginning of my bliss?
> Must here the burden fall from off my back?
> Must here the strings that bound it to me crack?
> Blest cross! blest sepulchre! blest rather be
> The Man that there was put to shame for me!

The procession to Golgotha has been a fruitful topic for tradition and fancy to work on. There is enough in the Scripture text, however, for our present purpose. "He bearing his cross went forth" (John 19:17), John tells us, and well for us that he does tell us, else we should gather from the other gospellers that Simon of Cyrene did all the cross-bearing for Him. But how then could the Scripture have been fulfilled which sets forth Isaac bearing the wood of the sacrifice as a chief type of the obedient Son? He must bear the cross which so soon was to bear Him. He must know the full measure of shame attached to the carrying of His own gibbet as well as the curse of hanging upon it. Not otherwise could He purchase for us the full weight of blessing and glory. Behold Him, then, moving heavily and wearily along His via dolorosa, His brow circled still, as it would seem, with the crown of thorns, His face welted with the smiting, His neck bound with a criminal's halter, His shoulders stooped with the weight of the beam upon which He must soon be stretched, until His exhausted energies slowed the procession beyond the patience of the soldiers, and they rudely impressed Simon to bear the cross after Jesus.

It was an unwilling burden at first which this African Jew bore, but later he spoke of it in the company of the saints in humble rapture, exhorting them as himself to fulfill in their lives the type of that cross-bearing, till not only was Simon known in all the church for that coveted service he had rendered their Lord, but his sons, Alexander and Rufus, were famed as the sons of the man who bore the cross after Jesus.

> Must Simon bear the cross alone,
>   And all the rest go free?
> No! there's a cross for every one,
>   And there's a cross for me.

So runs an old version of a familiar hymn: and indeed we may share Simon's honor, and "make up that which is behind of the sufferings of Christ for His body's sake" (Col 1:24, author's trans.) , by gladly accepting whatever loss, whatever reproach, whatever suffering may fall in the way of a complete following of the Lord. It will be no grief to us to have borne for His name's sake. Charles Simeon of England, who endured much at the hands of his fellows for the gospel's sake, was one day seeking consolation in his New Testament, and was so thrilled by this statement regarding his ancient namesake that he wrote, "It was enough! Now I could leap and sing for joy, as one whom Jesus was honouring with a participation in His sufferings. Henceforth I bound persecution as a wreath of glory round my brow." Here is a word of the Lord to remember: "Whosoever doth not bear his cross, and come after me, cannot be my disciple" (Luke 14:27) .

"JESUS OF NAZARETH THE KING OF THE JEWS" (John 19:19) ran the title which Pilate emblazoned above the cross of Christ in place of a crime advertisement. Since he had pronounced the acquittal three times, he could not placard a crime. What, I wonder then, was the mind of Pilate in placing this title over the head of Jesus? That it was no political recognition is a certainty. Yet it was on this score that the Jews had browbeaten Pilate into a betrayal of justice which his own soul abhorred, but which his self-interest demanded. He hated them for it, and, whatever undercurrents flowed in his thinking about Jesus, he knew that this title would be gall to them. It was an open taunt.

I am sure there was also some intentional acknowledgment of the Man he had so wronged. His kingliness was inescapable, and although Pilate was morally incapable of apprehending the high kingship which Jesus propounded to him, he was impelled, perhaps by way of unavailing compensation for his gross injustice, to recognize his victim's superiority: and the only way he knew to do it was to write Him up "the King of the Jews," in whatever sense.

It was written in Hebrew and Greek and Latin: in Hebrew, for all religion must bend before this King of the soul; in Greek, for learning must acknowledge Him "in whom are hid all the treasures of wisdom and knowledge" (Col 2:3) ; in Latin, for all power must bow the knee to this "only [true] Potentate, the King of kings, and Lord of lords" (1 Tim 6:15).

"Write not, The King of the Jews; but that he said, I am King of the Jews" (John 19:21). So protested the chief priests, the men who would not have this Man to rule over them. They would have His title changed to an indictment. But that is exactly what Jesus did *not* say! Whenever an attempt was made to elevate Him to the kingship of the nation, He consistently avoided it. He had other business on hand. Yet He was indeed their King. He was "born King of the Jews" (Matt 2:2), though cradled in a manger; He lived the kingliest life of all, while having no place to lay His head; He rode into Jerusalem in the lowly dignity of Israel's promised King; He died, not as a pretender to a crown, but as a true King. For once Pilate was right.

> In a manger,
> A stranger!
> Yet a star of matchless glory
> Heralded the royal story—
> "Born a King!"
>
> On a tree,
> One of three!
> But the Cross becomes a throne,
> Whence He sways our hearts alone:—
> He dies, a King!
>
> Victorious,
> All-glorious!

> Swaying the sceptre of infinite power,
> Waiting and hasting the Advent hour—
> He lives, a King!

The disposing of the remaining effects of one deceased is usually carried out with a degree of solemn emotion and tenderness. Not so in the case of our blessed Lord. The callousness with which the quaternion of Roman soldiers made the few garments of Jesus the stake in their game of dice, while He yet lived, and right under His eyes, is commentary enough on the hardness of the heart which knows not God. These men, in their ignorance and blindness, gambled within arm's length of what was at once the greatest tragedy and the greatest triumph of all history—the murder of the Son of God, and the atonement for a world's sin. We are living far closer to the unfoldings of God's mighty purposes than we know, yet how many flit about in trivialities, selling eternal gain for a cast of dice! Oh that men would look up from their sinful gaming, to see the face of the Crucified as He offers pardon and life to all!

"A man's heart deviseth his way: but the Lord directeth his steps" (Prov 16:9). These soldiers devised only according to their own selfishness, but the Lord was directing them into the fulfillment of His word. "They part my garments among them, and cast lots upon my vesture" (Psalm 22:18). So wrote David in his great psalm of the cross, which was so much in the mind of the Lord that day that He echoed its very words to speak His anguish and His victory; and which also was so involuntarily fulfilled in incident upon incident on that place called a skull. So the soldiers, without credit, were the servants of the Lord to give that prophecy its mate of accomplishment.

Many fanciful interpretations have been given to the "seamless robe," and much legend has been woven around it. It is not going beyond the bounds of propriety, however, to see in that untorn coat a symbol of the perfect righteousness of our Lord, for righteousness is commonly indicated in Scripture as a garment, and seamlessness certainly suggests perfection. The seamless coat presents a striking contrast to the garments of fig leaves which our first parents sewed together for themselves in their nakedness—garments which God did not accept. But think of that coat falling to a pagan Roman soldier who had taken part in the crucifixion of our Lord! Surely one must recognize in this a picture of the sinner being clothed with the spotless righteousness of Christ. "For he [God] hath made him to be sin for us, who knew no sin; that we might be made the righteousness of God in him" (2 Cor 5:21) . One wonders whether that Roman, who won his game of dice and carried off the seamless coat, did not someday hear Paul preaching this imputed righteousness, and read the type in his own possession, till he cried out with Isaiah: "I will greatly rejoice in the LORD, my soul shall be joyful in my God; for he hath clothed me with the garments of salvation, he hath covered me with the robe of righteousness, as a bridegroom decketh himself with ornaments, and as a bride adorneth herself with her jewels" (Isa 61:10) . Are we so clothed now?

> Christ's precious blood and righteousness
> My jewels are, my festive dress.
> Clad in this glorious robe of grace,
> Boldly I'll stand before God's face.

52

WORDS FROM THE CROSS

JOHN 19:25-30

In this chapter we consider the three "words from the cross" which John records:

1. The word of filial care (vv. 25-27)
2. The word of human suffering (vv. 28-29)
3. The word of divine triumph (v. 30)

OVER AGAINST the callous attitude of the gambling soldiers John invites our attention to an incident which relieves the darkness of the general scene. Three women, all named Mary, who at first stood afar off, beholding, have been drawn irresistibly to the cross of Jesus. Their loving devotion sets them in striking contrast to the quaternion of Roman legionnaires. This is surely no scene for tender women's eyes, but love will endure a sight without sickening which otherwise would be utterly repellent.

John also is there, the first of the apostolic band to recover from panic, and the only one to keep within sight of his Lord through that dreary night and morning. No doubt the sight of these three at the cross deeply moved this disciple, who, son of thunder by nature, had yet a heart as tender as a woman. We can well believe that he immediately set himself to watch over these sorrowing women who dared the scorn of the mocking crowds. With tender compassion would he lend the strength of his manhood to shelter that one especially whom the angel Gabriel had pronounced "blessed ... among women" (Luke 1:28), but who was now feeling the sharpness of the sword which prophetic Simeon had declared would pierce her soul.

Jesus did not fail to notice the grief-stricken women, His own

mother one of them. Neither did He ignore the gracious attitude of
His beloved disciple. His own agonies did not make Him insensible
of the griefs of others, nor did the cosmic work of redemption in
which He was engaged render Him negligent of more common duty.
It was here, then, in the midst of the pains of crucifixion, and with
the weight of a world's sin rolling in on His soul, that our Lord performed His last human service as a son. The high privilege of being
"the mother of our Lord" had not been without its price, and a heavy
price. Right in the beginning it had meant enduring ugly suspicion
of unchastity. It had involved the hasty flight into Egypt to escape
the murderous purpose of Herod. The anxiety of the growing enmity
against her holy Son had not been mitigated by understanding sympathy on the part of Mary's other children. Now at last the sword
had reached the quick of her own soul, every wound which she had beheld in her beloved Firstborn smarted in her own flesh, and anguish
overwhelmed her. The woman who had submitted to that price to
do the will of God must be cared for. It was by divine appointment
that the beloved mother and the beloved disciple were standing together by the cross, their hearts knit in a common grief. "Woman,"
said Jesus, so gently, "behold thy son!" (John 20:26), and to John,
"Behold thy mother!" (20:27).

In making this provision for His mother, our Lord accomplished
a difficult, delicate task, which is even hard to speak about. Mary
has been so extravagantly and blasphemously exalted by some sections of Christendom that the rest of us have reacted by scarcely giving
her the measure of honor due her lofty ministry. But some facts must
be kept in mind. She herself acknowledged God as her Saviour. She
recognized the need of purification, even after the birth of the holy
child, and obeyed the Law in that regard. It is our Lord's own attitude to her, however, which concerns us. He did not address her as
Queen of Heaven, Mother of God, or Saviour of the world. The
sacred record contains no instance of His ever calling her Mother!
Even at the tender age of twelve, her reproof of Him in the Temple
was answered by a reminder of His heavenly sonship. "My Father's
business" (Luke 2:49) was His concern. At the marriage feast of
Cana, He so gently repudiated her motherly authority over Him.
Later, when informed that she and His brethren were desirous of

speaking with Him, He defined the one basis of relationship with Him, namely, the will of His heavenly Father. In a similar strain He turned the blessing which an enthusiastic woman called down upon His mother to those who would "hear the word of God, and keep it" (Luke 11:28). In all this He was kindly but firmly disengaging the human ties between Himself and this blessed woman; and here at the cross He severed them forever. If ever a man will speak the word "mother" with all the passion in his heart, it will be in the article of death, but Jesus said, "Woman," and bade her look to John, not to Him, as her son. He must be to her Saviour, Lord, and God.

Our Lord began His ministry with a great hunger in the wilderness, and finished it with a burning thirst on the cross. Hunger and thirst represent the whole category of human wants to which Jesus Christ was no stranger. "For verily he took not on him the nature of angels: but he took on him the seed of Abraham. Wherefore in all things it behoved him to be made like unto his brethren, that he might be a merciful and faithful high priest" (Heb 2:16-17). It is good to remember that He who is the bread of life hungered; He who gives the living water thirsted; He who invites to rest was weary; He who opens the pathway to glory was put to shame; He who calls us to "all spiritual blessings in heavenly places" (Eph 1:3) suffered the curse; He who bestows life eternal went down into death. Be assured, then, that He will minister these divine benefits with a loving, understanding, sympathetic heart.

> Jesus knows all about our struggles,
>   He will guide till the day is done:
> There's not a Friend like the lowly Jesus—
>   No, not one!

Want is always an occasion of temptation, but it is always an opportunity to glorify God. When Jesus hungered in the wilderness, He was tempted to turn stones into bread for His own gratification, but instead He glorified God by waiting for the Father's provision. Likewise on the cross He glorified God by turning His thirst to the fulfillment of Scripture. "After this, Jesus knowing that all things were now accomplished, that the scripture might be fulfilled, saith, I thirst"

(John 19:28). The thirst was real, terribly real, but had there been no Messianic psalm which said, "In my thirst they gave me vinegar to drink" (Psalm 69:21*b*), He might have borne the parched throat and the burning fever in silence, as He did the thorns and the rod and the nails. "Glorify ye the LORD in the fires" (Isa 24:15), is an old command. Do we turn our fires of affliction into occasions to glorify the Lord?

Hunger and thirst speak of the longings of the soul. Our Lord had a continual thirst for the souls of men. Everywhere He saw men panting with an inward thirst to which the wells of this world were but as brine. His thirst was a yearning to give them the living water. How it satisfied Him to quench the thirst of the woman of Samaria with that living water, till His own hunger and thirst were forgotten! That, however, like other ministries in the days of His flesh, was but a preliminary to the larger task of opening the floodgates of life to all the world. To do that meant the cross. Only from His wounds could the healing waters gush forth, and the cleansing fountain. So He hastened to His baptism of suffering and death, like a hart panting for the water brooks. "I thirst!" He cried, and drank the sour wine of woe that He might claim the sweet wine of redeeming lost men.

It is reported that Queen Elizabeth of England, the great Queen Bess, when on her deathbed, said to her lady-in-waiting, "O my God! it is over. I have come to the end of it—the end, the end. To have only one life, and to have done with it. To have lived, and loved, and triumphed; and now to know it is over! One may defy everything else but this!" Can you not feel the pulse of defeat and despair? "All is vanity and vexation of spirit" (Eccles 1:14). All the pomp and glamour, all the power and glitter, were but hurrying the proud queen along a blind alley until she came to the dark end—the end, the end! Not so the "It is finished" (John 19:20) of the Son of God. His was a life of purpose, and the purpose had been accomplished; a life with a plan, and the plan had been perfected; a life with an aim, and the aim had been attained; a life with a task, and the task had been completed. "I have finished the work which thou gavest me to do" (John 17:4*b*). "O God, to us may grace be given to follow in His train!"

But specifically, what was the work that the Father gave Him to do? What is the finished work of Christ? It is the work of atonement, of propitiation, of reconciliation, of expiation. It had been typified and foreshadowed in many Old Testament events and established ceremonies, and foretold in many prophetic utterances. How shall sin be covered from the sight of a holy God? How shall divine wrath be turned back? How shall the sinner be brought nigh to God in full acceptance? How shall the debt be paid? Where shall the ransom be found to release the prisoner of sin? How can man be just with God? These were the questions that men's hearts were asking as God revealed to them the sinfulness of sin. All down the ages God Himself had been answering, in figure, in prophecy, in ceremonial, "Without shedding of blood is no remission" (Heb 9:22). "It is the blood that maketh an atonement for the soul" (Lev 17:11*b*). But what blood can avail for so mighty an accomplishment?

> Not all the blood of beasts on Jewish altars slain
> Could give the guilty conscience peace or wipe away the stain:
> But Christ the heavenly Lamb takes all our guilt away—
> A sacrifice of nobler name and richer blood than they!

That is the finished work—the shedding of that richer blood that covers my sin, gives me acceptance with God, releases me from bondage, delivers me from wrath, and makes me whiter than snow! To such a finished work do not try to add anything of personal merit, sacred rite, or carnal effort. Only believe! If the sacrifice of Jesus Christ on Calvary is not enough to save the soul, nothing that you or I can do or give will ever make up the deficit. But there is no deficit! "It is finished," and my soul is eternally secure in that which the Son of God wrought when He "loved me, and gave himself for me" (Gal 2:20*b*).

> Upon a life I did not live,
> Upon a death I did not die,
> Another's life, Another's death,
> I stake my whole eternity!

Where do you rest?

53

THE BURIAL

JOHN 19:31-42

In this chapter we have two movements:

1. The last stroke (vv. 31-37)
   a) The Scriptures honored
   b) The fountain opened
2. The last rites (vv. 38-42)
   a) Belated allegiance
   b) Calvary makes heroes

THE JEWS BEGAN the day of their blackest crime with punctilious religious scruples, and ended it with like religious care. Pilate must needs go out to them to hear their accusations against Jesus, for they might not enter the abode of the Gentile at the Passover season! Now that their thirst for the blood of the Nazarene had been satisfied, they must see that the crucified men were not left suspended to defile their holy days! So you see that religious scruples are not always accompanied by moral scruples. I have heard of obdurate criminals in penitentiary who were exceedingly careful not to eat meat on Fridays! Is your religion a cloak to cover unscrupulous conduct, or is it an armor of righteousness?

It looked as if our Lord were to suffer the further indignity of broken legs, but the Father shielded Him from that, for He had already sovereignly yielded up His spirit, and a divine restraint kept back the Roman soldiers from carrying out this assault on His body. The work of atonement had been done. There was no need of further shame or degradation. Yet an added witness was required, so "one of the soldiers with a spear pierced his side, and forthwith came there out blood and water" (John 19:34).

One cannot fail to mark the emphasis which John gives to this

252

incident. He writes as an eyewitness, having apparently returned to see the end after looking to the comfort of Mary, the mother of our Lord, in his own home; and of all the scenes of the crucifixion, this is the one which burned into his heart as having the greatest significance. He recalls two Scriptures which bear directly on the event. The first is a ceremonial command with prophetic intent, that no bone of the Passover lamb should be broken. The apostle John, as well as the later apostle Paul, saw in Christ the great Passover sacrificed for us, so that the care taken to keep the ceremonial lambs whole was a continual testimony to the Lamb of God, who, however bruised in His flesh, should yet suffer no fracture. Thus the type of the Passover was preserved.

Now the Scripture in Zechariah which says, "They shall look upon me whom they have pierced" (12:10*b*), is not to be fulfilled till the return of Christ in glory. But in order that He might be seen as the pierced One in the day of His glory, He must be pierced in the day of His humiliation. God was caring for the still far-off fulfillment of His Word nineteen centuries and more ahead of time. Not one jot or tittle of God's Word can pass away till all be fulfilled. Did you notice the accurate wording here also? The Scripture was *fulfilled* about no bone being broken, but with divine care it is stated, "Another scripture saith, They shall look on him whom they pierced" (John 19:37), for the piercing *then* was in view of the fulfillment of that Scripture *later*.

Such complete honoring of the prophetic word would be reason enough for emphasis, but the apostle, in his first letter, comes back to the thought of the blood and water, suggesting that there is special significance in that mingled tide. "This is he that came by water and blood, even Jesus Christ; not by water only, but by water and blood" (1 John 5:6). I think there is a double testimony here—physical and spiritual. Dr. A. T. Robertson holds, in agreement with some of the early Fathers, that we have here an effective answer to the old Docetic heresy, which denied that our Lord had a true human body. Then, following Dr. Stroud, most now regard the water and blood as indication that on the physical plane our Lord died of a broken heart; but as Dr. Campbell Morgan contends, not till He had accomplished His task and sovereignly permitted the rupture of the pericardium. Great Caesar's heart burst, according to Mark Antony, at sight of Brutus's treachery and ingratitude. Christ held His heart whole, bearing the full burden of His unparalleled sorrow, until His great "It is finished" was sounded forth, then gave His griefs leave to deal their blow. Then,

> He died of a broken heart for me,
> He died of a broken heart:
> O wondrous love, for you, for me,
> He died of a broken heart!

Many have been the attempts to explain the spiritual significance of the water and the blood. I have no doubt that this is the "fountain opened . . . for sin and for uncleanness" (Zech 13:1) . Andrew Bonar compares it to the blood and water which met and mingled in the ritual for the cleansing of the leper, regarding the blood as satisfaction for a broken law, and the water as obedience rendered to an unbroken law. Blood is for expiation, water is for cleansing. Blood is for purification in regard to guilt, water for purification in regard to defilement. The blood will speak to us of our justification, the water of our regeneration and sanctification. The whole provision is made on Calvary, by the offering "once for all" (Heb 10:10) of the body of the Lord Jesus. The blood would be incomplete without the water, for provision must be made for a transformed life after expiation of guilt has been realized; the water would be ineffectual without the blood, for sanctification cannot be wrought where sin is still imputed. So our Lord came, not by water only, as reformers do, but "by water and blood." An ancient and strange Jewish tradition has it that when Moses smote the rock twice at Kadesh, on the first blow it gushed blood and on the second blow it gave forth its waters. "And that Rock was Christ" (1 Cor 10:4) .

> Rock of Ages, cleft for me,
> Let me hide myself in Thee;
> Let the water and the blood,
> From Thy riven side which flowed,
> Be of sin the double cure,
> Save me from its *guilt* and *power*.
>
> RICHARD REDHEAD

That stroke of the lance was the last act which an enemy hand was allowed to perform on the sacred body. From that time, only the hands of His friends touched Him. Crises always bring their surprises, and the death of Jesus called forth the most unexpected men to His service. Two Sanhedrinists stepped forward to save the holy temple of the Lord's body from the burial of a criminal. One of these was the Arimathean, Joseph, rich, honorable, but timid. His noble soul had been drawn out to Jesus, in whom he had come to believe as the "Christ, the Son of the living God" (John 6:69), but his fear had kept him from open confession of the Messiah, in the hope that a more favorable tide would flow. The condemnation of the blessed One, however, spurred him to action. He frankly dissociated himself from the action of the Sanhedrin, and, bent on making late amends for his guilty silence, went openly to Pilate to beg the body of Jesus. Having obtained his request, he dared the enmity of the hierarchy to give his too-late acknowledged Master loving and honorable burial in his own rock-hewn tomb.

Nicodemus also! We have been accustomed to hear that this leader in Israel came to Jesus by night because he was afraid to come by day. It is not so stated in Scripture, and I have not been inclined to believe it. He had that night an undisturbed interview with the "teacher come from God" (John 3:2), and the foundation of a later faith was well and deeply laid. How and when Nicodemus came to true faith we do not know. We do remember that he raised a lone voice for justice when the council was determined to pass judgment on Jesus without any hearing. But whether they were lingering fears or lingering doubts, he cast them to the winds when he saw Jesus condemned, and bravely joined Joseph in lavish, loving care of the body, willing to be an outcast with Jesus.

Were these men late in their allegiance? Perhaps so, but they joined their Lord when the tide was at lowest ebb, when to join Him meant going "unto him without the camp, bearing his reproach" (Heb 13:13), when it meant counting loss all that before had been gain to them. They came, too, when not one of the known disciples made a move, or knew what to do, to secure the body of their Lord from the horrible indignity of the flames of Tophet. Perhaps these men were not heroes by nature, but Calvary made heroes of them.

And that stream of blood and water still makes heroes. I remember a very quiet young man who was brought to Christ in one of my former pastorates. So naturally timid was he that when news came from China of his engagement, one of his quick-witted friends remarked, "I wonder what he said when she proposed!" But that timid youth, after a sight of Calvary, was heroic in his determination to carry the gospel to the regions beyond, and he met his death "in the harness" in far interior China.

We read of the Israelites who came out of their hiding to chase the Philistines after Jonathan had got them on the run. But Joseph and Nicodemus stepped out for Christ when all seemed lost. Today the battle goes hard. How many are willing to turn from the easy way, and, putting on the whole armor of God, stand in the face of a sneering world that is trying to bury our Lord in the grave of outmoded religions? The resurrection morning must have found these two men happy that they had leaped to His side in the day of His humiliation. And we shall be glad that we stood with Him in the day of rejection when the trumpet heralds "the crowning day that's coming bye-and-bye."

54

THE EMPTY TOMB

JOHN 20:1-8

This chapter contains a study in seeing:

1. Casual seeing—Mary (vv. 1-2)
2. Observant seeing—Peter (vv. 6-7)
3. Understanding seeing—John (v. 8)

THERE WAS A LOT of good morning exercise in the early hours of that resurrection day! News from a breathless woman set two disciples running to the sepulcher, where they thought their beloved Lord lay.

Now here is a remarkable thing! Mary Magdalene hastened with her strange intelligence first to Simon Peter, the very disciple who had so foully denied the Lord. Despite his failure, there was something about rough Simon that made him the rallying point of the so bewildered group. Where did Mary go to find Peter? Where John was—and that was at his own home, where he had taken Mary, the mother of Jesus. John, then, had not cast off Peter for his base cowardice. He knew there had been coward enough in his own breast, and having obtained entrance to the place of danger and temptation and disaster for his fellow disciple, he humbly and gladly gave him refuge now in the more hallowed company of the mother of our Lord. It was there that Peter freely shed his tears of penitence, on the shoulder of his younger friend, and on the toil-worn hands of that blessed woman; and it was there that his conversion was so far accomplished that he began to strengthen his brethren, till they looked on him no more as the failure that he was, but as a support to their drooping spirits.

257

It was not good news that Mary Magdalene brought at first, for she had jumped to rash conclusions from very hasty observation—a dangerous thing to do in any circumstance, and especially in matters pertaining to the truth of God. She saw only the stone removed from the entrance to the tomb, and reported, "They have taken away the Lord out of the sepulchre, and we know not where they have laid him" (John 20:2*b*). With equally flimsy support, infidelity has repeated Mary's rash statement to this day, despite abundant evidence to the contrary. Peter and John did the wise thing—they went out to examine the situation for themselves.

"So they ran both together" (20:4*a*). But as the sepulcher comes in sight, see how John shoots ahead. Or is it Peter that lags? He is older, of course, and cannot hold the pace. Is that the reason? "What slowed Peter's feet? Not age, but a sudden shock of memory," declares Ralph Connor, and I think he may be correct. What right has he to take part in a search for the body of the Man he so deserted! But even as a panic of self-condemnation grips him, another memory arouses him. That look of recall flashes again upon his vision, and, with heart almost bursting with a passion to find his beloved Master, he renews his speed, slackening not again till he has pushed past John hesitating at the opening of the tomb, and leaped in.

There are three ways of seeing, and they all enter into this remarkable incident, indicated by three Greek verbs as well as by results. The first is very ordinary seeing, a sort of casual seeing what lies open to common view. It is expressed here by the Greek verb *blepo,* and is the kind of seeing that both Mary Magdalene and John did on their first coming to the tomb. With that quick glance Mary saw that the stone had been lifted away from the entrance. She saw that, but did not stop to consider how unusual it was. She did not look closely and reason, "How is it that the stone is not only rolled back from the opening, but lifted away?" Just that amount of observation would have corrected her conclusion that the tomb had been rifled. Body-snatchers were not engaged in the Herculean task of lifting gravestones out of their running grooves. Then came John with the same kind of seeing. He took a look into the sepulcher, and at first glance saw the body wrappings, perceiving only that they were empty. The body was gone—that was clear to the most careless look.

It was Peter who started the second kind of seeing, expressed by the verb *theoreo*. He did not hesitate at the entrance, but went immediately in, and scrutinized the situation. What did he see in his more critical examination? First, the body wrappings were lying there, apparently undisturbed, on the stone slab. Nothing is said of their being moved, thrown aside, or of the myrrh and aloes being strewn around. Then the napkin, which bound the head, was seen, not in a heap with the body wrappings, nor cast out of its folds, but lying separate, still folded, on the slab, apparently on the elevated portion, or pillow, where the head had lain. It was evident that no hasty rifling of the tomb had taken place. It looked as if the so-well wrapped body had just evaporated, leaving the graveclothes as they were, somewhat fallen together, but still in their folds and in their several places.

Before the sight, Simon Peter stood amazed and bewildered, not knowing what to make of it. Then it was that John ventured in and saw in a third way. The verb now is a part of *horao,* and tells us that the seeing was comprehensive, penetrating, understanding. "I see it," cried John, just as you and I have exclaimed when something that had baffled us for a long time at last penetrated our gray matter and we "saw through" it. John saw, outwardly, just what Peter saw, but the significance of it flashed through his mind. Before him were unmistakable evidences of resurrection, and he believed. He was the first believer in the resurrection, because he allowed the evidence of his eyes to tell its own story. I am not surprised that he rushed from the tomb, with wondering Peter after him. He would not seek the living among the dead. He must be a bearer of this good news, and await the risen Lord in scenes of life, not in places of death. Was there not a precious mother back there, who must immediately be informed that her divine Son was not death's victim, but its Conqueror, the Lord of life? And as John and Peter ran, the older disciple learned from his keener brother the parable of the empty tomb and the forsaken graveclothes.

Now tell me, how are your eyes? What kind of sight have you? Do you see casually, critically, or understandingly? How you see may win or lose you your kingdom. Legend has it that a certain king did not know which one of his three sons to appoint heir to the throne. He determined to test them. While out riding with them one day, he pointed to a crow sitting on a tree, and informed his sons that he would try their aim on that bird. "But before shooting your arrow," he said to his oldest, "tell me what you see." Rather puzzled, the boy began to describe the landscape. "You will not shoot just now," said the king. The second was asked to tell what he saw before trying his skill. "I see a crow sitting on the lowest limb of yonder tree in the midst of the meadow." He also was refused. "What do you see?" asked the king of his youngest. "I see the spot under which the crow's heart beats," said the lad. And the father answered, "You, my son, shall be king after me." He saw with understanding and purpose.

Mary saw casually, and reported falsely. Peter saw critically, but only on the surface, and was bewildered. John saw with the understanding, and believed. Elijah's servant saw a cloud as a man's hand; the prophet saw "abundance of rain" (1 Kings 18:41). We may be quick of sight, and observant in scrutiny, but blind in vision. "Anoint thine eyes with eye-salve, that thou mayest see" (Rev 3:18b). Spirit-anointed eyes are needed to discern the things of the Spirit.

> Open mine eyes, that I may see
> Glimpses of truth Thou hast for me:
> Place in my hand the wonderful key
> That shall unclasp and set me free.
> Silently now I wait for Thee,
> Ready, my Lord, Thy will to see:
> Open mine eyes, illumine me,
> Spirit divine!

It may be that we need a new kind of seeing with respect to the convulsions in the earth today. Our Lord reproved those of His day who could read the face of the sky, but could not "discern the signs of the times" (Matt 16:3b). Have we only military and political and economic eyes for these times? If so, we have surely advanced no further than the casual or critical seeing of Mary and Peter, and we shall have distorted views and sad bewilderment. But if we have understanding sight, we shall be singing:

Mine eyes have seen the glory of the coming of the Lord;
He is trampling out the vintage where the grapes of wrath are stored;

He hath loosed the fateful lightning of His terrible, swift-sword:
    Our God is marching on!

He has sounded forth the trumpet that shall never call retreat;
He is sifting out the hearts of men before His judgment seat:
Oh, be swift, my soul, to answer Him! be jubilant, my feet!
    Our God is marching on!

The seeing that saw the Lord risen from the dead that day will see the Lord coming in the clouds these days. "When these things begin to come to pass, then look up, and lift up your heads; for your redemption draweth nigh" (Luke 21:28).

55

THE RISEN LORD

JOHN 20:11-18

In this chapter we see:

1. Mary's attitude to Jesus:
   - *a)* In death she still calls Him "Lord"
   - *b)* In resurrection she still calls Him "Teacher"
2. Jesus' attitude to Mary:
   - *a)* Refuses worship "after the flesh"
   - *b)* Invites worship "after the spirit"

BY THIS TIME Mary Magdalene, hopelessly outrun by the men, had again reached the tomb, and when the disciples brushed past her, perhaps without noticing that she had returned, she allowed them to go their way with their amazing discovery, while she remained to indulge her now double grief in tears. For the first time she looked into the sepulcher, with a desperate hope that the body might still be there. That would have been comfort to her, for she had no thought of resurrection. With the body gone, that grave was a symbol of her world—a great void.

But the tomb was not empty, as she thought. Two heavenly visitants were there, watching over the place "where the body of Jesus had lain" (John 20:12*b*). Does God have a care for places? It is at least interesting to note that the angels were not standing outside the tomb to point anybody who sought proof of the resurrection to the empty place within. They were sitting inside, "one at the head, and the other at the feet" (20:12*a*), as if contemplating the wonder that the Lord of glory had for three days lain on that slab of stone, wrapped in those linen cloths. If God would thus send angels to the spot where the sacred body *had lain,* do you think that He is unmindful of the spot where the dust of your saintly beloved *now lies?* I was once at a funeral where Dr. H. A. Ironside, then pastor of the great Moody Church, officiated. I remember how deeply I was moved when, in his prayer at the grave, he spoke of the Holy Spirit remaining at that spot, watching over the interred body of that child of God till the day of "the redemption of . . . the [body]" (Rom 8:23). We spoke together of it on the way home, and he told me how as a child he was overcome by grief at having to leave his "grandma all *alone"* in the grave, but was greatly comforted when told that she was not alone. Since then he had learned more deeply the truth that the whole man is the charge of the Holy Spirit, "whereby ye are sealed unto the day of redemption" (Eph 4:30), so that He could not leave a body whose seal of resurrection He was. God has many sacred sites, and I am sure there are frequently angels hovering over those hallowed spots where lies the dust that one day will be clothed with immortality.

Mary had no eyes for angels. "My Lord" (John 20:13) was all her thought. I doubt if she saw the graveclothes, mute evidences of the resurrection, and she had no ears for the witness of angels either. Grief had so overwhelmed her, and the thought of the body having been taken away so possessed her, that even a sight of the risen Lord did not arouse her. It is possible to be so surrendered to one's sorrow that even angels from heaven could not comfort, nor the most manifest truth of the gospel find access to the heart. Although Mary entertained no thought except of a dead body, Jesus was nevertheless still to her "my Lord." A sight of Him dead was the only comfort she hoped for, yet she felt that He had so borne in on her soul that forever He would dominate her life. Is He really *Lord* to us, who know Him risen and alive forevermore?

Of Mary's love for the Lord, and the dominant place He held in her life and affection and thought there can be no doubt. See how her mind is so full of Him that she thinks everyone else must have Him uppermost and preeminent in their minds also, so that in addressing the gardener (as she thought), she used only the pronoun, as if everyone must know of whom she spoke: "Sir, if thou have borne him thence, tell me where thou hast laid him, and I will take him away" (John 20:15*b*). Some may smile at her naïveté, but can any

wonder at her passion of devotion, when He had wrought such deliverance for her, sin-bound, demon-possessed soul that she had been?
And if we would just stop to think deeply into His mighty salvation
work for us, and of His unnumbered mercies to us, we should vie with
Mary in her gratitude to the beloved Lord. I am stirred every time I
read Alexander Whyte's sermon on Mary Magdalene, especially the
culminating apostrophe: "Mary Magdalene! my sister, my forerunner
into heaven till I come, and my representative there! But, remember,
only till I come. Cease not to kiss His feet till I come, but give up thy
place to me when I come. For to whom little is forgiven, the same
loveth little. Give place then; give place to me before His feet!"

"Rabboni!" (John 20:16), she gasped, when His utterance of her
name roused her from her stupor of grief and called her to recognition: "My Teacher!"—and ran to take hold of Him. Imagine being
rebuffed by Jesus in such a moment! For that is just what happened.
"Touch me not; for I am not yet ascended to my Father" (20:17).
Yet a little later He was inviting His disciples to handle Him in evidence that He was not mere fleshless and boneless spirit. Some explain
that very simply by adducing that between the meeting with Mary
Magdalene and the later appearances Jesus ascended to the Father.
How many ascensions did He have, then? No, it is not so easily
explained.

The heart of the matter lies in that word, Rabboni. It was, on
Mary's lips, a word of love, of adoration, of ecstatic joy—a word of
faith, if you will; but it was a word signifying the old relation renewed, all things restored as before that dreadful day of crucifixion.
It was a wrong word, then, for all its tenderness and sweetness, indicating a wrong attitude. A week later, just the invitation to touch
Him brought from Thomas the rapturous cry, "My Lord and my
God!" (John 20:28). But allowance to take hold of Him would have
confirmed Mary in her error. She must learn to cleave to Him in a
new way. "Henceforth know we no man after the flesh," declared the
apostle Paul: "yea, though we have known Christ after the flesh, yet
now . . . know we him no more [after the flesh]" (2 Cor 5:16). Mary
would have Him in the old way, as the beloved Teacher, but she must
have higher titles for Him now, and learn how to realize His presence,
not as a Man in the flesh, but as the ever living and abiding Lord.

Had the Lord allowed Mary to satisfy her longing to clasp His feet as in former days, and so feel that all things were as before, it would have meant repeating the wrench and tearing open again the wound of her heart when He left them in bodily presence. His rebuff, then, was an act of great kindness. It was in order to give Himself to her in the fuller, richer, diviner way that He withheld Himself from her in the way of her thinking. Still does He sometimes refuse us the things we reckon most desirable, but it is that He might bestow better gifts upon us, and above all, Himself, in larger understanding and deeper communion.

We used to sing as children,

> I think, when I read that sweet story of old
> When Jesus was here among men,
> How He called little children as lambs to His fold,
> I should like to have been with Him then.
> I wish that His hands had been placed on my head,
> That His arms had been thrown around me,
> And that I might have seen His kind look when He said,
> "Let the little ones come unto Me."

For all the beauty of its sentiment, and the sweetness of its devotion, that lovely hymn is making the same mistake as Mary Magdalene. When we are wishing for the contacts of the days of His flesh, we are wishing for the very thing that Jesus denied her on the resurrection morning, wishing for something less than we have now. It is this very human desire for a worship in the realm of the senses that has tended to magnify the priestly office. The priest is Christ made tangible, and the word of forgiveness, vocal through him, seems more real. Yet is not that just Mary's fault?

Many years after Henry Newman went over to the Roman church, he gave as his reason this, "I wanted an horizon to my faith." Now that is exactly what true faith rejects. An horizon speaks of limitations within the bounds of sight; it belongs to the senses. Faith overleaps all horizon bounds and wings out to the infinities and the eternities. "We walk by faith, not by sight" (2 Cor 5:7), nor by touch, nor any of the senses. Our worship is spiritual, not sensual. We hold with the hands of faith a Saviour "whom *having not seen,* ye love; in

whom, *though now ye see him not,* yet believing, ye rejoice with joy
unspeakable and full of glory" (1 Pet 1:8, italics added). He is none
the less real, none the less near, for being beyond the reach of our
senses. Yea, rather,

> Speak to Him, thou, for He hears,
> And spirit with spirit can meet:
> Closer He is than breathing,
> And nearer than hands or feet.

Then we may pray also in words which were so often on the lips of
the godly founder of the China Inland Mission:

> Lord Jesus, make Thyself to me
> A living, bright reality;
> More present to faith's vision keen
> Than any outward prospect seen;
> More dear, more intimately nigh
> Then e'en the sweetest earthly tie.

56

THE WOUNDS OF THE SAVIOUR

JOHN 20:19-29

In this chapter we see how the wounds of Jesus become vocal:

1. The wounds of the Saviour speak peace (vv. 19-20)
2. The wounds of the Saviour demand service (vv. 21-23)
3. The wounds of the Saviour conquer doubt (vv. 24-29)

AFTER THE BATTLE of Marathon, where Greece crushed the power of Persia, Pheidippides, the mighty runner, threw down his shield, and ran like the wind to tell the good news in Athens. He burst into the Acropolis with the cry, "Rejoice, we conquer!" So it came to pass, we are told, that the Greeks made this their regular form of salutation: "*Chairete*, Rejoice!" With this salutation the risen Lord greeted the mourning women as they returned from the empty tomb. Since sorrow was the dominant emotion with them, joy was His gift to them. He came as herald of His own victory, to give "beauty for ashes, the oil of joy for mourning, the garment of praise for the spirit of heaviness" (Isa 61:3). We, too, with far larger implications than Pheidippides knew, can greet one another with, "Rejoice, we conquer!"

"Peace!" is the age-old salutation of the Hebrews, still used among them. With this word Jesus greeted His disciples on His first appearing to them as a group, and appropriately so, for they were huddled there behind a closed door, taken with fear. He who had stilled the tempest on the lake with His word of peace, now calmed the panic in their breasts, for He whom waves and winds obey can communicate His own peace to the troubled heart, even as He had said to these same men but a few days before, "My peace I give unto you" (John 14:27).

On this evening, however, the Lord brought with Him more than a wonderful power to infect others with His own poise and calm. He had with Him the tokens of peace. "He shewed unto them his hands and his side" (20:20). Luke indicates that the feet also were shown. Five open wounds were there, speaking "of sins forgiven, of hell subdued, and peace with heaven." By these He had secured to them and to us the peace that He bequeathed as He went out to the awful sacrifice. The scars no doubt served to confirm our Lord's identity to the disciples as the very One who had walked with them those precious years, and to assure them that He was alive from the dead, but that was momentary. The great, lasting, evangelical value of the wounds of Jesus lies in their being the marks of the sacrifice in which He became our peace.

> Five bleeding wounds He bears,
> Received on Calvary;
> They pour effectual prayers,
> They strongly plead for me:
> "Forgive him, O forgive," they cry,
> "Nor let that ransomed sinner die!"

In yet another sense did the risen Christ speak peace to His disciples that day. With the crucifixion all seemed to be over, and each contemplated the future with dread. Their old occupations would seem so futile, so meaningless, after the richer experience with Christ, yet what alternative was there? The Lord had a wonderful word of peace for them on that point. "Peace be unto you: as my Father hath sent me, even so send I you" (John 20:21). In these words the Lord Jesus was not indicating that His commission was now expired, and that He was sending out His disciples on a new venture. Rather, He said. "I received from My Father a commission which I still hold. Death has not ended nor abrogated it. I indeed finished a work on the cross for which the ages have waited. Now on the basis of that I carry on My commission, and under its terms I am sending you forth. You go, then, not on some new errand, but as lieutenants under the very command which I hold from My Father." It was the original plan, being carried out without diversion or change. He addressed them as a victorious King who was promoting subalterns to higher rank for new conquests.

All this new commissioning was done in close relation to the showing of His wounds. For they must know that it would be costly to follow such a Captain. Those scars in His hands and feet and side, received in the discharge of the duties of His high commission, stood as tokens, not only of peace with God for the sinner, but of the enmity of the world, and of the hardship which all must be prepared to endure who took up duty under that same divine appointment. A general who goes forth "conquering, and to conquer" (Rev 6:2*b*) does not promise his soldiers a round of entertainment, but bloody battles with fatigue and wounds and scars. But, on the other hand, the scars of battle which a general bears have a strange fascination for his men, becoming a challenge to dare and to endure in the stiffest campaign. Admiral Nelson's glass eye and stump of an arm put more fight into his men than all the signals he ever raised on his flagship.

> Lord, when I am weary with toiling.
>   And burdensome seem Thy commands,
> If my load should lead to complaining,
>   Lord, show me Thy hands,—
> Thy nail-pierced hands, Thy cross-torn hands,
> My Saviour, show me Thy hands.

> Christ, if ever my footsteps should falter,
>   And I be prepared for retreat,
> If desert or thorn cause lamenting,
>   Lord, show me Thy feet,—
> Thy bleeding feet, Thy nail-scarred feet,
> My Jesus, show me Thy feet.

*   *   *

> O God, dare I show Thee
> *My* hands and *My* feet?

B. T. BADLEY

Our Lord does not send us a-warring on our own charges, nor thrust us out to the service unequipped. Christ's soldiers are never sent out inadequately provided for. "Not by might, nor by power, but by my spirit, saith the LORD of hosts" (Zech 4:6*b*). "He breathed on them, and saith unto them, Receive ye the Holy Ghost" (John 20:22). Alexander Smellie calls this "a pre-libation of Pentecost— an Eschol cluster, that they might know how rich was the vintage

waiting for them." We live on this side of Pentecost. The full out-
pouring, the wealth of the vintage, is ours. Why, then, so little understanding of the Word, why so little victory in the life, why so
little power in service for our Lord? Is it because we have failed to
perceive and obey the active command in the word of bestowal,
"Receive ye the Holy Ghost"?

A particular operation attached to this breathing of the Spirit.
"Whose soever sins ye remit, they are remitted unto them; and whose
soever sins ye retain, they are retained" (20:23). Whatever this authority signifies, it can be exercised only as the Holy Spirit enlightens
and directs. It must be related to the discernment of spirits, which is
definitely a gift of the Spirit, and ought to operate in the whole realm
of church fellowship, in receiving and expelling and restoring. Peter
exercised it in the case of Simon Magus of Samaria, and in regard to
the sin of Ananias and Sapphira. Paul taught the Corinthian church
first to retain and later to remit the sin of the adulterer in their midst.
Whatever excommunication may be necessary, restoration is the end
in view. "Brethren, if a man be overtaken in a fault, ye which are
spiritual, restore such an one in the spirit of meekness" (Gal 6:1).

In yet another connection our Lord showed His wounds. Thomas
was not present that first Sunday. It must have been something of
unusual importance that kept him from assembly that day of all days,
when reports were multiplying of the empty tomb, the empty graveclothes, the angels, and even appearings of the Lord Himself! Or was
he just stubborn in his grief, and sought neither to give nor to receive
consolation? At any rate, his absence that day cost him a whole week
of misery. Your absence from church is costing you far more than
you know!

It is strange how people will react toward something they have
missed. It is, I suppose, the old story of "sour grapes." Thomas put
on a very hard-boiled exterior when his fellow disciples came with
their wonderful, joyful news. "So you saw the wounds, did you? It
might have been an optical illusion. You cannot always trust your
eyes, you know. No, gentlemen, I demand double evidence. In addition to seeing, I must touch the wounds and make sure there is no
fake." So Thomas enjoyed his misery till the next Lord's Day, when
he fortunately agreed to be present at the meeting.

Then came the Lord with His greeting of peace, and immediately addressed Himself to that one recalcitrant member. I hope you, brother pastor, preach some sermons with certain individuals in mind. The sermon that day was the same as the Sunday before, preached again for the sake of this one, and with special application. "The wounds of the Saviour" was the topic. And those wounds spoke that day! What a melting of the hard heart, what a yielding of the stubborn will, what a chasing of unbelief, until Thomas made the biggest, grandest confession of them all, but in few words: "My Lord and my God!" And he worshiped there.

Dr. A. J. Gordon gives us this: "The law of God by the hammer of affliction or by the smitings of judgment may break the heart. But broken ice is just as cold as solid ice. And we have seen worldly hearts all shattered and bruised to pieces by calamity, yet remaining as frigid as an iceberg. We do not undervalue law work in preaching, but oh! it is grace work that melts. And the wounds of Christ are just as powerful to melt the heart as to heal it."

57

FOLLOW THOU ME

John 21:1-22

In this chapter our study closes with the following thoughts:

1. Recreation—with breakfast served (vv. 1-14)
2. Inquisition—with love confessed (vv. 15-17)
3. Commission—with an apostle reinstated (vv. 18-22)

You would have done it yourself. Here they were, old timers in the fishing game finding themselves by the dear old lake. They had not cast a net in a dog's age, and they had just passed through a time of nervous strain that left them quivering and tense. What would ease the tension and restore them to normal more quickly than a night on the beautiful lake, in the cool breezes, with the gentle excitement of the old occupation? Peter did not have to coax that crowd to go fishing with him!

Recreation has its place in the life of a servant of the Lord. There is a tradition about John to the effect that when he was bishop in Ephesus he had a hobby—pigeons. On one occasion an Ephesian Christian came down from hunting in the mountains and passed John's house when he was playing with one of his pigeons. The Christian gently chided the old bishop for spending his time so frivolously. John looked at his critic's bow, and remarked that the string was loosened. "Yes," said the huntsman, "I always loosen the string of my bow when it is not in use. If I kept it tight all the time it would quickly lose its rebound and fail me in the hunt." "And I," replied the aged apostle, "am now relaxing the bow of my mind, that it may the better shoot arrows of divine truth." It may be only legend, but the lesson has abiding values. I do not blame those fishemen-disciples for going fishing that night. Nevertheless, they need some deeper lessons than the profit of recreation.

For one thing, they must learn to await the Lord's commands instead of planning their own course. Since that first day that Jesus had said to them, "Follow me," none of their self-conceived projects had succeeded. This was now the second time that they had tried a fishing trip on their own, and it is Luke who tells us about the failure of the first one. A whole night, and not a bite! But that time and this, when they cast on the Lord's orders, they drew a haul to make any fisherman rub his eyes. Be not surprised if the Lord allows your own enterprise to mock you after you have heard His call to follow Him, for after that you are not your own master. "Whatsoever he doeth shall prosper" (Psalm 1:3*b*) is for him only who has come to this:

> I was not ever thus, nor prayed that Thou
> Should'st lead me on;
> I loved to choose and see my path, but now
> *Lead Thou me on!*

To another kind of fishing were they called, and the mastery of the Lord in the lesser fishing was a parable of His mastery in the greater. The master Fisherman is the Master of fishers of men, and He who could command shoals of fish for a lesson to His disciples will order our service with a degree of success which may not always be apparent, but which will draw His "well done" at the end of the day. Certainly the 153 fish of that morning haul were promise of the three thousand souls in the Pentecost morning ingathering so soon after.

The next hour was to be a solemn, heart-searching one for the disciples, and particularly for one, Simon Peter. It was an act of great thoughtfulness on the part of the risen Lord to serve breakfast first, for these men were hungry and tired after the night's toil. Do you ever stop to think that those same nail-scarred hands spread *your* breakfast table? And do you give thanks? Besides, the informality of the morning meal, eaten on the shore as the sun began its daily climb, set the men at ease in the presence of their Lord, whose conquest of death had struck them with a sense of awe before Him.

I do not think the Saviour's three questions to Peter were asked in rapid succession, but they broke in on the conversation at intervals.

Between questions, the fallen but rapidly rising disciple had time to think, and the previous question had time to work. The two Greek words for "love" used in this passage have often been indicated, and because the development of the whole action hangs on their use I make no apology for introducing them again. Look at the three rounds.

FIRST ROUND—Question: "Simon, son of Jonas, lovest thou me more than these?" (John 21:15*a*). The Saviour speaks of a lofty, worshipful, sacrificial kind of love, that sees infinite worth in its object and will carry its devotion even unto death. Had not Peter professed such a love for his Lord? And had he not boasted of a steadfastness and a loyalty and a devotion that would stand even if all his fellow disciples failed? In the light of such a question, how despicable seemed that squalor of denial! It was a humbled Peter who answered.

Answer: "Yea, Lord; thou knowest that I love thee" (21:15*b*). The odious comparisons were omitted. He would no more boast superiority over his brethren. Even the kind of love which the Lord referred to seemed too lofty for him to affirm, failure that he was. He would tell the Lord that he had delight in Him, that he had heart affection for Him, and leave it at that. Besides, he would appeal to the Lord's own unfailing knowledge of the heart of every man, rather than to any demonstration of his love.

Command: "Feed my lambs" (21:15*c*). Love is the basis of all true service. Now it is almost instinctive to love the lambs, the little ones. But our ministry to Christ's lambs is not to be on the basis that we "simply adore these little tots," but on the ground of our love for *Him*. We shall not love *them* any less for that!

SECOND ROUND—Question: "Simon, son of Jonas, lovest thou me?" (21:16*a*). Peter did not expect it a second time, for the conversation had been flowing on in other channels. He called to remembrance how those challenges in the high priest's palace had come the same way—suddenly and unexpectedly. The Lord dropped the comparison phrase this time, but He was pressing the same big word for love which seemed out of Peter's reach.

Answer: "Yea, Lord; thou knowest that I love thee" (21:16*b*). The identical words as in the previous answer, again appealing to the Lord's perfect knowledge, and pleading, as it were, that the Lord would not press that too lofty word on his so humiliated and broken spirit.

Command: "Shepherd My sheep" (21:16c, author's trans.). That was going to make heavier demands on love than the former task. The instinctive love that little folks command would not help him here. He would have to deal with many thoroughly developed kinks and strongly established perversities. Then there would be more than the feeding to do. All the tasks of shepherding would be involved, and these would prove taxing at times on the patience. Yes, Peter and all pastors had better see to their love for Christ, and have Christ's own love established in the heart, for there will be times when the sheep will exhaust all our own store of love, so that only if the love of Christ constrain us shall we come through on the victory side. I think I see in this commission a warning to Peter that he had better rise to the love which his Master's word signified, for his own would not be equal to the task.

THIRD ROUND—Question: "Simon, son of Jonas, lovest thou me?" (21:17a). So a third time, in the midst of the conversation. It was measure for measure. Here was a balancing of the account. His love is questioned for every denial he had uttered, and alas, his protestations of love are not nearly as effusive and assertive as his denials. It is just as well. He will declare his love more convincingly yet. But this third time is a change. The Lord is using Peter's own word, and questioning even the heart affection that the so reproved apostle has been so humbly affirming. That was the sting—not merely the three times over.

Answer: "Lord, thou knowest all things; thou knowest that I love thee" (21:17b). It was the impatience of a broken heart. This time the distracted penitent made a double appeal: first to the Lord's perfect knowledge, as before, and then to His experimental knowledge, as much as to say, "Despite all my failure, Thou hast not walked with me these years without seeing many evidences of my heart affection for Thee." And I think the Lord smiled upon Peter, for He did know.

Command: "Feed my sheep" (21:17c). And he did, and then passed it on to us also: "Feed the flock of God which is among you. . . . And when the chief Shepherd shall appear, ye shall receive a crown of glory that fadeth not away" (1 Pet 5:2-4).

There was one word more for Peter. It was the word which the Lord had spoken to him by this same lake in the beginning of the gospel: "Follow me" (John 21:19). He had started to do so, and had become so sure of his ability to follow that he boasted that prison and death would not stand in the way of his following. It was idle boasting then. But now the boasting and the prayerlessness and the sinful sleep and the cursing and all the rest were buried in the grave of Jesus; now the three denials had been canceled by the precious blood and balanced by a threefold confession of love; and now he could begin again. "Follow me." This time, without boasting aforetime, he would really follow to prison and to death. He would die for his Lord, not in the impetuosity of youth, but in the maturity of age, and by that say, not *philo*, I love, but *agapao*, I love. What John does, or Andrew, or any of the others, will not be his business, except to be a helper of their faith and love and service. As for him, he has heard the master word which will control all his future days, "Follow thou me."

> I heard Him call, "Come, follow,"—that was all;
> Earth's joys grew dim, my soul went after Him:
> I rose and followed—that was all.
> Will you not follow if you hear His call?